Strategic Studies Institute
and
U.S. Army War College Press

NUCLEAR WEAPONS SECURITY CRISES:
WHAT DOES HISTORY TEACH?

Henry D. Sokolski
Bruno Tertrais
Editors

July 2013

The views expressed in this report are those of the authors and do not necessarily reflect the official policy or position of the Department of the Army, the Department of Defense, or the U.S. Government. Authors of Strategic Studies Institute (SSI) and U.S. Army War College (USAWC) Press publications enjoy full academic freedom, provided they do not disclose classified information, jeopardize operations security, or misrepresent official U.S. policy. Such academic freedom empowers them to offer new and sometimes controversial perspectives in the interest of furthering debate on key issues.

*****

*****

Comments pertaining to this report are invited and should be forwarded to: Director, Strategic Studies Institute and U.S. Army War College Press, U.S. Army War College, 47 Ashburn Drive, Carlisle, PA 17013-5010.

*****

CONTENTS

Foreword v
    Henry D. Sokolski and *Bruno Tertrais*

Preface..vii
    Henry D. Sokolski

Introduction

1. The Unexpected Risk: The Impact of Political Crises on the Security and Control of Nuclear Weapons 3
    Bruno Tertrais

Part I: Case Studies

2. A "Nuclear Coup"? France, the Algerian War, and the April 1961 Nuclear Test 25
    Bruno Tertrais

3. Securing Nuclear Arsenals: A Chinese Case Study 65
    Mark A. Stokes

4. Controlling Soviet/Russian Nuclear Weapons in Times of Instability 87
    Nikolai Sokov

5. Political Transitions and Nuclear Management in Pakistan 145
    Feroz Hassan Khan

Part II: Lessons Learned

6. The Conundrum of Close Calls: Lessons Learned for Securing Nuclear Weapons 191
    Reid B.C. Pauly and Scott D. Sagan

7. Nuclear Command and Control in Crisis: Old Lessons from New History 205
    Peter D. Feaver

8. Securing Nuclear Arsenals in Times of Political Turmoil: "Top 10" Lessons Learned 227
    Gregory F. Giles

9. Beyond Crises: The Unending Challenge of Controlling Nuclear Weapons and Materials 253
    Matthew Bunn

About the Contributors 279

FOREWORD

This volume is the 16th in a series of edited volumes of contracted research the Nonproliferation Policy Education Center (NPEC) has published in cooperation with the Strategic Studies Institute of the U.S. Army War College. It is the product of a joint effort between NPEC and Bruno Tertrais of the Fondation pour la Recherche Stratégique.

The volume features research done over the past 2 years. This work addresses the possibility of nuclear weapons and materials falling into the hands of unauthorized actors during political crises. It uses specific historical case studies as the basis from which to draw lessons for the future. Funding for this project came from the Carnegie Corporation of New York, and the U.S. Department of Defense.

Much of the work to prepare the book for publication was done by NPEC's research associate, Kate Harrison, and the staff of the Strategic Studies Institute, especially Dr. James Pierce and Rita Rummel. This book would not have been possible without their help. Finally, we owe heartfelt thanks to the project's authors and reviewers, who contributed their time and ideas.

> HENRY D. SOKOLSKI
> Executive Director
> The Nonproliferation Policy
>   Education Center
>
> BRUNO TERTRAIS
> Senior Research Fellow
> Fondation pour la
>   Recherche Stratégique

PREFACE

NUCLEAR SECURITY HISTORY: WHY IT COMMANDS OUR ATTENTION

Of all the projects my center, the Nonproliferation Policy Education Center (NPEC), has undertaken, none has generated as much high-level attention as the contents of this volume—four histories of disturbingly close calls when governments came close to losing control of their nuclear arsenals during political crises. Certainly, the number and seniority of current and former officials attending the rollout of this research by my center and the Fondation pour la Recherche Stratégique was impressive: an Assistant Secretary of State; the national intelligence officer in charge of Southwest Asia; a former International Atomic Energy Agency (IAEA) deputy director for safeguards; two former members of the National Security Council; and several senior staffers from State, Defense, Energy, and the Central Intelligence Agency (CIA).

The officials' interest in these histories is understandable. Accounts of nuclear security crises that have taken place outside of the United States have generally been cloaked in secrecy. Also, the drama associated with these crises is significant. At the height of the Cultural Revolution, a Chinese long-range nuclear missile was fired within the country, and the nuclear warhead it was carrying detonated. A French nuclear device was exploded in Algeria during a coup. When the Soviet empire collapsed, shots were fired at a Russian crowd intent on rushing a nuclear weapons-laden plane straining to remove a stash of nuclear weapons to a safer locale. Pakistani governments have been routinely pushed aside by a powerful nuclear-armed military. But expert observers worry that in the future, Pakistan's powerful military might be divided against itself or held hostage by some faction that seizes control of some portion of Pakistan's nuclear assets. How could one not be interested to learn more?

Yet, for all of this, it is unclear just what these stories teach. It certainly would be a mistake to assume that they impart a list of specific policy prescriptions. With each case—the Algerian coup of 1961, the collapse of the Soviet Union, the Chinese Cultural Revolution, and the series of Pakistani crises dating back to the 1980s—the circumstances were so unique it is difficult to draw recommendations that would be very useful today.

The reasons why are nonintuitive. First, the technical challenges each government encountered and the fixes they employed to maintain control over their arsenals were not only different in each instance, but arguably unique to the era when the crisis occurred. Whatever specific technical solution a government might have employed to prevent a past nuclear security crisis, then, is not necessarily the one another government would be advised to use today.

Second, and far more important, each and every nuclear security crisis is and will always be driven by a unique set of human actors, individuals, or groups whose thoughts and intentions, both then and now, are largely beyond anyone's ability to precisely pin down. This presents an immediate historical challenge: How does one determine or prove what key individuals thought or intended to do in the past when it may be in their interest now to embellish or lie? This matters enormously, since no matter how "secure" one tries to make nuclear weapons assets procedurally or technically, individuals with enough authority or access can elect to override or find ways around such protections. The political and organizational solutions employed successfully in the past, therefore, may or may not work in the future.

Such uncertainty is bewildering, because enhancing the nuclear security of existing nuclear weapons arsenals and nuclear weapons-usable materials and plants is a high priority. Hundreds of tons of military and civilian nuclear weapons-usable materials are added to the world's total every year, and the number of new civilian nuclear plants continues to grow. It would be a relief to know that these materials and plants could be rendered safe against theft, seizure, or sabotage. Of course, one can do better or worse at providing nuclear security, but the history of close nuclear security calls suggests that as long as there are assets that can be diverted to make nuclear weapons or sabotaged to produce environmental disasters, there will be no absolute fix to prevent the worst. There is, however, a silver lining to this history that more than justifies our fascination with it: The more we learn about past nuclear crises, the healthier our dose of fright. At a minimum, this history reinforces the imperative to avoid such crises in the future. Certainly, had any of the past nuclear security crises detailed in this book gone differently—had the rebel faction of the French military seized the nuclear device that was to be tested in Algeria, had the nuclear-armed missile the Chinese fired and exploded during the Cultural Revolution hit a city, had the Russians lost control of the weapons they were evacuating from remote bases to hostile local forces, or had the Pakistani government ever lost control of its weapons to irredentist forces—each of these governments would likely have collapsed.

In addition to detailing the nuclear security crises that took place during the French Algerian coup of 1961, the Chinese Cultural Revolution, the collapse of the Soviet Union, and Pakistan's persistent political instability since the 1980s, this volume showcases an analysis of this history by a series of distinguished nuclear experts and practitioners. The hope is that history and its lessons will help in support of preparations for the next Nuclear Security Summit, planned for the Netherlands in 2014.

Next year, my center plans to publish an additional volume of historical research it has commissioned on known instances of large amounts of nuclear materials useful to make bombs that have gone unaccounted for (known as material unaccounted for [MUF]). Several cases will be examined. These will include the loss and possible theft by Israeli agents of at least 100 kilograms of weapons-grade uranium in the 1960s from a nuclear plant in Pennsylvania; the scores of bombs' worth of plutonium gone unaccounted for in Japan and Europe since the 1980s; the hundreds of bombs' worth of weapons-grade materials gone unaccounted for from U.S. nuclear weapons plants operating during the Cold War; and the challenges of accounting for South Africa's past production of nuclear weapons uranium. Given the continued military and civilian production of such materials today and the efforts to cap them, this history should also be instructive.

HENRY D. SOKOLSKI

INTRODUCTION

CHAPTER 1

THE UNEXPECTED RISK: THE IMPACT OF POLITICAL CRISES ON THE SECURITY AND CONTROL OF NUCLEAR WEAPONS

Bruno Tertrais

The past 2 decades have seen an increase in nuclear dangers. Arsenals have been operationalized in India and Pakistan, and China seems to be augmenting its own. North Korea has crossed the nuclear threshold, and Iran seems to be on the way to do so itself. Four hitherto undisclosed—and illegal—nuclear programs were discovered: Iraq in 1991, Iran in 2002, Libya in 2003, and Syria in 2007. Pakistani and North Korean nuclear expertise and technology transfers were also uncovered. Al-Qaeda and other jihadist groups showed an interest in gaining access to nuclear weapons and materials, and some attacked nuclear-related facilities in Pakistan.

The security and control of nuclear weapons is thus more important than ever, as witnessed by the political success of two Nuclear Security Summits in Washington (2010) and Seoul (2012). Despite disagreement over budget priorities, the topic enjoys a rare level of bipartisanship in the United States.

Much has been written about nuclear accidents and nuclear crises, but much less about the impact of political crises in nuclear-capable states.[1] The goal that Henry Sokolski and I set in undertaking this project was to shed light on the following issue: How do nuclear-capable states behave in times of major political crises?

Our project focuses more specifically on "nuclear security" and "control of use." According to the U.S. Department of Defense, *nuclear security* covers procedures, facilities, and equipment designed to avoid loss of custody, theft, and diversion of nuclear weapons, as well as other unauthorized actions, vandalism, and sabotage. *Control of use* covers both use control (components and codes) as well as command and control (organizational and communications procedures and capabilities).[2]

At first glance, all nuclear-armed countries today seem to have well-established procedures and institutions to ensure nuclear security and control of use. In Western countries, as well as in India and Israel, the primacy of civilian and political officials over nuclear oversight and control is apparently well entrenched.[3]

However, the global picture of nuclear security and control is much less rosy than it seems. First, things are more complex than they appear in countries such as Russia, China, and Pakistan, where the military has a stronger and sometimes key role.

- In Russia, there is not one but three "Chegets" (strategic communication devices): one for the president, one for the defense minister, and one for the chief of general staff. Some claim that the agreement of all three authorities (plus that of one of the strategic forces commanders) is needed to launch a nuclear strike.[4] But most informed sources state that any of the three can launch a nuclear strike.[5] What seems clear in any case is that nuclear use does not technically require any input from the Russian president. (This was the case in the Soviet Union.)[6] A well-known Russian expert has stated that "real control over nuclear weapons has never been in the hands of the political leadership. It has always been under the control of the defense minister and the General Staff."[7] He wrote more recently that "It is not clear whether the system is fail-safe from the action of reckless military commanders."[8] Indeed, other testimonies have stated that, technically, the ability to launch nuclear weapons exists well below the upper echelons of Russian political and military power.[9]

- In China, procedures remain unclear, but it seems that any decision to use nuclear weapons would be made by a combination of top party and military leaders.[10]
- In Pakistan, despite the prime minister's chairmanship of the National Command Authority, few doubt that the military would have the final say in the use of nuclear weapons, especially since the "Employment Control Committee" involves the main armed forces leaders.

Second, the history of nuclear security and control is fraught with lax procedures and insufficient measures compounded by human mistakes.[11] Even in Western nuclear powers, the establishment of solid command and control procedures took time and has often been insufficient, in no small part because the elaboration of nuclear deterrence procedures is submitted to a fundamental dilemma. Survivability and readiness call for dispersion, movement, and pre-delegation. But security and control call for concentration, no movement, and code retention. The problem is that, to use Peter Feaver's apt characterization, procedures tend to err on the side of "always" (i.e., always be fired when directed) rather than on the side of "never" (i.e., never be fired if not ordered by a proper authority).[12]

Pre-delegation existed at least in the United States and in the United Kingdom (UK) in the 1950s.[13] In the United States, combination locks on nuclear warheads appeared only in the late-1950s. In 1960, the U.S. Joint Committee on Atomic Energy discovered that security measures designed to prevent the theft or unauthorized use of U.S. nuclear weapons in Europe were limited to a single 18-year-old sentry armed with a carbine.[14] This led to the development and introduction of Permissive Action Links (PALs). But it did not solve the North Atlantic Treaty Organization (NATO) nuclear security problem. In the mid-1970s, tactical nuclear weapons in Germany were so poorly secured that a small group of terrorists could have easily stolen them. In the early-1980s, about half of the U.S. arsenal in Europe was still equipped with old four-digit combination locks. In France, early command and control arrangements were, to say the least, rudimentary: General Charles de Gaulle thought that he had a sufficiently recognizable voice so that his military commanders would know it was him giving the order.[15] In Western countries and in the Soviet Union, "nuclear briefcases" were introduced only in the 1980s. Until the early-1990s, American (and Soviet) nuclear-powered ballistic missile submarine (SSBN) commanders were still technically able to launch their missiles without any input from outside.[16] UK SSBN commanders still can. The UK WE-177 free-fall bombs that were withdrawn in 1998 "were armed by turning a bicycle lock key."[17]

Thus, it can hardly be taken for granted that the next nuclear powers will be "born" with solid security and control procedures. In fact, if Scott Sagan is to be believed, "there are compelling reasons to predict that many would-be proliferators will develop nuclear arsenals that are considerably less safe than those of current nuclear powers."[18]

In addition, nuclear institutions are as likely as any other complex organization to undergo what experts call "normal accidents," despite—and sometimes, experts argue, because of—efforts to build in redundancies and safeguards to take into account technical failures and human frailties.[19]

We suspect that such existing weaknesses, which are inherent to any complex human organization, could be magnified if a major institutional or political crisis was to occur in a nuclear-armed country. At best, this means that nuclear weapons or technologies could fall into the wrong hands (state or nonstate actors), with the risk of regional instability, political blackmail, and nuclear accidents. At worst, such a crisis can mean a nuclear explosion or a nuclear war.

Indeed, the list of serious nuclear security and control incidents, failures, and lapses is a rather long one. Some of the most egregious include the following:[20]

- In April 1961, control of the French nuclear site in Algeria and of a nuclear device that was located there became the object of competing loyalties as a coup d'état unfolded in Algiers.[21]
- In October 1962, during the Cuban Missile Crisis, a security guard at a Duluth, MN, military base mistakenly took a bear for an enemy intruder and sounded the alarm. This triggered air-raid klaxons in the region. However, at the nearby Volk Airfield, due to a faulty system, the nuclear attack alert was sounded, causing nuclear-armed F-106A to scramble for takeoff.[22]
- Two days later, North American Air Defense (NORAD) radar picked up an unidentified object flying in space; because this happened

at the same time that a test tape had been introduced in the equipment, the NORAD command post mistakenly thought that a missile had been launched from Cuba, targeted against Florida.[23]
- In December 1963, when U.S. President Lyndon B. Johnson took office, the director of the White House Military Office discovered that no one had updated the authenticator codes for 6 months.[24]
- In September 1966, the Chinese Cultural Revolution led to internal strife within the nuclear program. The center of Chinese nuclear research and development (R&D) was split between two factions.[25]
- In October 1966, the newly created Second Artillery Corps (the Chinese strategic missiles force)—inspired by calls from radicals to accelerate the nuclear weapons program—conducted a dangerous test of a nuclear-tipped missile, which flew over population centers, to demonstrate revolutionary spirit. This was seen by some as an unauthorized test.[26] Throughout 1966-67, the Second Artillery Corps was rife with rivalries and power struggles.[27]
- At the same time, the Lop Nor testing site was also the focus of a competition for power.[28] Around December 1966, the Party boss of Xinjiang is believed to have made an indirect threat to seize the site. A December 1967 test was seen to have been a "fizzle" due to a hasty detonation.[29]
- In the mid-1970s, U.S. Senator Sam Nunn discovered that the NATO nuclear base he visited was guarded by units composed of demoral-

ized soldiers with stories of regular alcohol and drug consumption.[30]
- Until 1977, the U.S. Strategic Air Command (SAC) reportedly used intercontinental ballistic missile (ICBM) launch procedures that bypassed the normal coding mechanisms.[31]
- In November 1979, the insertion of an exercise tape into a NORAD computer triggered a threat assessment conference and an air defense alert, including the launch of the National Emergency Airborne Command Post.[32]
- In March 1981, U.S. President Ronald Reagan's authenticator codes disappeared in a Federal Bureau of Investigation (FBI) evidence bag after he was shot.[33]
- A few months later in May 1981, French President François Mitterrand was so moved by his election that he forgot the launch codes, given to him by his predecessor, at home in the suit he was wearing the day before.[34]
- In 1988, after General Zia Ul-Haq's sudden death, the new Pakistani president (1988-93) Ghulam Ishaq Khan, decided to retain the nuclear program's secret files under his control instead of turning them over to the prime minister. He turned them over to the military when forced to retire in 1993.[35]
- In the 1990s, the so-called A. Q. Khan network managed to copy three Pakistani nuclear warhead designs. The first one, of Chinese origin, was given to at least one country (Libya). The two others–plans for more sophisticated devices–were digitalized by the network and may have been transferred to other states or entities.

- In January 1990, rebels fighting Moscow's rule in Azerbaijan stormed the perimeter at an army base and tried to steal the nuclear weapons stored there.[36] This triggered a massive, hurried, and partly improvised withdrawal of tactical nuclear weapons stationed in the smaller Soviet Republics.[37]
- In the spring of 1991, a communication error resulted in Ukrainian officers receiving an order to make a loyalty oath to Russia. This led the Kiev leadership to intervene to block the withdrawal of tactical nuclear weapons and take steps to gain access to launch control systems of strategic weapons.[38]
- In August 1991, during the attempted coup against him, Mikhail Gorbachev was deprived of his "Cheget," while Defense Minister Dmitry Yazov (one of the putsch leaders) lost his own in the turmoil.[39] At some point, the coup leaders were in possession of all three Chegets.[40]
- In late-1991, Ukraine sought to prevent Russia from being able to launch nuclear weapons still stationed on its soil. Subsequently, Ukraine ordered a study of the possibility of bypassing the launch codes.[41]
- In July 1993, Russian Defense Minister General Pavel Grachev abruptly took possession of the Cheget belonging to Marshal Yevgeniy Shaposhnikov, the commander in chief of the Commonwealth of Independent States (CIS).[42]
- In October 1993, during an attempted coup in Moscow, militarized squads of supporters of the Supreme Soviet attacked the General Staff building, which hosts the Russian nuclear command and control center.[43]

- In January 1995, the launch of a Norwegian sounding rocket triggered the activation of Russia's strategic emergency command, control, communications, and intelligence (C3I) system ("Kazbeck") and of the Chegets. Oslo had notified the Russian Foreign Ministry of the impeding launch, but launch notification had gotten lost in the meanders of the post-Soviet bureaucratic disorder: It had failed to reach the appropriate on-duty personnel.[44] Given the unusual size and trajectory of the rocket, some Russian officials genuinely feared, for several minutes, a strike that might have been an Electro-Magnetic Pulse (EMP) attack.[45]
- In November 1995, during Russian President Boris Yeltsin's heart attack, his Cheget was illegally taken away from him by General Alexandr Korzhakov, his chief of presidential security, who reportedly declared, "Whoever has the button has the power."[46]
- In April 1999, after a NATO Summit, U.S. President Bill Clinton left behind his military aide carrying the "football." The aide had to walk back to the White House by himself in a hurry.[47]
- Around 2000, Clinton misplaced his presidential authentication card. The loss was discovered only after several months, when it was time to update the codes.[48]
- In August 2007, a U.S. B-52H strategic bomber mistakenly carried six nuclear-tipped Advanced Cruise Missiles (ACM) from Minot Air Force Base (AFB) to Barksdale AFB. The nuclear warheads were supposed to have been removed.
- Since the late-2000s, Pakistani terrorists have attacked several military installations sus-

pected of holding nuclear weapons-related facilities or research.⁴⁹
- In January 2010, European anti-nuclear activists penetrated the inner perimeter of a NATO nuclear base in Belgium.⁵⁰

We selected four case studies: China, France, Pakistan, and the Soviet Union. The time frame of each case study varies, ranging from a few days for France (the 1961 attempted military coup) to several decades for Pakistan. But we believe that these four countries are good examples of the sort of risks that we are talking about.

In addition, we noted that all four of them had experienced severe political upheavals, including *coups d'état* (Pakistan in 1958, 1977, and 1999); attempted coups (France in 1961, the Soviet Union in 1991, and Russia in 1993); major institutional crises (France in 1958 and China in 1966-68); and even break-ups (France in 1962 and the Soviet Union in 1991). By comparison, the five other countries that have developed nuclear weapons (the United States, the United Kingdom, South Africa, India, and North Korea) have been much more stable from an institutional point of view. But this still means that *out of nine states that built nuclear weapons, four are known to have undergone severe political crises affecting nuclear security and/or control of use in one way or another, thus, nearly 50 percent.* These states include the three countries (China, Pakistan, and the Soviet Union/Russia) where the military traditionally has played a strong role in the political system. In two cases (France in 1961 and China in 1967), there is evidence that political turmoil and threats against testing sites resulted in the hurried detonation of nuclear devices.

When we began this project, we knew that others had cleared the path before us. In 1978, Lewis

Dunn published a seminal article entitled "Military Politics, Nuclear Proliferation, and the Nuclear 'Coup d'Etat'."[51] He pointed out that most of the potential proliferators had experienced attempted or successful military coups and, among other insights, suggested that "in the many politically unstable, coup-vulnerable, future N-th countries, access to nuclear weapons could become a sought-after source of power and bargaining leverage."[52] In 1987, Leonard ("Sandy") Spector devoted a chapter in his book, *Going Nuclear*, to the effect of political instability on nuclear control.[53] There have also been many detailed historical studies on nuclear security, at least for the Union of Soviet Socialist Republics (USSR) and Pakistan.

The added value of the case studies presented here is threefold. First, not all cases have been well covered by the existing literature (France in 1961, in particular). Second, new evidence and new sources have become available over the years. Third, and most importantly, we asked our authors, who are all experts in the nuclear programs of the countries we chose, to focus on one key question: How did political instability affect nuclear security and use control?

Our project does not claim to give the definitive historical account or to shed light on all the incidents that may have taken place in these four countries.[54] But it brings new insights and sometimes contradicts conventional wisdom. Tertrais (for France) and Khan (for Pakistan) make the case that the nuclear risks stemming from political instability and attempted coups were less than many believed. In contrast, Sokov (for the Soviet Union/Russia) and Stokes (for China) raise intriguing questions and describe troubling and not well-known episodes.

Leonard Spector's 1987 conclusions were fourfold. First, he argued that "Nuclear weapons ... can indeed change hands as political control abruptly shifts over the territory where they are located." Second, he suggested that "It is not implausible that a radical, anti-status-quo government can sweep into power and inherit significant nuclear assets." Third, he believed that "Preventing the inheritance of nuclear assets is likely to be costly and complicated, and in some cases, it may not be possible at all." Finally, Spector argued that, "Though a radical government has never inherited nuclear arms, there is historical precedent for the key elements of this scenario."[55]

Subsequent events since 1987 (in the Soviet Union, in Russia, and in Pakistan) have proven him right.[56] As will be seen, our study supports and bolsters these early conclusions. We draw lessons about the behavior of governments, institutions, and leaders regarding nuclear security and control of use during major political crises. Our project is useful for thinking in advance about the next major political crisis involving a nuclear-capable country such as Iran or North Korea; a mature nuclear power such as Pakistan, China, or Russia; or a future nuclear-capable state such as Saudi Arabia, Egypt, or Algeria. The project also brings insights to how to improve nuclear security and control of use.

It is tempting to say that organizations and procedures have, on balance, behaved fairly well throughout the nuclear age. After all, since 1945, there has never been either a nuclear explosion in anger, or a known transfer of an operational nuclear device. Perhaps political and military officials have taken better care of nuclear weapons than many have feared. There may have been progress—both through experience, information sharing, and improved technology—in the way nuclear arsenals have been controlled.

But one should guard against optimistic conclusions. The U.S. history of nuclear security over the past 2 decades, for instance, is less than stellar, even though the United States has the longest experience with and arguably the best know-how to deal with such issues. For example, in addition to the incidents listed above, the transcripts of the meeting that took place in the White House Situation Room immediately after President Reagan was shot in 1981 should give pause to optimists.[57] This would not come as a surprise to pessimistic organization theorists, who demonstrate that more technology does not necessarily mean more safety, and that effective learning from past incidents is very difficult, if not impossible.[58] Finally, nuclear security procedures and controls are only as strong as their weakest part, and, as in most other organizations, that is often the human element. This starts at the top. As U.S. expert Bruce Blair puts it, "No system of safeguards can reliably guard against misbehavior at the very apex of government."[59]

The history of the Cold War also shows that a few individuals, sometimes even one single person, stand between the risk of nuclear tragedy and return to normalcy. In April 1961, General Jean Thiry, the commander of the French nuclear testing grounds in the Sahara, decided to refuse to obey the rebels who had taken over Algiers and wanted him to give them control of a nuclear device that was ready to be tested.[60] On October 27, 1962, Vassili Arkhipov, a Soviet officer on board an attack submarine near Cuba, may have saved the world by refusing to launch a nuclear-tipped torpedo against U.S. forces. In November 1983, in the midst of acute Soviet paranoia about Western military intentions, NATO decided to tone down a major exercise entitled Able Archer-83, by taking out the direct participation of high-ranking civilian and military U.S. officials. This may have been in response to warnings by a KGB double agent, Oleg Gordievsky, that some in Moscow believed a Western nuclear attack was imminent.[61] In August 1991, the chiefs of the three Soviet strategic services decided to cut off the coup leaders from the nuclear Command, Control, and Communications (C3) system in order to avoid any dangerous or reckless decisions.[62] Strategic Forces Commander General Y. P. Maksimov also decided to visibly lower the alert level of Soviet mobile missiles, allegedly in order to reassure Washington.[63]

Experience, wisdom, sound procedures, and technological improvements may have contributed to the absence of a nuclear explosion or to the transfer of nuclear weapons. But the absence of nuclear use cannot rely only on loyalty, cool-headedness, good management practices, and technical fixes. It is possible that, "To have so successfully prevented accidental nuclear explosions, tens of thousands of obscure soldiers must have taken much greater care than is taken in any other situation involving human agents and complex mechanical systems. To bypass every opportunity to buy or build nuclear weapons, hundreds of terrorist leaders must have shrunk from exploring those opportunities."[64] But even if that was true, are we willing to bet that it will continue to be the case for the next 60 years? We would do so at our own peril.

ENDNOTES - CHAPTER 1

1. On the risk of nuclear accidents and crises stemming from organizational issues and human failures, two pioneering studies are Bruce G. Blair, *The Logic of Accidental Nuclear War*, Washington, DC: Brookings Institution Press, 1991; and Scott D. Sagan, *The Limits of Safety: Organizations, Accidents, and Nuclear Weapons*, Princeton, NJ: Princeton University Press, 1993.

2. According to the U.S. Department of Defense, "surety" includes safety, security, reliability, and control of use. See section 5.4.1 - DoD and DOE Safety Programs, "Chapter 5: Nuclear Safety and Security," in *The Nuclear Matters Handbook*, Expanded Version, available from *www.acq.osd.mil/ncbdp/nm/nm_book_5_11/ chapter_5.htm*. Our project covers, broadly speaking, the second and fourth categories.

3. For a good summary of existing procedures in each country, see Hans Born *et al.*, eds., *Governing the Bomb: Civilian and Democratic Accountability of Nuclear Weapons*, Oxford, UK: Oxford University Press, 2010.

4. Richard Rhodes, *The Twilight of the Bombs: Recent Challenges, New Dangers, and the Prospects of a World Without Nuclear Weapons*, New York: Alfred A. Knopf, 2010, p. 93.

5. Peter Vincent Pry, *War Scare: Russia and America on the Nuclear Brink*, Westport, CT: Praeger, 1999, pp. 85, 151; and J. Michael Waller, "Changing the Nuclear Command," *Insight on the News*, Vol. 17, No. 7, February 19, 2001.

6. Details on the exact Soviet command and control arrangements remain unclear. One account suggests that the General Secretary had the authority to order the use of nuclear weapons and that the actual execution of the order was subordinated to a direct command by the General Staff. David E. Hoffman, *The Dead Hand: The Untold Story of the Cold War Arms Race and Its Dangerous Legacy*, New York: Doubleday, 2009, p. 149. Another account states that the "permission command" (i.e., the political authorization) was intended to be formed jointly by the president, the minister of defense, and the chief of the general staff, but that the "direct command" could technically be given without such a permission command (though it required concurrent decisions by the general staff and the strategic rocket forces). See Blair, *The Logic of Accidental Nuclear War*, pp. 72, 86.

7. Alexei Arbatov, quoted in Pry, *War Scare*, p. 147.

8. Alexei Arbatov, "Russia," in Born *et al.*, *Governing the Bomb*, pp. 73-74. See also Pry, *War Scare*, pp. 150-151; and Waller, "Changing the Nuclear Command."

9. Pry, *War Scare*, pp. 150-153.

10. Bates Gill and Evan S. Medeiros, "China," in Born *et al.*, *Governing the Bomb*, pp. 147, 149-150.

11. This project applies only to nuclear weapons, not fissile materials stockpiles.

12. Peter D. Feaver, "Command and Control in Emerging Nuclear Nations," *International Security*, Vol. 17, Winter 1992-93.

13. The U.S. North American Air Defense (NORAD) command had the authority to fire nuclear weapons in combat without the specific approval of the president. In addition, most U.S. nuclear-armed air defense interceptors were single-seat aircraft, which precluded the implementation of the "two-man rule," the only existing security feature at the time, since PALs had not yet been introduced. In addition, SAC had the authority to launch a retaliatory strike after verifying that an enemy nuclear strike was under way in circumstances when the president was not available.

14. Peter Stein and Peter Feaver, *Assuring Control over Nuclear Weapons: The Evolution of Permissive Action Links*, Cambridge, MA: Center for Science and International Affairs, Harvard University, 1987.

15. Testimony of Admiral Sabbagh in Université de Franche-Comté, Institut Charles de Gaulle, ed., *L'Aventure de la Bombe: De Gaulle et la dissuasion nucléaire (The Adventure of the Bomb: De Gaulle and Nuclear Deterrence)*, Paris, France: Plon, 1984, p. 336.

16. The ability of Soviet SSBN commanders to fire their missiles without a coded input from a higher authority is disputed by Blair. See Blair, *The Logic of Accidental Nuclear War*, pp. 97-98, 160.

17. "British nukes protected by bicycle lock keys," BBC Press Release, November 15, 2007, available from *www.bbc.co.uk/pressoffice/pressreleases/stories/2007/11_november/15/newsnight.shtml*.

18. Sagan, *The Limits of Safety*, pp. 266-267. Reasons given include the fact that some new nuclear-capable nations would not be able to afford modern safety features; the weight and power of military services in some of these countries (an echo to Lewis Dunn's preoccupations mentioned above); and the existence of strong pressures to keep their nuclear arsenals on a high state of readiness (something that, however, did not materialize, as far as is known, for India and Pakistan).

19. Analysts suggest that this is due to two structural characteristics of many organizations' operating dangerous technologies: "interactive complexity" (which produces unanticipated failures); and, "tight-coupling" (which causes the failures to escalate out of control). See Sagan, *The Limits of Safety*.

20. This list includes neither nuclear weapons accidents per se (e.g., Palomares, 1966; Thule, 1968) nor false alarms created by purely technical "glitches," such as those that happened in the United States in June 1980 or in the Soviet Union in September 1983.

21. See Chap. 2 by Tertrais in this volume.

22. Sagan, *The Limits of Safety*, p. 99.

23. *Ibid.*, pp. 130-131.

24. David H. Hackworth, "Hell in a Handbasket," *Maxim*, January 2001.

25. See Chap. 3 by Stokes in this volume.

26. *Ibid.*

27. John Wilson Lewis and Litai Xue, *Imagined Enemies: China Prepares for Uncertain War*, Stanford, CA: Stanford University Press, 2008, pp. 176-178.

28. *China Builds the Bomb*, Stanford, CA: Stanford University Press, 1988, pp. 201-205.

29. Leonard S. Spector, *Going Nuclear*, Cambridge MA: Ballinger, 1987, pp. 32-37.

30. Hoffman, *The Dead Hand*, p. 381; Philip Taubman, *The Partnership: Five Cold Warriors and Their Quest to Ban the Bomb*, New York: Harper, 2012, p. 200.

31. Bruce G. Blair, "Keeping Presidents in the Nuclear Dark (Episode #1: The Case of the Missing Permissive Action Links)," *Bruce Blair's Nuclear Column,* Center for Defense Information, February 11, 2004.

32. Sagan, *The Limits of Safety*, pp. 228-230.

33. Blair, "Keeping Presidents in the Nuclear Dark."

34. Jacques Séguéla, "La clé atomique" ("The Atomic Key"), *Le Nouvel Observateur (The New Observer)*, January 5-11, 2006; Victoria Gairin, "Derrière les murs du Château" ("Behind the Walls of the Castle"), *Le Point*, March 29, 2012. The same misadventure reportedly happened to U.S. President Jimmy Carter, whose suit did go to the dry cleaner. Hackworth, "Hell in a Handbasket."

35. See Chap. 5 by Khan in this volume.

36. Andrew and Leslie Cockburn, *One Point Safe*, New York: Doubleday, 1997, pp. 9-12.

37. See Chap. 4 by Sokov in this volume.

38. *Ibid.*; and Pry, *War Scare*, p. 113.

39. Arbatov, "Russia," p. 74.

40. Pry, *War Scare*, p. 85; and Jonathan Stevenson, *Thinking Beyond the Unthinkable: Harnessing Doom From the Cold War to the Age of Freedom*, New York: Viking, 2008, p. 205.

41. See Chap. 4 by Sokov in this volume. See also William Potter, "Ukraine's Nuclear Trigger," *The New York Times*, November 10, 1992.

42. Pry, *War Scare*, p. 197.

43. *Ibid.*, pp. 175-176.

44. Arbatov, "Russia," p. 59; Pry, *War Scare*, pp. 217-218, 224, 234.

45. Pry, *War Scare*, pp. 218-230.

46. *Ibid.*, pp. 196-197.

47. Hackworth, "Hell in a Handbasket." The author mentions several other episodes of accidental or deliberate separations between the President and the "football."

48. John Donvan, "President Bill Clinton Lost Nuclear Codes While in Office, New Book Claims," *ABC News*, October 20, 2010.

49. Shaun Gregory, "The Terrorist Threat to Pakistan's Nuclear Weapons," *CTC Sentinel*, Vol. 2, No. 7, 2009; "Terrorist Tactics Threaten Nuclear Weapons Safety," *CTC Sentinel*, Vol. 4, No. 6, 2011.

50. Hans M. Kristensen, "U.S. Nuclear Weapons Site in Europe Breached," *FAS Strategic Security Blog*, February 4, 2010.

51. Lewis A. Dunn, "Military Politics, Nuclear Proliferation, and the 'Nuclear Coup d'Etat,'" *The Journal of Strategic Studies*, Vol. 1, No. 1, May 1978.

52. *Ibid.*, p. 46.

53. Spector, *Going Nuclear*.

54. For instance, the Pakistani study does not cover the sale or transfer of Pakistani weapons designs.

55. Spector, *Going Nuclear*, p. 58.

56. Spector also wondered about the fate of the South African nuclear program when the apartheid would collapse. See *Ibid.*, p. 59.

57. See Richard V. Allen, "The Day Reagan Was Shot," *Hoover Digest*, No. 3, July 30, 2001.

58. See Sagan, *The Limits of Safety*, pp. 207-210.

59. Quoted in Rhodes, *Twilight of the Bombs*, p. 95.

60. See Chap. 2 by Tertrais in this volume.

61. There is no certainty about the role that Gordievsky may have played. See Benjamin B. Fischer, *A Cold War Conundrum: The 1983 Soviet War Scare*, Washington, DC: Central Intelligence Agency, July 7, 2008; Pry, *War Scare*, p. 38.

62. Mikhail Tsypkin, "Adventures of the 'Nuclear Briefcase': A Russian Document Analysis," *Strategic Insights*, Vol. III, Issue 9, September 2004.

63. Rhodes, *Twilight of the Bombs*, p. 94. It should be noted that there are diverging views about the role of Maksimov. Pry argues that the missiles were in fact recalled to the garrison in order to ensure that their crews could be directly supervised, at a time when the coup leaders had put the Soviet nuclear forces on alert even before declaring a new government. See *War Scare*, p. 83, 156.

64. Theodore Caplow, *Armageddon Postponed: A Different View of Nuclear Weapons*, Lanham, MD: Hamilton Books, 2010, p. 38.

PART I:
CASE STUDIES

CHAPTER 2

A "NUCLEAR COUP"?
FRANCE, THE ALGERIAN WAR,
AND THE APRIL 1961 NUCLEAR TEST

Bruno Tertrais

The author would like to thank Pierre Abramovici for having provided him with some of the source materials (interviews) he used for his book, Jeffrey Lewis for having provided him with a copy of the Brennan article (which is almost impossible to find), and Marie-France Lathuile and Anne Pasquier for their assistance in researching for this paper. He is grateful to Samy Cohen, Brian Jenkins, Henry Sokolski, Maurice Vaïsse, and Randy Willoughby for their thoughtful reviews and comments.

The strategic literature about the risk of nuclear proliferation and of nuclear terrorism sometimes mentions a little-known episode of French colonial history: a nuclear test that took place in April 1961 while four generals mounted a coup in Algiers against the nascent Fifth Republic. The first mention of this episode in publications devoted to international security issues appears to have been a 1968 short journal article by Donald Brennan and Leonard Spector's pioneering book, *Going Nuclear* (1987). To the best of this author's knowledge, no detailed analysis of the 1961 events has ever been published.[1]

Conventional wisdom—various citations of the episode that appear in the literature, mostly based on the two aforementioned accounts—has it that France decided to detonate the nuclear device rather than run the risk of having it captured by the rebel forces. At the same time, one of the foremost experts in the field of terrorism, Brian Jenkins, argued in a recent book — based on conversations with former French officials — that he became convinced that the story was bunk and that experts should cease mentioning it as an example of the risks of nuclear terror.[2]

This chapter seeks to reconstruct the 1961 events and the intentions of the various parties involved to the fullest possible extent. To that effect, it relies heavily on sources that have become available since the 1968 and 1987 studies were published. These include two well-documented books on the Algiers coup published in 2011, on the occasion of the 50th anniversary of the coup, one by historian Maurice Vaïsse and the other by journalist Pierre Abramovici. The sources also include two books on the history of the French nuclear program published a few years ago, one by analyst Jean-Damien Pô and the other by historian André Bendjebbar.[3] This chapter also relies, crucially, on personal testimonies of key actors.[4] Sources used in this chapter also include information about the history of French nuclear testing made public (through publication or leaks) in France at the occasion of the 1995-96 final series of tests and about recent controversies regarding the human and environmental effects of testing in Algeria. Finally, the sources include information provided to the author by the French Atomic Energy Commission (Commissariat à l'Energie Atomique [CEA]).[5]

The chapter will in particular address two sets of questions. One is about the timing of the April 1961 test. Was it in any way affected by the ongoing political events in Algeria? If yes, what did the French authorities seek in altering that timing? The other set of questions relates to the assessment of the actual risks that existed during the coup. Was there ever a real risk of the device passing under the control of the rebels? If yes, could they have used it in any way?

As will be seen, what happened during those days in Algeria is complex and supports a more subtle interpretation than either the traditional version of the story or the more recent Jenkins debunking of it—neither of which can be considered as an accurate summary of the events. Both Brennan and Jenkins relied on a small number of testimonies of unnamed former officials: a senior official of the French nuclear establishment (Brennan) and French intelligence officials (Jenkins).

The goal of this chapter is to draw lessons for possible future contingencies in which a nuclear-capable country is threatened from inside and the control of nuclear materials or weapons may be at risk. More broadly, the chapter passes judgment on whether or not this episode is worth giving as an example of the risk of nuclear terrorism.

THE CONTEXT

When General Charles de Gaulle arrived in power in May 1958, he inherited two legacies of the Fourth Republic (1945-58): One was the rebellion in the French departments of Algeria, which was worsening; the other was France's burgeoning nuclear program, which was coming to fruition. In the last days of the Fourth Republic (on April 11), a nuclear test had been scheduled for 1960 by Chairman of the Council [of Ministers] Félix Gaillard.

The two issues rapidly became connected. De Gaulle sought both to transform France's nominal nuclear capability into a full-fledged operational nuclear force, and to solve the Algerian question one way or the other in order to pursue an ambitious foreign policy agenda: He knew that the only way to do that would be to change the territory's status. But these orientations put him on a collision course with a large segment of the French military. Many did not want France to withdraw from Algeria, and most were not interested in an independent nuclear deterrent.[6]

Of these two issues, Algeria in early-1961 was certainly the most important in the eyes of the French armed forces. About 480,000 French military personnel—mostly conscripts—were stationed there to take part in the campaign launched in 1957 to "pacify" the territory in light of growing unrest, rebellion, and terrorism.

In September 1958, 96 percent of Algerian voters had said "yes" to the adoption of the new French constitution. However, a call to boycott the vote had been issued by the Algerian National Liberation Front (Front de Libération Nationale). De Gaulle did not believe that the full integration of Arab and Berber populations into France was sustainable in the long run. In September 1959, he stated that three paths were open to Algeria: full independence, full integration, or—his obvious preference—an "association" with the French Republic.

Even though he had not declared support for independence, de Gaulle probably knew all too well that, having now made clear that he did not favor the status quo, he faced the possibility of a military action against him—by the same group of officers who had helped him return to power. In May 1958, a short-lived coup in Algiers (today often referred to as the "putsch d'Alger") was partly manipulated by the Gaullists. They emphasized the possibility of a coup in Paris itself—a scenario that was indeed very much in the cards and entitled Operation RESURRECTION — which led to the downfall of the Fourth Republic and to the return of de Gaulle to power. At that time, the military believed that he would ensure that France would hold on to its North African territories — not mistakenly, since de Gaulle had not come to power with a clear picture of the Algerian endgame.

In the months following his return to power, de Gaulle removed the leaders of the May 1958 movement — Generals Edmond Jouhaud and Edouard Salan — from their positions in Algiers. On September 16, 1959, he alluded for the first time to the possibility of "self-determination" for Algeria.[7] In January 1960, a short-lived insurrection (semaine des barricades) led by opponents to de Gaulle's policy, took place in Algiers and Paris.[8] It was triggered by the recall to France of General Massu, another leader of the 1958 movement. In March, General Maurice Challe, who had been appointed by de Gaulle as the head of all French forces in Algeria in December 1958, was replaced. In December, massive demonstrations in favor of independence took place throughout Algeria. De Gaulle began referring to the hypothetical possibility of an "Algerian Republic."[9] On January 8, 1961, 75 percent of the French approved by referendum the self-determination of the Algerian territories. In April, De Gaulle mentioned for the first time the possibility of "a sovereign Algerian State."[10] This statement and others finally convinced those among the French military who sought to oppose Algerian independence that the dice were cast. General Challe took the leadership of a military conspiracy to stop the political process leading to Algerian independence.

Meanwhile, Algeria had been chosen as early as July 1957 as the location for the first French nuclear tests, due to the existence of large inhabited regions in the south of the territory with geologically favorable conditions. A 108,000-square kilometers (km) inhabited zone was designated as military grounds and named the Sahara Center for Military Experiments (Centre Saharien d'Expérimentations Militaires, CSEM). Starting in October and throughout 1957, the CEA and the armed forces built the necessary facilities near Reggan, a small town of about 8,000 inhabitants (see Figure 2-1).[11] The base and testing grounds were placed under military command. Up to 10,000 civilian and military personnel were stationed in and around Reggan.[12]

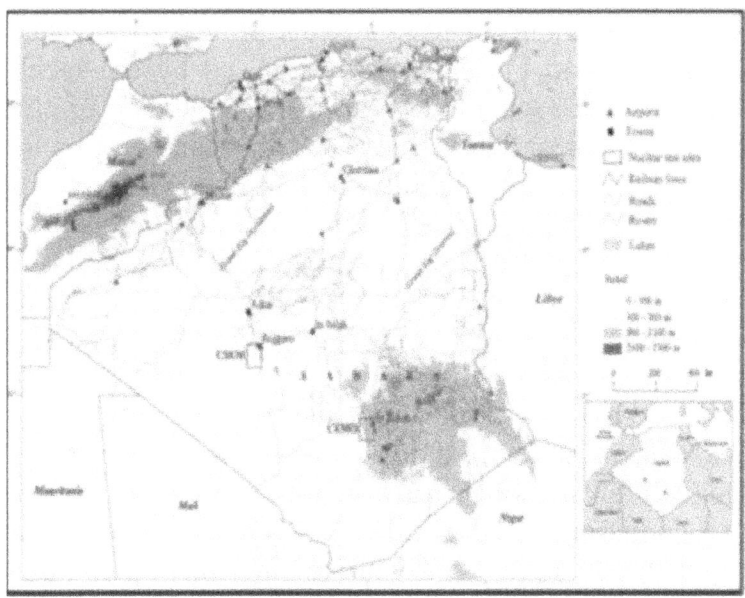

Figure 2-1. The Location of the Reggan Test Site (CSEM).

The French testing site had complex command arrangements:
- The CSEM was in charge of the site itself, which comprised four locations: offices in Reggan; technical facilities, housing, and logistics at the "base-vie" 15 km from the town; the Hamoudia observation and command post some 35 km from the "base-vie"; and the "ground zero" area another 15 km away. The CSEM was headed by a colonel, and reported for operational purposes to the Paris-based Joint Special Weapons Command (Commandement Interarmées des Armes Spéciales [CIAS]), a ministry of defense structure.[13] However, for territorial defense and law and order maintenance, the CSEM reported to the Sahara area command.[14]
- The tests themselves were the responsibility of a unit called the Operational Group of Nuclear Experiment (Groupement Opérationnel des Expérimentations Nucléaires, [GOEN]), which included both military and civilian experts. Led by a general who was also the head of the CIAS, this separate and temporary unit reported both to the ministry of defense and to the CEA. It included a joint dedicated military force, the 621st Special Weapons Group (Groupe d'Armes Spéciales), which regrouped all military personnel assigned to the GOEN. There was a dedicated communication link between the GOEN and the CIAS headquarters.

Neither of these two units reported directly to Algiers, upon which they depended only for their supplies.

THE EVENT

The Coup.

The rebellion began during the night of Friday-Saturday, April 21-22, 1961. The leaders were Challe and his predecessor in Algeria, General Raoul Salan, as well as Generals Edmond Jouhaud and André Zeller. They could count on the support from the onset of at least six regiments of the French armed forces.[15] By Saturday, April 22, in the morning, Algiers was fully in the hands of the rebels, who made a radio proclamation announcing their success and sent the loyalist leaders to the south of the territory.[16] By then, Challe and his acolytes could count on the support of about 25,000 military personnel.[17] Paris became awash with rumors of an imminent military action against the metropolitan territory.[18]

This sequence of events happened just as the Reggan base was preparing for the fourth French nuclear test. Codenamed "Gerboise verte" ("Green Jerboa"), this explosion of a fourth plutonium fission device ("R1") was planned to be the last atmospheric test in the Sahara before the base moved on to subterranean tests in a different location in Algeria.

Evidence exists that the rebels were fully aware of the upcoming test and sought to exploit the circumstances to their benefit. But was the timing of Gerboise verte affected by the political events? And, if yes, what did the French authorities seek in altering the timing of the test?

There is no doubt that the detonation of the R1 device had been organized well in advance. One source mentions a March 3 press article that announced the fourth French nuclear test, "probably for April."[19] At the occasion of the test, an exercise had been planned as early as February.[20] The idea was to benefit from the test to study the conditions of fighting in a nuclear environment. (The previous test of December 27, 1960, had also involved such an exercise). According to the CEA, the "operation order" for the test had been given on March 30; it stipulated that the test would take place on or after April 24, but the date had later been changed to May 1, since the technical preparation of the device needed more time.[21]

The Events in Paris and Reggan (Saturday, April 22, to Monday, April 24).

De Gaulle learned of the coup in the early hours of Saturday, April 22. At 9:00 a.m., he met with Prime Minister Michel Debré, who left the Elysée at 11:20 a.m.[22] It was during this meeting, or immediately afterward, that de Gaulle decided to move forward the date of the test, since a conversation with the Reggan authorities took place at 11:30 a.m.[23] De Gaulle believed that the coup would not last more than 3 days.[24] This is an important element: It means that he sought to influence the events through the test. At 5:00 p.m., a special meeting of the Council of Ministers decided to impose a state of emergency taking effect at midnight. On Sunday evening, a telegram was sent to the French ambassador in Morocco, requesting him to notify King Hassan of the imminence of the test, clearly referring implicitly to the ongoing coup.[25]

News of the coup reached Reggan on Saturday, April 22, around 9:00 a.m.[26] However, two contradictory orders were received in the next 24 hours.[27] One was given by Paris, ordering that the device be tested. It was possibly a telegram signed by de Gaulle himself.[28] Standard procedure was that a green light was given by the Elysée, and that the Reggan authorities decided on the exact day of the test.[29] But another order was given by Challe from Algiers, requesting that the test be delayed.[30] The putsch leaders may have been warned of the impending test by the Notice to Airmen (NOTAM) delivered by Thiry.[31] More precisely, according to a key witness — Professor Yves Rocard, one of the fathers of the French program — Challe called General Jean Thiry, the commander of the CIAS/GOEN, who knew him well (they were both fellow air force generals). Rocard told Thiry: "Refrain from detonating your little bomb, keep it for us, it will always be useful."[32]

The CSEM and GOEN personnel were culturally inclined to be faithful to de Gaulle, since their mission was the nuclear program.[33] But Thiry was hesitant about which party to support. His exact mindset is difficult to assess. Some claim that he initially decided to side with the rebels before changing his mind 24 hours later. Others state that he was impressed with Challe's order but that, in his phone conversation with Challe, remained deliberately vague and uncommitted about his intentions.[34]

There are differing accounts of the exact chronology of events:
- There is uncertainty about when the order to proceed with the test on (or after) Monday, April 24, was given by Paris. A key witness, Jean Bellec, who was then an officer stationed at Reggan, claims that on Saturday, April 22, at 11:30 a.m., after having conferred with Paris, the CSEM and GOEN made the decision to test on April 24.[35] However, a CEA document suggests that on April 22, "it was contemplated to

proceed with the test as soon as possible" but that it is only the next day, Sunday, April 23, that the formal order was given to detonate the device "on or after the 24th."[36]
- It is also uncertain when the final decision to proceed with the test on Tuesday, April 25, was given by Thiry. Bellec claims that the decision was made on April 23, because of unfavorable wind conditions expected for April 24.[37] However, another source based on the recollection of another key witness, Pierre Billaud, has Thiry, "probably in the morning of the 24th," deciding to proceed with the test on April 25.[38]

The weather was a nontrivial consideration in Thiry's calculations and his final decision to test on April 25 at dawn:
- With each day, the temperature was rising on the site — this part of the Sahara is one of the hottest places in the world — and the measurement instruments were becoming unreliable. There was a risk that the test would be rendered scientifically useless, so it could not be postponed too long.[39] The DAM personnel on the site were "haunted by the deterioration of operational conditions due to excessive heat, and wanted to proceed with the detonation early."[40]
- To ensure the best optical measurements, and also because of the heat, French atmospheric tests in the Sahara had to be conducted at dawn (the four tests all took place between 6:00 a.m. and 7:00 a.m.), and technical preparations no doubt took at least several hours. So, in the absence of a decision the day before, another 24 hours would be lost.

- At the same time, another meteorological element had to be taken into account when making the final decision: wind patterns. Sources converge to suggest that the forecast for April 24 was unfavorable, but more favorable for April 25.[41]

But there is little doubt that political considerations were a key factor. Jean Viard, the director of the technical team, feared that the device could have been used by Algiers as a bargaining chip against Paris.[42] This is supported by the testimony of Bellec, who writes that concern existed that the rebels could use the device as an instrument of "blackmail, at least through the media."[43]

The atmosphere at the base during those days is described in various testimonies as "changing," "uncertain," or "turbulent." On April 22, news reports gave the impression that most of Northern Algeria had passed under the control of the rebels.[44] A reflection of the uncertainty reigning on the site is that bulletins delivered to base personnel quoted both the statements provided by Algiers and those sent by Paris.[45] In the afternoon of April 23, it had been learned that General Gustave Mentré, commander of the French forces in the Sahara region, had sided with the rebels; he put additional pressure on Thiry to refrain from testing the device.[46] Mentré's Algiers-based command issued orders to the effect that all units in the region — including the CSEM — obey Challe's orders.[47] Thus, Thiry hesitated. Billaud suggests that, at this point, he may have used the unfavorable weather forecast as a pretext for waiting to see where, so to speak, the political winds were blowing.[48]

Uncertainties about the Loyalties of On-site Troops.

Another element was in play. There were doubts about the loyalty of the on-site military units, and some of them "more or less openly advertised their sympathy with the rebellion."[49] It was rumored on the base that some of the units had been relocated to the Sahara because of their sympathy for the cause of "Algérie française."[50] A total of 424 soldiers had been sent to Reggan for a military exercise to take place during the test.[51] Colonel Celerier, head of the CSEM, decided to have the armored forces stationed for a long duration under the desert sun in the disguise of an exercise. The uncertainty about the loyalty of some elements on the base played both ways: not proceeding with the test for fear of a fight on the base, or proceeding with the test as quickly as possible to get rid of the device.

Viard and other CEA personnel on the site urged Thiry to proceed with the test for both weather and security reasons.[52] Billaud recounts that the Elysée intervened twice to hasten the test, obviously, according to him, for political reasons.[53] In normal times, only one "green light" was needed from the Elysée. It is unknown whether the Paris authorities, who had cracked the code used by the rebels for their radio communications, were aware of Challe's call to Thiry.[54]

On Monday, April 24, Celerier still feared an action by the armored units, who the night before had hailed the news of a possible coup in Paris itself.[55] According to Abramovici, this consideration was paramount in the decision to test as quickly as possible.[56] If one assumes that the decision to test on the morning of April 25 had not yet been confirmed, it is certain at that point (on April 24) that it was.

Early in the afternoon, soldiers participating in the exercise were ordered to take their positions near the ground zero site near Hamoudia.[57] In the evening, the base personnel were informed that the test would take place the next morning.[58]

In an episode that seems more of a Mel Brooks parody than a James Bond movie, when it came to transporting the device to the tower some 50 km away, Jean Viard decided to have the heavily guarded official convoy leave without anything on board, while a CEA engineer, Pierre Thierry, transported the physics package in his modest 2CV (deux chevaux) car.[59] But the weather conditions then took a bad turn, with sand winds blowing all over the testing grounds.[60]

The Test (Tuesday, April 25).

At 3:00 a.m. on April 25, communications with Algiers were cut off by Reggan in order to ensure that the news of the test would be announced by Paris and not by the rebels.[61] At 6:05, the device was detonated. The test was immediately made public by Paris through a bland government communiqué that made no reference to the most particular circumstances under which it was done.[62]

In Algiers, the Sahara command of General Mentré continued to send telexes to his troops, urging them to support the coup.[63] But that same morning, unknown to base personnel, Mentré met with Challe in Algiers and came out of the meeting convinced that the putsch was doomed. He flew to the base on the evening of the same day — not to seize control of it, but to hide himself from Paris.[64] Two hours later, at 11:00 p.m., it was announced at the base that the coup had failed.[65]

Unknown to the Reggan loyalists, the coup had in fact failed the previous night, just as they were getting ready for the final countdown: In Algiers, around 2:00 a.m., the four generals had decided to give up and had separated.[66]

Evidence Behind the "Political" Nature of the Timing.

There is little doubt that the timing of the test was at least partly political. In addition to de Gaulle's orders, various testimonies mentioned above concur that concern was high among the military and civilian leadership at the site. One of the main figures of the French nuclear program, Yves Rocard, writes that the decision was meant to "clean the site of any atomic bomb and divert the rebellion's attention away from it."[67] Likewise, the CEA engineer in charge of the device, Pierre Billaud, says that "political circumstances" dictated of the decision to test on April 25.[68] Moreover, the change in weather conditions (the sand winds) did not deter Thiry from giving the final go-ahead.

The yield of the device provides another clue. Various official sources refer merely to a yield of less than five kilotons, the same vague characterization as that of the two previous tests (Gerboise blanche and Gerboise rouge).[69] It seems clear, however, that the test was a partial failure. But there is no evidence behind Brennan's 1968 anonymous source's assertion that the device had been "optimized" to ensure detonation even if it meant a lower yield.[70] The official report for the CEA activities of 1961 is unusually modest regarding the results of Gerboise verte, an indication of the fact that they were somewhat disappointing.[71] An early account suggested a yield of less than one kiloton.⁷² The unpublished memoirs of Pierre Billaud state that the delivered energy was 5 percent of what had been planned, and put the yield at 0.7 kiloton instead of the anticipated 15 kilotons.⁷³ There is, in fact, some uncertainty at the CEA itself about the yield delivered (probably due to the fact that weather conditions precluded a precise measurement). A classified report gives several different values, ranging from 0.7 to 1.2 kilotons—for an anticipated yield of 6 to 18 kilotons.⁷⁴

An additional element in support of the fact that Gerboise verte was a partial fizzle is the high residual activity of Pu239 and Pu240 on the site, which were estimated in 2005 as being much higher than the activity stemming from the two previous tests (which were also of low energy).⁷⁵

According to several testimonies, the reason behind this failure is that the neutron initiation of the fission reaction failed to take place properly.⁷⁶ One of the main goals of Gerboise verte was to test a new implosion architecture and a new architecture of the physics package, allowing for better safety.⁷⁷ Two different explanations exist about what exactly took place, but they complement each other and support, each in its own way, the hypothesis of a hasty—and thus political—decision to test. According to Pô, the final preparation of the device, as far as the neutron initiation was concerned, had not yet taken place in Reggan when the order to test was given by Paris.⁷⁸ As mentioned above, before the coup the CEA had moved the planned date of the test to May 1 because the device was not ready. According to Pierre Billaud—who was in charge of the test—the weather was the main culprit: Because of the heat and strong sand winds, the neutron flux was delivered 5 micro-seconds too early, which explains the low yield delivered.⁷⁹ As stated above, the atmospheric conditions unexpectedly turned bad the day before or the night preceding the test. In normal circumstances, says Billaud, the test should have been postponed.[80] Thiry had the authority to stop the process, but he did not do it.

To sum up, orders from Paris, uncertain political conditions on the base, and the increasing heat in the region pushed for a test as soon as possible. These factors prevailed against orders from Algiers. Unexpected sand winds, which endangered the scientific value of the test, were not enough for Thiry to reverse his decision.

What Did the Loyalists Seek?

What did de Gaulle seek in moving forward the date of the test? Was it really to avoid the capture of the weapon, as stated in the Brennan article?

In fact, available evidence overwhelmingly suggests that moving the date was to make a symbolic show of authority in the eyes of the French population, the armed forces, and the world. Several sources converge in this regard. One is an early and well-informed account of the coup.[81] The others are three key witnesses who were close to de Gaulle and were interviewed by Abramovici in the 1990s for his book. According to then-Defense Minister Pierre Messmer, de Gaulle sought to "give a lesson to the rebels" and "send a message to the rest of the world." Colonel Pierre Dabezies, who was then an assistant to Messmer, said that de Gaulle's purpose was to "show who the boss was." Bernard Tricot, then an assistant to the president, remembers that de Gaulle "wanted to send a message to Algiers. He requested the shot to be made earlier than planned so that it was made clear that

France never abdicated."[82] Logic also supports this thesis. Had de Gaulle feared a capture of the weapon, he would have ordered the device to be scuttled and the test to take place immediately.[83] The fact that the military exercises scheduled during the test, as well as simultaneous "cold" nuclear experiments, took place as originally planned, is another clue that the process was hasty but not hurried.[84]

However, Thiry's "tactical" decision to test on Tuesday, April 25, and maintain it despite last-minute unfavorable wind conditions was at least partly driven by on-site security considerations (the fear of a capture), though increasing heat on the site was also a factor. If so, one question remains: If security was uncertain and the weather was getting hotter and hotter, why did Thiry decide that the test would take place only on Tuesday, April 25, and not on Monday, April 24, since he apparently had the authority to do so, and was requested to test as early as possible, on or after April 24? There are two possible explanations. First, the winds were not expected to be favorable in the early hours of April 24 (an explanation consistent with the CEA document and Bellec's testimony). Second, Thiry may still have been uncertain about his political loyalties during the whole day of Sunday, April 23 (an explanation consistent with Bendjebbar's account, based on Billaud's testimony).[85] These two explanations are not incompatible.

Whatever the reality, what Paris had sought to convey is that it was business as usual that day, Tuesday 25, 1961, at the Reggan test site.[86]

The Aftermath.

The coup ended rather quickly. In the evening of April 23, de Gaulle made a major speech on television, and the government mobilized the population in support of the Paris authorities. He resorted to Article 16 of the new constitution, giving him full powers—in effect, a form of legal counter-coup.[87] Faced with limited support in Algeria and even less in the metropolitan territory, the generals gave up during the night of April 24-25. De Gaulle had been right: The coup had lasted 3 days. In the end, the nuclear event of 1961 appears as the perfect symbol of de Gaulle's consolidation of power. For beyond its security and diplomatic value, the nuclear program was also, to some extent, an instrument to control the armed forces.[88]

It is interesting to note, in this regard, that two of the leaders of the 1961 coup, Generals Salan and Jouhaud, were vocal opponents to the nuclear program.[89] While they might not have guessed that nuclear weapons were going to consolidate the primacy of the politicians over the military, they perfectly understood that de Gaulle's priorities—building an independent deterrent and withdrawing from the NATO integrated military command—conflicted with an enduring, politically and financially costly "pacification" operation in Algeria.[90] De Gaulle's historical speech of November 3, 1959, to the armed forces had heralded the withdrawal from the NATO integrated command and drawn the contours of a new defense policy, without once mentioning Algeria; what he had hoped for that day was to stir patriotism and encourage French soldiers to think beyond their obsession with what was then called the "pacification" of Algeria.[91] It was, as a historian put it, "either Algeria or the Bomb."[92]

The choice, for de Gaulle, was "trading Algiers for Mururoa," as another one writes.[93]

The 1961 event is also connected in several respects to the decision taken less than a year later to propose the popular election of the President of the Republic (who was until then elected by a college of 81,000 elected officials). First, a direct election would shelter de Gaulle against another attempted military coup—or any other form of sudden eviction from power. Second, one of the reasons behind the 1962 reform was the legitimacy de Gaulle believed he needed to have the sole authority over the employment of nuclear weapons.[94]

The Evian Agreements for the independence of Algeria were signed in March 1962. They stipulated that France would continue to use the Sahara as a nuclear testing ground for 5 years.

QUESTIONS

So, was there ever an actual risk of the device being put under the control of the rebels? If yes, could they have used it in any way?

Was the Device Ever at Risk?

The way the events unfolded, it seems that the device was never really at risk of being controlled by the rebels.[95] For sure, Thiry hesitated for 24 hours, but had he refused to test (he could have, and may have argued that weather conditions were not appropriate), would it have been enough for Algiers to claim control of the bomb? Moreover, this would not have changed anything to the outcome of the coup 1 day later. As far as the insider threat is concerned, there is no evidence that some of the units present in Reggan had the willingness to seize the device, whatever their personal inclinations regarding the coup. Finally, the fact that the test took place in the early hours of the morning, which was standard procedure for technical reasons, is another indication that there was no clear and present danger to the security of the device. Had Thiry's prime objective been to scuttle it in order to prevent its capture, and thus disregard the scientific aspects of the experiment, the test could have taken place at any time.

There is no evidence either that the Algiers generals ever intended to devote the resources needed for a capture of the device. The control of the Sahara, with its vast oil riches and the presence of a nuclear testing and missile proving grounds, would have been an important strategic objective for any power seeking to establish itself in the French Algerian territories. However, nothing indicates that the timing of the coup depended on the planned test or that the control of the testing site was a key objective of the rebels. The question of the fate of the R1 device was probably discussed by Algiers as an afterthought, an opportunity to be seized.[96] In this respect, the 1961 event is very different from the 1991 attempted Soviet coup, when control of nuclear weapons was a central point.[97]

Would It Have Been Possible for the Generals to Take Control of the Device by Force?

If the generals had decided that the device was a key objective, an option would have been for them to ask some of the military forces in Reggan to capture it. As stated, some of the on-site military personnel were clearly sympathetic to the cause of the generals.[98] However, this could have meant a bloody and uncertain battle at the base itself. Moreover, one would have to assume that these units had direct means of communication with Algiers.

Another option would have been for Algiers to organize a dedicated operation to seize the whole testing grounds by force. As stated, the Reggan base was operationally under the control of Paris but organically depended on Algiers for its supplies, which came by air.[99] However, the success of such a move would have meant a significant diversion of rare military resources by the rebels, flying forces — say, one regiment of 1,000-1,500 men — about 1,000 miles south of the coast. (The six regiments that the rebels could count on were needed to control the main coastal cities.) Security at the base was not heavy: Dedicated forces apparently included only a company of soldiers and one platoon of gendarmes (as well as another company in Adrar, some 50 km away from Reggan).[100] The security culture was said to be rather lax (probably because the isolation of the site was its first line of defense).[101] But here, too, such an attack would have meant the risk of fighting at the base itself.[102]

Moreover, the rebels would not necessarily have known whether the elements of the device were stored in Reggan or already transported to the testing grounds. In Reggan, the physics package and the conventional explosives were stored in different locations, at a distance of 200 to 300 meters from each other. The operation would not have been a simple one.[103] Thus, even if the control of the base had been a key objective, by far the best option for the rebels would have been to wait for the coup to succeed and have most of the French forces present in Algeria — including those at the testing site — be under their command.[104] There is not much the CEA experts could have done against that, except, maybe, to sabotage elements of the device to render it inoperable.

If They Had, Could They Have Used the Device?

Even if the rebels had been able to get hold of a functional device, either physically by force or legally by succeeding in their enterprise, they would hardly have been able to use it as a weapon had they wanted to.[105] Assembly was planned to be made by an automated process; a new mechanism would have had to be designed. This automated assembly mechanism was located in the testing tower itself near Hamoudia, some 50 km away from the storage areas (see Figure 2-2). The key to initiate the mechanism was under military control.[106] Also, R1 was a device, not a weapon: Even if assembled, it was not meant to be transported and detonated at will.[107] Thus, the rebels would also have had to design a new mechanism for its remote detonation.

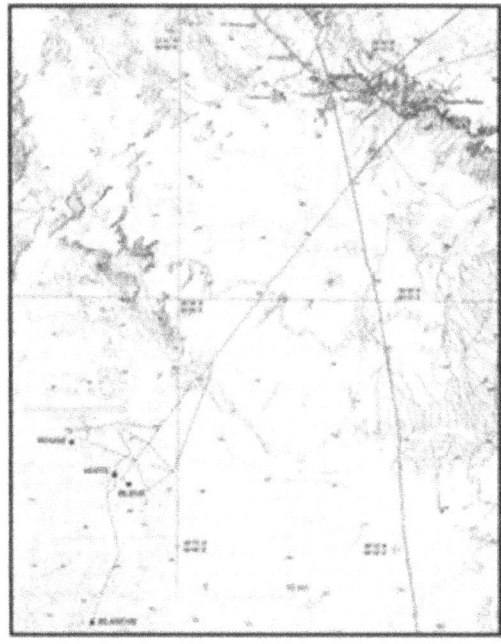

Figure 2-2. The Location of the Four French Tests in Reggan.

More realistically, the control by the rebels of the elements of the device would have been an instrument of political blackmail — as many on the base feared — or more simply and more likely, a testimony of their control over the most potent symbol of French power.[108] According to Pierre Billaud, General Challe's counter-order to Thiry was probably meant to "affirm his control over the Sahara."[109] Just imagine the Paris media announcing, "The rebels have the Bomb!" It would have been, in a sense, poetic justice: the ultimate revenge of the generals against de Gaulle.[110] Whether this would have affected the outcome of the coup in any way remains open to speculation.[111]

LESSONS

How much and how far is this episode worth using in support of the idea that nuclear terrorism is a real danger? Can any parallels be drawn with the foreseeable evolution of contemporary nuclear-capable states?

Lessons that can be learned from this episode include the following:
- The possibility of a nuclear device falling into unauthorized hands (either physically or legally) is not a far-fetched scenario. The very case of France presents other interesting hypotheses. If de Gaulle had not come to power, and the previous regime had completely collapsed in the years 1958 to 1960, control of the first French device by the armed forces, for instance, could have been an important political stake. Also, given that the 1962 Evian Agreements allowed France to continue nuclear testing on its Algerian territory for 5 years, which it did

until 1966, tensions with Paris could have led the Algerian authorities to attempt to seize a device as a bargaining tool (or even perhaps as a short cut to nuclear status).[112]
- The control of nonweaponized devices can become a key political objective for competing armed factions in a situation of political instability. This could happen in countries such as Iran, North Korea, Pakistan, and China. Indeed, particularly interesting scenarios include a secessionist movement in the restless regions of Baluchistan or Turkestan, which respectively host Pakistan and China's testing sites.
- At the same time, a scenario such as the one in 1961 is more likely to happen in an emerging nuclear-capable state with a nascent program and rudimentary means than in a mature nuclear power such as China. Hypothetical future nuclear-armed countries such as Iran, Egypt, and Saudi Arabia could also present risks of dangerous scenarios in case of domestic political turmoil. Iran and Egypt, in particular, would deserve special attention, given the importance of armed forces in their respective political systems.
- An interesting question is whether and how much the technical context would make a difference. Technology diffusion (as well as a greater global sensitivity to nuclear surety concerns) suggests that security of devices and installations such as testing sites, as well as communications between authorities and nuclear installations, could be much better in, say, Iran in 2021 than what they were in France in 1961. For the same reason, contrary to what

happened in 1961, several countries would be able to follow the events in real time by satellite means, and possibly influence the crisis.
- Complex command arrangements for military nuclear activities can prove to be problematic in crisis situations, creating legitimacy conflicts or uncertainties about who controls various nuclear commands and institutions.[113] The personal role of key leaders can make a difference (in this case, that of de Gaulle in Paris and Thiry in Reggan).
- Nuclear weapons can become instrumental in the consolidation of the primacy of civilian power over the military, the primacy of the executive over the legislative branch, and the popular legitimacy of the head of the state. What happened in France was, in a sense, the reverse of what happened later in Pakistan, where control of nuclear weapons reinforced the armed forces' primacy over the civilians.

ENDNOTES - CHAPTER 2

1. Donald G. Brennan, "The Risks of Spreading Weapons: A Historical Case," *Arms Control and Disarmament*, Vol. 1, 1968; and Leonard S. Spector, *Going Nuclear*, Cambridge, MA: Ballinger Publishing Company, 1987, pp. 25-33.

2. "The rumor survived for decades, and I myself was guilty of repeating it until further inquiries with French officials, who had knowledge of these events, put the story in the category of 'never happened.'" Brian Jenkins, *Will Terrorists Go Nuclear?* New York: Prometheus Books, 2008, p. 144.

3. Maurice Vaïsse, *Comment de Gaulle fit échouer le putsch d'Alger (How de Gaulle Foiled the Coup in Algiers)*, Paris, France: André Versaille, 2011; Pierre Abramovici, *Le putsch des généraux: De Gaulle*

contre l'armée, 1958-1961 (*The Generals' Coup: De Gaulle Against the Army, 1958-1961*), Paris, France: Fayard, 2011; Jean-Damien Pô, *Les moyens de la puissance: Les activités militaires du CEA, 1945-2000* (*The Means of Power: The Military Activities of the CEA, 1945-2000*), Paris, France: Ellipses, 2001; André Bendjebbar, *Histoire secrète de la bombe atomique* (*Secret History of the Atomic Bomb*), Paris, France: Le Cherche Midi, 2000.

4. These include, in particular, Yves Rocard, *Mémoires sans concessions* (*Memories without Concessions*), Paris, France: Grasset, 1988; Jean Bellec, "Vie au Sahara"("Life in the Sahara"), *Site Personnel de Jean Bellec* (*Personal Site of Jean Bellec*), available from *www.kerleo.net* (undated); personal testimony to Pierre Abramovici provided to the author; Pierre Billaud, "Souvenirs d'un pionnier de l'armement nucléaire français" ("Recollections of a Pioneer of French Nuclear Weapons"), available from *pbillaud.fr*, 2009; personal communications between Pierre Billaud and the author; personal testimony to Pierre Abramovici provided to the author. Rocard was in charge of the CEA's scientific programs. Bellec was a civilian engineer and an officer at the base. Billaud was a CEA military engineer in charge of coordinating the conception of the French device. He was adjoint technique (technical deputy) at the Département des techniques nouvelles (Department of New Techniques); on the day of the test, he was the chief CEA representative in Reggan.

5. Available French presidential archives do not provide any detail on the episode.

6. See Bruno Tertrais, "'Destruction Assurée': The Origins and Development of French Nuclear Strategy, 1958-1981," in Henry D. Sokolski, ed., *Getting MAD: Nuclear Mutual Assured Destruction, Its Origins and Practice*, Carlisle, PA: Strategic Studies Institute, U.S. Army War College, 2004, p. 62.

7. Allocution by General de Gaulle, Paris, France, September 16, 1959.

8. During this episode, one of de Gaulle's ministers suggested, half-jokingly, it seems, to use the first French device, which was to be tested in Reggan a few days later, against the insurgents in Algiers. Alistair Horne, *A Savage War of Peace: Algeria 1954-1962*, Revised Ed., London, UK: Papermac, 1987, pp. 365-366.

9. Speech by General de Gaulle, Paris, France, November 4, 1960.

10. Press conference by General de Gaulle, Paris, France, April 11, 1961.

11. The base command and the command of the 11th regiment of military engineers were located in the town of Reggan.

12. Ministère de la défense (Ministry of Defense), Délégation à l'Information et à la Communication de la Défense, Dossier de présentation des essais nucléaires et leur suivi au Sahara (Delegation Information and the Communication of the Defense: Presentation File of Nuclear Testing and Monitoring in the Sahara), Paris, France: January 2007, p. 1.

13. The Joint Special Weapons Command had been created in 1951 by General Charles Ailleret to oversee the development of the French nuclear program.

14. Pierre Denis, *L'armée française au Sahara* (*The French Army in the Sahara*), Paris, France: L'Harmattan, 1991, p. 236.

15. Abramovici, *Le putsch des généraux*, p. 196; Vaïsse, *Comment de Gaulle fit échouer le putsch d'Alger*, p. 151.

16. The Algiers officials were sent under guard to In Salah, about 300 km from Reggan.

17. Vaïsse, *Comment de Gaulle fit échouer le putsch d'Alger*, p. 72.

18. Direct action against Paris was indeed planned, but this part of the coup had been neutralized by French authorities as early as April 22 in the morning.

19. Quoted in Bendjebbar, *Histoire secrète de la bombe atomique*, p. 326. This is consistent with Vaïsse's book, which states that the test had been "planned for a long time." Vaïsse, *Comment de Gaulle fit échouer le putsch d'Alger*, p. 78.

20. Various testimonies refer to the name of the exercise as "Hippocampe vert" (Green seahorse). Official documents do not use this name and mention two distinct operations: the "Garigliano" offensive maneuver and the "Bir-Hakeim" defensive maneuver. One armored squadron (reinforced by one armored platoon), one reconnaissance squadron, and one mechanized company were to participate. See *Rapport sur les essais nucléaires français 1960-1996*, Tome I, *La genèse de l'organisation et les expérimentations au Sahara*, (*Report on the French Nuclear Test, 1960-1996, Vol. I, The Genesis of the Organization and the Experiments in the Sahara*), CSEM et CEMO, p. 229-235. (This text is a classified report leaked in 2010.) This "Groupement des essais tactiques" (Tactical Tests Group) had been formed on February 15 and represented a total of 424 soldiers. See Denis, *L'armée française au Sahara*, p. 238. At least 195 soldiers from the 12th armored regiment, with five Patton M47 tanks, had been called from Germany to participate in the event. The date of February is also given by a soldier who participated in the exercise. See Christophe Labbé and Olivia Recasens, "Le secret des irradiés du Sahara" ("The Secret of the Irradiated of the Sahara"), *Le Point*, August 2, 2002. The episode has given rise to a controversy about the possible exposure of French troops to dangerous levels of radiation. The story was first been made public by Vincent Jauvert, "Sahara: les cobayes de 'Gerboise verte'" ("Sahara: Guinea Pigs of 'Green Jerboa'"), *Le Nouvel Observateur* (*The New Observer*), February 5-11, 1998.

21. CEA document communicated to the author.

22. The minutes of de Gaulle's agenda are reproduced in Vaïsse, *Comment de Gaulle fit échouer le putsch d'Alger*, pp. 48-49.

23. Personal testimony of Bellec to Abramovici. See also Abramovici, *Le putsch des généraux*, p. 307. (Abramovici mistakenly mentions the date as April 21 instead of April 22.) Another version has Pierre Messmer, the then-defense minister, ordering to "maintain the planned date," without asking for de Gaulle's authorization. This rather self-serving testimony does not match with the evidence presented in this text, unless Messmer referred to the date of April 24 as originally planned before the putsch. See the personal testimony of Messmer in the report of a roundtable held in June 1992, Groupe d'études français d'histoire de l'armement nucléaire (French Study Group of the History of

Nuclear Weapons), *Les expérimentations nucléaires françaises* (*The French Nuclear Experiments*), Paris, France: Institut d'histoire des relations internationales contemporaines (Institute of the History of Contemporary International Relations), Institut de France, 1993, p. 110.

24. De Gaulle's belief that the coup would last no more than 3 days was conveyed to his advisor Jacques Foccart: "It's a matter of three days." Quoted in Yves Courrières, *La guerre d'Algérie*, Tome 4, *Les feux du désespoir*, (*The War in Algeria*, Vol. 4, *The Fires of Despair*) Paris, France: Fayard, 1971, p. 308.

25. Text quoted in Vaïsse, *Comment de Gaulle fit échouer le putsch d'Alger*, p. 178.

26. Personal testimony of Bellec to Abramovici.

27. Pô, *Les moyens de la puissance*, pp. 139-140.

28. Bendjebbar, *Histoire secrète de la bombe atomique*, p. 329.

29. Personal communication by Pierre Billaud to the author, September 16, 2011.

30. Jacques Fauvet and Jean Planchais, *La fronde des généraux* (*The Revolt of the Generals*), Paris, France: Arthaud, 1961, p. 145.

31. The NOTAM explanation is given by Pierre Billaud. See Billaud, "Souvenirs d'un pionnier de l'armement nucléaire français," and personal testimony of Billaud to Abramovici.

32. Rocard, *Mémoires sans concessions*, p. 322.

33. Jean Bellec, "Vie au Sahara."

34. According to Rocard, he told Challe : "Yes, yes, we'll see." Rocard, *Mémoires sans concessions*, p. 232.

35. Abramovici, *Le putsch des généraux*, pp. 307-308. The book mentions April 21, but the rest of the paragraph suggests that he means April 22.

36. CEA document communicated to the author. Standard procedure was that Thiry had the authority to determine the time of the test, not its date, but he could postpone it. See *Rapport sur les essais nucléaires français 1960-1996*.

37. Personal testimony of Bellec to Abramovici.

38. Bendjebbar, *Histoire secrète de la bombe atomique*, p. 329. Billaud's own account is that he and Viard went to see Thiry "around the 23rd" in order to convince him to go ahead. See Billaud, "Souvenirs d'un pionnier de l'armement nucléaire français."

39. Bendjebbar, *Histoire secrète de la bombe atomique*, p. 328. Billaud's account mentions the risk of a "complete paralysis of the instruments." Billaud, "Souvenirs d'un pionnier de l'armement nucléaire français."

40. Personal testimony of Billaud to Abramovici.

41. CEA document communicated to the author; and Bellec, personal testimony.

42. Pierre Billaud's testimony quoted in Bendjebbar, *Histoire secrète de la bombe atomique,* p. 329; Billaud, "Souvenirs d'un pionnier de l'armement nucléaire français."

43. Bellec, "Vie au Sahara."

44. Abramovici, *Le putsch des généraux*, p. 308.

45. Bellec, "Vie au Sahara."

46. Personal testimony of Bellec to Abramovici.

47. In January 1961, the Sahara Joint Command (Commandement Interarmées au Sahara) had been relocated from Algiers to Reggan, but the decision had not yet been implemented.

48. Personal testimony of Billaud to Abramovici.

49. Abramovici, *Le putsch des généraux*, pp. 307-308; and Billaud, "Souvenirs d'un pionnier de l'armement nucléaire français."

50. Bellec, "Vie au Sahara."

51. Denis, *L'armée française au Sahara*, p. 238.

52. Pierre Billaud's testimony quoted in Bendjebbar, *Histoire secrète de la bombe atomique*, p. 329; Billaud, "Souvenirs d'un pionnier de l'armement nucléaire français"; personal communication of Pierre Billaud to the author, September 15, 2011; personal testimony of Billaud to Abramovici.

53. Personal communication to the author, September 16, 2011.

54. The information about Paris having cracked the code used by the rebels was given to Brian Jenkins by Constantin Melnik, the prime minister's intelligence coordinator. Personal communication of Brian Jenkins to the author, March 15, 2012.

55. Personal testimony of Bellec to Abramovici.

56. Abramovici, *Le putsch des généraux*. pp. 307-308.

57. Testimony of Jean-Francis Rommès, "Le peloton Patton sous Gerboise verte" (The Patton Platoon under Green Jerboa), *Moruroa Mémorial Des Essais Nucléaires Français* (*Moruroa Memorial of French Nuclear Tests*), available from *www.moruroa.org*.

58. Testimony of a soldier quoted in the television documentary *L'Algérie, de Gaulle, et la Bombe* (Algeria, de Gaulle, and the Bomb), directed by Larbi Benchiha, Aligal Production, and France Télévision, 2010.

59. This version is mentioned in the testimony of a CEA engineer, Claude Ayçoberry quoted in Pô, *Les moyens de la puissance*, pp. 139-140. The 2CV was a popular Citröen car, initially produced in 1948 with a view to encourage the transition of the French peasantry to modern vehicles. There are varying accounts of the episode. One states that the package was delivered in one of the utility 2CVs that belonged to the military; see Abramovici, *Le putsch des généraux*, p. 308. Another suggests that the 2CV was indeed driven by CEA personnel, but that choice of the transportation mode was simply dictated by the legendary suspension

mechanism of the car, which had been designed to fit the rocky roads of the French countryside, and thus provided guarantees of safety given the delicate nature of the package (personal testimony of Bellec to Abramovici).

60. An official 2001 report blandly states that the weather conditions "were not conducive to a proper exploitation of the data." Office parlementaire d'évaluation des choix scientifiques et technologiques (Parliamentary Office of Science and Technology Options), *Rapport sur les incidences environnementales et sanitaires des essais nucléaires effectués par la France entre 1960 et 1996 et éléments de comparaison avec les essais des autres puissances nucléaires* (*Report on Environmental and Health impacts of Nuclear Testing by France between 1960 and 1996 and a Comparison with Tests of Other Nuclear Powers*), Assemblée nationale (National Assembly), February 5, 2001, p. 27.

61. Personal testimony of Bellec to Abramovici.

62. Bendjebbar, *Histoire secrète de la bombe atomique*, p. 326.

63. Bellec, "Vie au Sahara."

64. Abramovici, *Le putsch des généraux*, p. 308. Vaïsse seems to imply that Mentré's choice was made on the 24th; see Vaïsse, *Comment de Gaulle fit échouer le putsch d'Alger*, p. 73. However, Mentré himself later reportedly claimed, during his trial, that he had switched his allegiance back to Paris on April 25. Incidentally, he also claimed at that occasion that he had been instrumental in ensuring that the test was conducted. See Spector, *Going Nuclear*, p. 30.

65. Personal testimony of Bellec to Abramovici.

66. Vaïsse, *Comment de Gaulle fit échouer le putsch d'Alger*, p. 83.

67. Rocard, *Mémoires sans concessions*, p. 232.

68. Personal communication with the author, September 15, 2011.

69. There is little official, unclassified information available about French test yields. A comprehensive parliamentary study published in 2001 gives less than five kilotons for the second, third, and fourth tests. Office parlementaire, *Rapport sur les incidences environnementales et sanitaires des essais nucléaires effectués par la France*, p. 26. The same data are given in Ministère de la défense, *Délégation à l'information et à la Communication de la Défense*, p. 1. The government communiqué of April 24, 1961, stated that the explosion was of a "low energy," but this did not mean anything in itself: Five kilotons could be considered "low energy" as compared with the first French test (70 kilotons).

70. Brennan, "The Risks of Spreading Weapons," p. 60. Nor is it clear that this means anything from the technical standpoint.

71. It says that it "allowed the [Military Applications Division of the CEA] and the armed forces to build on the lessons learned at the occasion of the previous explosions, in particular regarding the functioning of the device, its overall effects...." See CEA, *Rapport annuel 1961* (Annual Report, 1961), quoted in Bendjebbar, *Histoire secrète de la bombe atomique*, p. 330. This was not a lie, since the CEA team discovered, at this occasion, unanticipated and valuable information about the behavior of the plutonium sphere during the implosion. Billaud, "Souvenirs d'un pionnier de l'armement nucléaire français," and personal communication with the author, September 15, 2011. In addition, Gerboise verte included progress in the instrumentation of the tests. See, *Rapport sur les essais nucléaires français 1960-1996*, p. 242. The 1961 report also mentioned lessons learned about the "essential characteristics that military equipments and materials must have to ensure an efficient protection of personnel," an obvious reference to the live exercise. Contemporary presentations of the test are balanced. The CEA claims that "the experiment was conducted in a quasi-nominal fashion and almost all the scheduled measurements were acquired" (CEA document communicated to the author). A 1998 official documentary simply mentions Gerboise verte as having been "disappointing" (Histoire des essais nucléaires français, Etablissement de communication et de production audiovisuelle des armées, 1998).

72. Brennan, "The Risks of Spreading Weapons," p. 59.

73. Billaud, "Souvenirs d'un pionnier de l'armement nucléaire français." The author gives slightly different—but not inconsistent—data about the yields in another chapter of his memoirs (0.5-1 kiloton delivered for 10-15 kilotons anticipated).

74. *Rapport sur les essais nucléaires français 1960-1996*, pp. 118, 229, 231.

75. International Atomic Energy Agency, *Radiological Conditions at the Former French Nuclear Test Sites in Algeria: Preliminary Assessment and Recommendations*, 2005, pp. 11-12.

76. Pô, *Les moyens de la puissance*, p. 139; Billaud, "Souvenirs d'un pionnier de l'armement nucléaire français"; and Bellec, "Vie au Sahara."

77. Billaud, "Souvenirs d'un pionnier de l'armement nucléaire français."

78. Pô, *Les moyens de la puissance*, p. 139.

79. Personal communication with the author, September 15, 2011. The same design ended up being successfully tested in 1963. Billaud, "Souvenirs d'un pionnier de l'armement nucléaire français."

80. Personal communication with the author, September 15, 2011.

81. Fauvet and Planchais, *La fronde des généraux*, pp. 231-232.

82. E-mail conversation with Pierre Abramovici, April 9-10, 2012.

83. Historians of the Algerian war have called the test "an extraordinary demonstration of the realities of Gaullist power" (Horne, *A Savage War of Peace*, p. 459), one that "showed the whole world that the Government's authority extended to the far ends of the Sahara," (Fauvet and Planchet, *La fronde des généraux*, p. 232).

84. Two cold experiments involving small amounts of plutonium were separately conducted that day under the code

name "Augias 2." *Rapport sur les essais nucléaires français 1960-1996*, p. 118.

85. A third explanation, that the engineers were requesting more time to prepare the device, would be inconsistent with Billaud's testimony, according to which they were arguing for an early detonation because of heat and security concerns.

86. Pierre Messmer, who was defense minister at that time, claimed in a seminar held in 1992 that, to the best of his knowledge, there had been no pressure from the rebels for the test to not take place. See *Les expérimentations nucléaires françaises*, p. 110. See also above the quotation of former French officials by Brian Jenkins (although contrary to Messmer, the officials in question had perhaps not had access to the relevant information).

87. France remained under Article 16 until October 1961.

88. See for instance Tertrais, "'Destruction Assurée': The Origins and Development of French Nuclear Strategy, 1958-1981."

89. On Salan and the nuclear program see Abramovici, *Le putsch des généraux*, pp. 130-131. Zeller too was against the Bomb, but more for ethical reasons (personal communication by Bernard Zeller, September 13, 2011).

90. "How is the atom bomb going to help us pacify Algeria?" wondered Jouhaud in 1958. "L'heure d'un choix," *L'Air*, December 15, 1958, quoted in Samy Cohen, "France, Civil-Military Relations, and Nuclear Weapons," *Security Studies*, Vol. 4, No. 1, Autumn 1994, p. 163.

91. Jean Lacouture, *De Gaulle*, Tome 3, *Le Souverain* (*De Gaulle*, Vol. 3, *The Sovereign*), Paris, France: Seuil, 1986, p. 80.

92. Vaïsse, *Comment de Gaulle fit échouer le putsch d'Alger*, p. 110.

93. Lacouture, *De Gaulle*, p. 469. Mururoa is the location chosen later for most of the French nuclear tests in the Pacific.

94. On this, see, Tertrais, "'Destruction Assurée': The Origins and Development of French Nuclear Strategy, 1958-1981."

95. The base was never under the control of the rebels, contrary to what Spector hypothesized in 1987. See Spector, *Going Nuclear*, pp. 25, 30. The misuse of some French sources in this part of the Spector book was noted by political scientist Samy Cohen in "France, Civil-Military Relations, and Nuclear Weapons," pp. 177-178.

96. Pierre Billaud recounts that his flight to Reggan was particularly unusual. Flying over the Mediterranean, the plane received an order from Paris to return to its base. Then it received another order, this time to land in Algiers instead of going straight to the test site. Billaud and his colleague George Tirole (who were the only two passengers) had their identities checked by a rebel unit, which then let them go to Reggan. Whether or not this was a cumbersome attempt to stop or delay the test is unclear. See the testimony of Pierre Billaud in Bendjebbar, *Histoire secrète de la bombe atomique*, pp. 327-328; and Billaud's own account. No mention of the date of the flight is given, but Bellec mentions Billaud's arrival on Sunday 23.

97. The author is grateful to Samy Cohen for this suggested comparison.

98. It is unclear whether specific units were actually clearly siding with the rebels. As stated above, several sources state that armored units were sympathetic to the generals' cause. See for instance Pô, *Les moyens de la puissance*, p. 139; and Abramovici, *Le putsch des généraux*, p. 307. The testimony quoted by Pô refers specifically to a unit that was present for the exercise planned during the test; however, these troops had no contact with the base personnel and were probably largely unaware of what was going on. See Rommès, "Le peloton Patton sous Gerboise verte." Abramovici mentions armored units and Legion étrangère units.

99. Pô, *Les moyens de la puissance*, p. 139.

100. Yves Rocard goes as far as saying that the site "did not even have a single machine gun to defend it"—a dubious assertion. Rocard, *Mémoires sans concessions*, p. 232.

101. Bellec, "Vie au Sahara."

102. Whether or not French forces would have gone as far as spilling "blood for the bomb" is dubious. Vaïsse notes the prevailing culture of the French military included a strong repugnance to the idea against fighting against one another (*Comment de Gaulle fit échouer le putsch d'Alger*, pp. 292-294). More likely, a confrontation on the site would have had one side ceding to the other before actual fighting could have taken place.

103. Antoine Schwerer, "Auprès de ma bombe," unpublished manuscript, March 1990, p. 49.

104. Another possibility would have been to seize the device before it reached Reggan, assuming it was not yet on the site.

105. This is a theoretical discussion. It is hard to conceive a scenario in which such use would have made sense, apart from proceeding with the test at a moment of their choice to demonstrate their control of the Sahara.

106. Schwerer, "Auprès de ma bombe," pp. 49, 65. The "final 35 minutes" of the assembly process were automated, according to a CEA engineer interviewed by the French public radio, broadcasted on March 17, 1960, Archives of the Institut National de l'Audiovisuel (National Audiovisual Institute).

107. One account suggests that the core of the device had not yet been delivered to the Reggan base when the coup took place. The head of Radio-Alger, André Rossfelder (appointed by the rebels in the first hours of the coup) claims that he was informed in the evening of April 22 that the device—without its detonator—which was due to be transferred to Reggan, was a in a military warehouse in the port of Algiers. When he sought to have the story confirmed, he was told by a military official that this was a mistake and the device had already been delivered to Reggan. While Rossfelder does not hypothesize about the veracity of the events, he seems to suggest implicitly that the Algiers generals had deliberately allowed the core to be transferred to Reggan. André Rossfelder, *Le onzième commandement* (*The Eleventh Commandment*), Paris, France: Gallimard, 2000, pp. 497-499.

108. According to the testimony of Zeller's grandson, the idea of nuclear blackmail did not square well with the mentality of the four generals. Personal communication of Bernard Zeller to the author, September 13, 2011.

109. Personal communication to the author, September 15, 2011.

110. The notion of poetic justice is suggested by Rossfelder (*Le onzième commandement*, p. 498). One thing the rebels could have done is proceed with the test according to their own timetable, to demonstrate their control of the site, but this would have meant acquiring the cooperation of the CEA personnel.

111. The details of the Reggan events remained secret for several weeks, and there is no evidence that the United States, for instance, was aware in real time of what was going on at Reggan in April 1961. No mention of the episode is made in the studies of U.S. archives done by French experts. See Vincent Nouzille, *Des secrets si bien gardés: Les dossiers de la Maison-Blanche et de la CIA sur la France et ses présidents 1958-1981* (*The Secret So Well Kept: Records of the White House and CIA on France and Its Presidents 1958-1981*), Paris, France. Fayard, 2010; and Vaïsse, *Comment de Gaulle fit échouer le putsch d'Alger*. No U.S. official analysis of the events has been found by this author. A declassified 1964 CIA study contained comments on each French test, but the description is excised in the declassified version. See, Central Intelligence Agency, *The French Nuclear Weapon Program*, OSI-SR/64-10, March 27, 1964, available from *www.foia.cia.gov/docs/DOC_0001522915/DOC_0001522915.pdf*. Brian Jenkins had access to other previously classified documents and confirms that no mention of the test appears in any of them. Personal communication with the author, March 2012.

112. A report drafted by Professor Thomas Schelling for the Kennedy administration in October 1962, recounting delivery possibilities for new nuclear powers, states that "a fishing boat or a cheap airplane might have been an adequate means of delivery for, say, the Algerian Nationalists against Marseilles, or Castro's Cuba against Baltimore and Miami," quoted in Francis J. Gavin, "Same As It Ever Was: Nuclear Alarmism, Proliferation, and the

Cold War," *International Security*, Vol. 34, No. 3, Winter 2009-10, p. 22; perhaps this scenario was inspired by the April 1961 events and the subsequent Evian Agreements.

113. As stated above, the CSEM reported both to Paris (Joint Staff) and Algiers (Sahara Command), and the GOEN reported both to the Ministry of Defense and the CEA.

CHAPTER 3

SECURING NUCLEAR ARSENALS: A CHINESE CASE STUDY

Mark A. Stokes

INTRODUCTION

Nuclear warhead stockpile security has long been a concern of the major powers. Of particular concern is the potential theft of nuclear warheads and associated materials, or a breakdown in command and control authority over their use during periods of domestic instability. Since the inception of its program in the 1950s, the Chinese Communist Party (CCP) has granted nuclear warheads special political significance. The value of nuclear weapons resides not only in their international deterrent/coercive significance, but also in the domestic power and political legitimacy that a faction enjoys with control over the means of mass destruction. Domestic instability in the People's Republic of China (PRC) during the initial stages of nuclear warhead production could serve as an illustration of how one nuclear power has absorbed lessons from threats to the security of a warhead stockpile.

China's Great Proletarian Cultural Revolution, which began in 1966 and ended by 1976, is the prominent case in which political instability could have resulted in the loss of control of China's limited nuclear weapons stockpile. The domestic chaos that characterized this period coincided with a significant deterioration of relations with the former Soviet Union. Perceived domestic and external threats likely shaped the highly centralized approach to securing the national nuclear warhead stockpile that the Chinese People's Liberation Army (PLA) continues to employ until today.

During the initial stages of China's program, its system of storage and handling nuclear warheads was relatively integrated with its civilian nuclear research and development (R&D) and production complex. Concerns over domestic stability and external threats to China's initial nuclear capabilities contributed toward the institutionalization of a highly centralized storage and handling system involving strict political control through the Central Military Commission (CMC), rather than the General Staff Department (GSD). The power of the CMC stems from its political subordination to the CCP Central Committee, rather than to legal state authority.

Furthermore, the experience of the Cultural Revolution may have contributed to a relative emphasis on security over operational effectiveness that has characterized China's nuclear strategy until today. Since the production of China's first nuclear device in 1964, warheads have been managed in peacetime through an independent organization, known as 22 Base, which is separate and distinct from operational missile bases and subordinate launch brigades. From the time of China's initial production of a nuclear device in 1964 until 1979, 22 Base, subordinate to the PLA's National Defense Science and Technology Commission, exercised control over the country's nuclear warhead stockpile. The organizations responsible for the means of delivery, primarily the Second Artillery Corps and to a lesser extent the PLA Air Force, exercised no peacetime control over the nuclear weapons stockpile. It was not until after the political chaos of the Cultural Revolution subsided that the CMC directed the 22 Base's subordination under the Second Artillery Corps. However, even then, security considerations remained paramount. Within the Second Artillery, an organizational structure that maintained a clear division between the management of the nuclear warhead stockpile and missile operations was established and maintained until today.

Based on limited historical data, this case study outlines the potential effects that the domestic political instability the Cultural Revolution had on the security of China's nuclear weapon inventory during its initial stages. The case study begins with an overview of China's early plans for its warhead storage and handling system, then addresses the chaos of the Cultural Revolution and how security considerations may have led to a decision to move storage functions to the Qinling Mountain area south of the Shaanxi city of Baoji and west of the historic city of Xian. While the literature to date has highlighted the role of defense industrial scientists and engineers, little attention has been given to key PLA personnel responsible for the security aspects of the program. The case study then examines how the turmoil of the Cultural Revolution may have influenced the PLA's current system of warhead storage and handling.

ESTABLISHMENT OF CHINA'S INITIAL WARHEAD STORAGE AND HANDLING FACILITY

An examination of PLA units and senior officers responsible for the formation of China's warhead storage and handling system begins with Jia Qianrui [贾乾瑞], Hong Youdao [洪有道], and Yao Shumei [姚书梅]. The National Defense Science and Technology

Commission units supporting the nuclear program included 20 Base in Jiuquan, Gansu province; 21 Base in Lop Nor, Xinjiang province; and 22 Base near Haiyan, Qinghai province. Base 22 was assigned responsibility for warhead storage and handling. In 1958, Mao Zedong commissioned a little known infantry school based in Shangqiu, Henan Province, to survey sites for missile and nuclear warhead testing and storage. The Shangqiu Infantry School commandant Major General Jia Qianrui [贾乾瑞] and student affairs director Hong Youdao were responsible for the warhead storage site survey, with the former eventually becoming the father of China's warhead security.

The regiment under 22 Base responsible for security of the 221 Factory was the 8126 Unit, with the 8122 Unit responsible for warhead storage. Originally under direct supervision of the CMC, the storage facility was near a village known as Shangwuzhuang [上五庄], which may now host the 56 Base's warhead storage regiment.[1] The first storage tunnel reportedly was completed in 1964, the same year as China's first nuclear test, and subordinated to the National Defense Science Commission in 1965. The political commissar during the 22 Base's formative years was Yao Shumei, who served in the position until the base's subordination to the Second Artillery in 1979.[2]

THE CULTURAL REVOLUTION AND NUCLEAR WARHEAD SECURITY

The PRC's modern system for storage and handling of nuclear weapons was shaped by the events of the Cultural Revolution. A key event in nuclear warhead security was the "223 Incident," an uprising in February 1967 in Qinghai Province, the center of nuclear weapon R&D and location of initial storage facilities. The Cultural Revolution and concerns over competing loyalties within the PLA affected China's nuclear weapons program and, more specifically, warhead storage and handling.

The Cultural Revolution was launched by CCP Chairman Mao Zedong, ostensibly to broaden and deepen Socialist goals. However, Mao appeared intent upon consolidating his power in the wake of failed economic policies under the Great Leap Forward and silencing critics within the leadership. Among the most prominent of Mao's targets included Liu Shaoqi, Deng Xiaoping, and eventually Defense Minister Lin Biao, Mao's chosen successor. In May 1966, Mao called for removing "revisionists" through class struggle and appealed to youthful Red Guards, revolutionary factions within industry and other societal organizations. By early-1967, Mao's senior staff directed the Cultural Revolution to be extended into the PLA, enforced in large part by political commissars within the PLA and encouraged by Minister of Public Security Xie Fuzhi. The formal phase of the Cultural Revolution ended in 1969, but purges continued until the death of the military leader Lin Biao in 1971. Political instability continued until Mao's death in 1976.

The Cultural Revolution had direct effects on China's nuclear weapons complex during its infant stage of development. In September 1966, engineers within the nuclear weapons program, specifically, the China Academy of Engineering Physics (CAEP, or "Ninth Academy") 221 Factory near the Qinghai town of Haiyan, split into rival factions, one supporting more radical elements of the Cultural Revolution. In October 1966, the newly established Second Artillery Corps, inspired by radical calls to accelerate the nuclear weapons program, conducted a risky test of a Dongfeng-2 medium-range ballistic missile (MRBM) equipped with a 12kt nuclear device. The missile and its nuclear payload overflew populated areas between Gansu and its landing zone in western Xinjiang Province.

Red Guards advanced the cause of nuclear weapons, explicitly suggesting a linkage between the creative force of radicalism and that unleashed by the atomic bomb. Although the device detonated as planned, the test demonstrated the lack of an effective command and control system at the time. By conducting what appeared to some as an unauthorized test by the Second Artillery within the confines of China, the test appeared to raise the frightening prospect of an unauthorized launch against one of China's neighbors. To quote Nie Rongzhen, the leader of the nuclear weapons program and ostensibly under pressure from radical elements within the party, "It was a somewhat risky assignment, because if by any chance the nuclear warhead exploded prematurely, fell after it was launched, or went beyond the designated target area, the consequences would be too ghastly to contemplate."[3]

By January 1967, internal strife intensified, leading to attempts at a forcible takeover of the program. One radical group from a key military institute in Harbin, led by Mao Zedong's nephew (Mao Yuanxin), attempted a forcible occupation of nuclear facilities, but was intercepted upon orders from Nie Rongzhen. In February, Xinjiang Military Region Commander Wang Enmao threatened to forcibly take control over Base 21 at Lop Nur if Mao did not act to restrain the Red Guards. In Qinghai, a radical faction within the 221 Factory accused leaders of revisionism, and participated in the occupation of Qinghai Province's primary newspaper building in Xining. On February 23, 1967, Beijing authorized military control of newspapers and radio stations and ordered the Qinghai Military District Commander, Liu Xianquan, to occupy the provincial newspaper, *Qinghai Daily*, which had been taken over by Red Guards. Liu Xianquan's Deputy Commander, Zhao Yongfu, used armed force when seizing the building, killing 169 civilians and injuring 178. Known as the "223 Incident," the crackdown spread throughout other parts of the city the following day, with a dozen casualties at the Qinghai Ethnic College.[4]

On March 5, 1967, Premier Zhou Enlai, at the urging of CMC Vice Chairman Nie Rongzhen [聂荣臻], authorized martial law in Qinghai, and assigned the PLA to take control of the 221 Factory. Jia Qianrui was placed in charge of a five-member committee to oversee the joint military command responsible for enforcing martial law.[5] After 3 months, the situation was sufficiently stable for the test of China's first hydrogen bomb on June 17, 1967. However, localized fighting between Red Guard elements and PLA operational units continued across the country through the summer of 1967. PLA officers gradually became the dominant component of the CCP Politburo and assumed leadership positions in most of China's provinces.

While insufficient information exists to determine the specific factors influencing the decision, senior leaders in Beijing directed preparations for relocating production and storage to more secure areas inside China's interior shortly after the 223 Incident. By 1969, Jia Qianrui and Hong Youdao initiated the relocation of the 22 Base's central nuclear warhead storage functions to Taibai County, Shaanxi Province.

A number of factors may have led to the move. First, Taibai County may have been designated as the ultimate location of China's nuclear weapons stockpile as early as 1958. Taibai County had been identified as a candidate reserve storage site in the 1958 survey, and this may have been a factor in the establishment of Taibai County in the early-1960s. Taibai Mountain is the highest peak in China east of its three western-most provinces of Tibet, Qinghai, and Xinjiang. Taibai Mountain reaches 3,767 meters (12,358 feet) in height, and is formed of large granite rock.

Details regarding construction of the Taibai tunnel complex are unavailable at the current time. However, construction of underground facilities in Taibai County coincided with a PLA Rail Corps project to construct a railway linking Baoji with Chengdu and a third line of nuclear production facilities near Mianyang in the late-1950s and early-1960s. The Baoji-Chengdu Railway was completed in 1961, although work continued throughout the 1960s to electrify the system. The Baoji-Chengdu line was considered a major feat, not only because it was China's first electric rail, but because of the tunnels that sliced through the Qinling mountains south of Baoji. Of most significance was a 2.3-km tunnel passing through Qinling Mountain and a series of spiral tunnels just southwest of Baoji, the largest city near the Taibai complex. The rail also supported a major ballistic missile engine and component research, development, and production complex, known as the 067 Base, which was established in 1965 in the mountainous county adjacent to Taibai.

A second explanation could be concerns over the relative proximity to the industrial complex that was the source of unrest and the possibility of nuclear warheads falling into unauthorized hands. Located in deep mountain valleys, the Taibai underground complex has been equipped with an advanced physical protection system. In addition to a battalion dedicated to perimeter security, security measures have become increasingly sophisticated, including real-time video monitoring, infrared security, computerized warhead accounting systems, temperature and humidity controls, firefighting equipment, fingerprint and other access control, and advanced communications linking sites within the complex. Since its establishment during the Cultural Revolution, the command center in the area of Taibai appears to serve as the operational hub of the 22 Base's warhead storage and handling system. Known as the Hongling Command Cell, the watch center likely is co-located with a storage facility, and overseen by one of the 22 Base's deputy chiefs of staff. One recent *PLA Daily* article indicated that Second Artillery underground storage facilities may double as reserve operational command centers.[6]

Another possible explanation for the move is the deterioration of relations with the Soviet Union in 1969, and concerns over the possibility of a Soviet strike against China's nuclear weapons complex.[7] Situated farther away from the Soviet border, Taibai County likely was considered more survivable than Qinghai. In addition, a larger facility may have been required to facilitate the growth in delivery platforms and initial operational capability of the DF-2 (CSS-1), which was initially tested in 1966.

Regardless, the Cultural Revolution and national political turmoil that could have affected control over the nuclear warhead stockpile came to a head in 1969. Since 1967, Mao had increasingly relied upon the PLA to re-establish order and consolidate his continued control over the party. Claiming the need to be prepared for a potential Soviet attack, Lin Biao, defense minister and anointed successor to Mao in April 1969, issued an independent order to move the PLA into a higher state of readiness on October 18, 1969, ostensibly without clearance from Mao. The move, viewed as tantamount to a coup, infuriated Mao, who had relied heavily on the PLA as a guarantor of his position. Any move to take control of nuclear weapons and leverage their political value as the basis for usurping Mao's power may have been a disturbing prospect. The ensuing political competition between Mao and Lin Biao ended when Lin was killed in a plane crash in Mongolia in September 1971.

CHINA'S NUCLEAR WARHEAD STORAGE AND HANDLING SYSTEM TODAY

China's nuclear weapons program had a powerful patriotic, political, and revolutionary appeal during the opening phase of the Cultural Revolution. In order to salvage the program from the political chaos of the time, Zhou Enlai and Nie Rongzhen relied heavily upon isolation of 22 Base from other parts of the PLA, even the force responsible for ballistic delivery of nuclear weapons (the Second Artillery Corps). A premium was placed on political integrity and loyalty.

Political upheaval in China, at least on the scale similar to the Cultural Revolution, is unlikely, yet possible. The Cultural Revolution shaped China's approach to nuclear warhead storage and handling, including extraordinarily stringent personnel reliability standards, direct reporting to CMC authority (especially the civilian Chairman and Vice Chairman) rather than General Staff Department, and continued centralization of nuclear warhead storage.

Since its relocation to Taibai and subordination to the Second Artillery in 1979, the 22 Base has continued to serve as the CMC's custodians for the national central nuclear warhead stockpile. The base's mission includes warhead reliability and safety; storing and transporting warhead components; training missile base personnel in warhead storage, maintenance, assembly, and mating; maintaining a support infrastructure for warhead management; and operating a communications system that supports its mission.

Each of the Second Artillery's six army-level missile bases replicates 22 Base functions on a smaller and perhaps modified scale. Missile bases, separate and distinct from 22 Base, possess only a limited number of warheads at any given time. The emphasis on centralized security, a legacy of the Cultural Revolution, makes the mobility of nuclear warheads critical to the Second Artillery's nuclear deterrent and warfighting capability. A separate regiment under the 22 Base is responsible for circulating warheads back and forth between the central storage complex in Taibai and six smaller storage facilities subordinate to each missile base. Only a relatively small handful of warheads appear to be maintained at each base's storage regiment for any extended period of time.[8] Given the Second Artillery's high degree of reliance on the nation's rail and highway system for its nuclear deterrent, a failure in the transport network is cause for concern. Transfer units conduct armed escort missions and rely on dedicated communications and surveillance networks for security.[9]

Although the Taibai nuclear warhead facility has existed for 40 years, Second Artillery engineering units have been engaged in a national engineering project in the Qinling Mountain region between

Taibai and the western foothills adjacent to Tianshui City (Gansu Province) over the past 10 to 15 years. The storage complex is supported by a Second Artillery civil engineering regiment subordinate to the 308 Engineering Command, based south of Taibai in the city of Hanzhong, and by an installation engineering group in Luoyang. At least one 22 Base study implied a requirement for upgrades to older underground facilities for health reasons. Other engineering projects also have been taking place in the area.

Because of their extremely destructive nature, nuclear warheads require strict safety, reliability, and security measures to guarantee that they are never accidently or intentionally detonated without the authorization of the most senior political authorities.[10] Along these lines, the 22 Base bears the responsibility for engineering analysis and environmental testing to ensure the safety and reliability of China's nuclear weapon stockpile. The reliability and safety of nuclear warheads and materials have become sensitive issues in Chinese politics. Veterans from four units associated with the testing, storage, and maintenance of nuclear warheads in the 1960s and 1970s have submitted legal claims to the government related to radiation-linked health problems.[11] Located in Taibai County, the 22 Base's training regiment appears to train not only base personnel, but also the missile base warhead units.[12]

Today, the specific regimental-sized organization under the 22 Base's authority that is responsible for warhead reliability and safety is the 96411 Unit, also known as the "Equipment Inspection Institute." Since at least 2005, the institute has focused on improving its warhead surveillance capabilities. Engineers regularly "pulse" components inside the 22 Base storage complex to ensure safety and reliability.[13] The institute also works with the China Aerospace Science and Technology Corporation (CASC) and PLA General Armaments Department (GAD) warhead-related laboratories housed in CAEP facilities.[14] In the past, 22 Base engineers have worked with their CAEP counterparts to extend the service life of warheads associated with DF-2 (CSS-1), DF-4 (CSS-3), and DF-5 (CSS-4) ballistic missiles.[15]

Furthermore, since the end of the Cultural Revolution, the CMC has had a dedicated command, control, and communications network for warhead management and directing nuclear strikes. It is unknown if the 22 Base communications regiment is responsible for only internal communications related to central storage and handling or if it plays a role in the overall command and control for China's nuclear operations.

CONCLUSION

A preliminary examination of the 1967-69 crisis within the nuclear industry and political-military system more broadly indicates that the Cultural Revolution shaped Beijing's contemporary approach to nuclear warhead storage and handling. With the bulk of its nuclear warhead stockpile nestled deep in secure mountain palaces, the 22 Base's physical protection system appears to be founded upon more than "guns, gates, and guards." The legacy of the Cultural Revolution may have influenced the establishment of one of the most secure warhead stockpile in the world. However, any stockpile is only as secure as the broader political system that it supports. No amount of physical security can shelter a nuclear arsenal from political chaos at the highest levels of government. Beyond this, the centralization of the stockpile forces managers to rely heavily on the nation's rail system and other means of transportation. With warheads most vulnerable to theft or accident during transportation, the system's reliance on mobility creates opportunities for incidents and terrorist action.

Based on the experience of chaos during the Cultural Revolution, the CMC prioritizes security and safety over operational readiness in its nuclear warhead storage and handling system. A centralized warhead management system has clear benefits. One advantage is reduced vulnerability to the loss of political control over a given region. However, assuming China's nuclear strategy remains one of minimal deterrence and retaliation, centralized storage and handling also can be vulnerable to a disarming first strike. As a result, China's warhead storage and handling system is designed to survive a first strike and retain sufficient operational capability for retaliation. Deterrence relies upon ambiguity surrounding the precise locations of the base-level storage facilities and launch sites and the numbers of warheads maintained at any given time.

The experience of the Cultural Revolution led toward the separation of civilian industry and the storage and handling functions of 22 Base. A cost of doing so may have been problems with warhead safety and reliability associated with the lack of follow-up support after delivery of new warheads to the Second Artillery. In a 1991 assessment, Second Artillery Equipment Department analysts lamented the excess prioritization of missiles over nuclear warhead stockpile management. In addition to inadequate launch battalion training on live warheads, few engineers from the Second Artillery unit tasked with stockpile reliability had hands-on experience in inspecting warheads. Analysts have recommended a major program to improve China's nuclear stockpile management, especially as a new generation of warheads would be entering the operational inventory.[16] In 2006, 22 Base began contracting with senior warhead designers and specialists in at least 10 nuclear-related institutions throughout China, including the CAEP, China Institute of Atomic Energy, and China Institute of Radiation Protection (CIRP).[17]

The legacy of the Cultural Revolution and the relative emphasis on security over operational effectiveness could result in self-imposed constraints on the size of China's arsenal. The precise size of China's nuclear warhead inventory is unknown. However, a highly centralized system for warhead storage and handling could lead toward a preference for a smaller arsenal. The Second Artillery's missile brigade infrastructure has expanded significantly over the past 15 to 20 years, including the engineering of an expanded number of underground facilities supporting missile brigade operations. A Project 2049 Institute survey of the specific units responsible for the warhead storage and handling system offers no clear sign of a significant increase in China's nuclear stockpile.

Finally, the CMC likely has relied on the Second Artillery as its exclusive custodians of the national nuclear warhead stockpile. Unlike the Air Force, Navy, and Military Regions, the Second Artillery reports directly to the party's CMC rather than through the General Staff Department. The Chairman and Vice-Chairman of the CMC have authority due to their positions within the party, and not necessarily to senior state positions.

For added security, warheads are mated with missiles assigned to brigades only in elevated readiness conditions and perhaps, on occasion, for training purposes. The Cultural Revolution legacy of centralizing the storage and handling of nuclear weapons, as well as the practice of keeping warheads separate from delivery vehicles, raises questions regarding a new generation of nuclear submarines that are to be equipped with a JL-2 submarine-launched ballistic missile that would patrol with armed warheads. Whether or not 22 Base, and perhaps regional bases, would manage warheads to be mated with JL-2 missiles for use on Navy Type 094 submarines remains unknown. In addition, warheads appear to have been managed separately from China's civilian fissile material protection, control, and accounting system. Who manages China's fissile material remains unknown.[18]

Given nuclear warheads' status as a liability, their safety and security is a common interest of the United States and the PRC, and one of the few practical issues worthy of cooperation between our two defense establishments through the Cooperative Threat Reduction (CTR) or other programs. Most public discussion on nuclear safety and security to date appears limited to the civil nuclear energy sector, despite efforts to place the issue on the defense agenda.[19]

ENDNOTES - CHAPTER 3

1. Among various sources, see "Retired Soldiers of China's Nuclear 22 Base" [中国核军事二十二基地退役战士], *Petition to the Dazu County Government*, June 21, 2007. Also see "Regarding the Problem of Health Support for 1972 Military Retirees" [关于72年退伍军人生活保障问题], Chongqing City Government website, September 14, 2006, available from *www.cq.gov.cn/PublicMail/Citizen/ViewReleaseMail.aspx?intReleaseID=17027*. For reference to the 1958 Shangqiu test site survey team, see John Wilson Lewis and Xue Litai, *China Builds the Bomb*, Stanford, CA: Stanford University Press, 1988, p. 175. For an account of soldiers involved during the early stages of China's nuclear weapons program experienc-

ing radiation sickness in their later years, see Michael Sheridan, "Revolt Stirs among China's Nuclear Ghosts," *Times Online*, April 19, 2009, available at *www.timesonline.co.uk/tol/news/world/asia/article6122338.ece*. Not covered, however, are court cases introduced by 22 Base soldiers involved in warhead storage and handling.

2. Declassified U.S. intelligence community reporting from 1971 indicates that a central storage facility for warheads was located "in a ridge about 12nm from the Koko Nor weapons fabrication complex." See *Communist China's Weapons Program for Strategic Attack*, NIE 13-8-71 (declassified), October 28, 1971. This reporting added that "some of this space is probably used for nuclear weapons inspection and retrofit." The report suggested that launch bases included facilities for the checking out and mating of the warhead, as well as possibly for "separate or temporary storage." It was uncertain if the Chinese would keep nuclear warheads stored at launch bases or in a central stockpile, then transporting them to the bases only in a crisis situation. A logistics system would be able to rapidly deploy warheads from base-level storage sites to launch positions as the missiles were being readied. The reporting notes that warheads could be stored near launch sites or even on missiles.

3. Nie Rongzhen, "How China Develops Nuclear Weapons," *Beijing Review*, April 29, 1985, pp. 15-19.

4. Roderick MacFarquhar and Michael Schoenhals, *Mao's Last Revolution*, Cambridge, MA: Harvard University Press, 2006, pp. 179-180.

5. For additional background about the impact of the Cultural Revolution on the nuclear weapon development program, see John Wilson Lewis and Xue Litai, *China Builds the Bomb,* Stanford, CA: Stanford University Press, 1988, pp. 202-206. In addition to a brief discussion of the warhead storage base functions, one account asserts that the Taibai storage complex had been planned as early as 1960, with Taibai County formed in 1961 for the nuclear storage mission. See "The Leaker: Cruise Missiles Point toward Hainan Target Zone, Target is Obvious" [漏斗子：巡航導彈劍指海南靶區，針對性太明顯了], *China.Com Blog*, December 28, 2009, available from *big5.china.com/gate/big5/zzh1125.blog.china.com/200912/5644340.html*.

6. Base-level storage facilities for nuclear and probably conventional warheads, missiles, associated subsystems, components, and fuels are generally referred to as "equipment inspection" regiments. Each regiment oversees at least three battalion-level facilities, known as "equipment inspection sites," which conduct testing and diagnostics of warheads in underground facilities, usually in mountainous regions. Each site can have as many as seven subordinate subunits, indicating that a missile base's warhead inspection and missile depot system could have as many as 21 sites. Companies subordinate to battalions are responsible for tasks such as missile management, security, and site management. Among various sources, see Liang Pengfei and Xia Hongping, "Second Artillery Technical Service Regiment Support Battalion Studies Practical Developments" [第二炮兵某团技术勤务营学习实践科学发展观活动见闻], *PLA Daily*, November 17, 2009, available from *chn.chinamil.com.cn/2009jbzsc/2009-11/17/content_4080730.htm*.

7. See the declassified "Memorandum for the President from Secretary of State William Rogers, The Possibility of a Soviet Strike against Chinese Nuclear Facilities," September 10, 1969, in William Burr, ed., *The Sino-Soviet Border Conflict, 1969: A National Security Archive Electronic Briefing Book*, June 12, 2001, available from *www.gwu.edu~nsarchiv/NSAEBB/NSAEBB49/sino.sov.19.pdf*.

8. For an explicit reference to the centralization of warhead storage, see Yu Jixun, ed., *Second Artillery Campaign Science*, Beijing, China: PLA Press, 2004, pp. 242-244. Each missile base also has regiments responsible for training, transportation, warhead storage and inspection, repair and maintenance, and communications. A specialized 13-member warhead expert working group assists The Second Artillery's leadership in stockpile management policy. The Second Artillery Headquarters Department also oversees a Nuclear Security and Control Bureau.

9. For a reference to the transportation infrastructure and the rail battalion of the special transportation regiment, see Larry M. Wortzel, *China's Nuclear Forces: Operations, Training, Doctrine, Command, Control, and Campaign Planning*, Carlisle, PA: Strategic Studies Institute, U.S. Army War College, May 2007, p. 22; and Xia Hongqing, "Second Artillery Service Regiment Rail Transport Company: Growing Up with the Flag" [第二炮兵某勤务团铁运

连：党旗伴我成长], *PLA Daily*, July 1, 2002, available from *www.pladaily.com.cn/gb/pladaily/2002/07/01/20020701001045_army.html*.

10. For a comprehensive overview of warhead reliability, safety, and security issues, see Richard L. Garwin and Vadim A. Simonenko, "Nuclear Weapon Development without Nuclear Testing?" paper prepared for the Pugwash Workshop on Problems in Achieving a Nuclear-free World, October 25-27, 1996, London, England.

11. See "Retired Soldiers of China's Nuclear 22 Base" [中国核军事二十二基地退役战士], Petition to the Dazu County government, June 21, 2007. Also see "Regarding the Problem of Health Support for 1972 Military Retirees" [关于72年退伍军人生活保障问题], Chongqing City Government website, September 14, 2006, available from *www.cq.gov.cn/PublicMail/Citizen/ViewReleaseMail.aspx?intReleaseID=17027*.

12. The 96423 Unit's political commissar, Feng Danli [冯丹利], was associated with a Second Artillery training regiment "deep in the mountains," probably in Qilichuan village. See Zhang Guangtian, "96401 Unit Helps Establish a New Farming Village in Qilichuan" [96401 部队援建七里川村新农村建设], *PLA Daily*, June 18, 2008; and Zhu Weishe, "Picture" [图片], *PLA Daily*, April 18, 2009, available from *www.chinamil.com.cn/site1//zbxl/2009-04/18/content_1730645.htm*.

13. The institute is directed by Wang Guoqing [王国庆], with Dr. Kong Xiangyu [孔祥玉] also playing a major role. Wang Yongxiao and Wang Feng, "Inspection and Transportation on Target: China's Strategic Missile Unit's Special Operations Troops" [装检押运报靶：中国战略导弹部队的特种兵], *China News Network*, June 21, 2006.

14. The specific CASC institute responsible for warhead and re-entry vehicle structural design is the China Academy of Launch Technology (CALT, or CASC First Academy) 14th Research Institute, or Beijing Institute of Special Electro-Mechanics [北京特殊机电研究所]. For background on CIRP, see *www.cirp.org.cn/*. CAEP hosts five PLA GAD laboratories that focus on issues such as shock wave and detonation physics [冲击波物理与爆轰物理], computational physics [计算物理], high-density, high-

temperature plasma [高温高密度等离子体], and surface physics and chemistry [表面物理与化学].

15. See "CMC and State Council Invites High Tech Expert to Beidaihe—Yang Weixin [中央、国务院邀请到北戴河休假的高技能人才—杨维新], *Government Labor Bureau*, August 6, 2004, available from *www.lm.gov.cn/gb/training/2004-08/06/content_42314.htm*. Presumably working in conjunction with CAEP's Institute of Electronic Engineering, Yang developed a fuze control system [引控系统] and advanced "synchronous detonation" components. The 524 warhead design for the DF-3 was allegedly first tested in 1968, the 515 design for the DF-21/JL-1 in 1974, and the 506 warhead design for the DF-5 were first tested in 1976.

16. See *Lessons from the Gulf War for Second Artillery Force Development* [海湾战争对二炮武器装备建设的启示], Beijing, China: Second Artillery Headquarters Equipment Department, May 1991.

17. For reporting on efforts to advance the educational level of institute engineers, see Han Haifeng, Wei Cunren, and Wang Yongxiao, "Second Artillery Equipment Inspection Institute Overcomes Difficulties to Promote Doctoral Candidates to Grasp Core Control Issues" [二炮装检所破格提拔博士攻克核心控制领域难题], *PLA Daily*, February 8, 2008, available from *mil.news.sina.com.cn/2009-02-07/0805541171.html*. Senior CAEP advisors to the 22 Base include Xu Zhilei [徐志磊]. As a senior figure in the development of China's second-generation nuclear warheads, Dr. Xu was a recipient of one of China's highest prizes for defense science and technology (S&T) achievement for design and manufacturing of the fissile core of a nuclear device, known as the "pit." In the 1980s, Xu was appointed as chief designer for the miniaturized warhead subsystem on two new intercontinental ballistic missiles (ICBMs). Concurrently, Xu functioned as deputy chief designer for the DF-31 program. Other key CAEP engineering consultants include Peng Xianjue [彭先觉] and Tang Xisheng [唐西生]. Liu Senlin [刘森林] from the China Institute of Atomic Energy has also served as a warhead safety and reliability consultant. Cooperation between the Second Artillery 22 Base and the civilian nuclear industry would appear to be a departure from extreme stovepiping in the past. For a discussion of bureaucratic barriers to cooperation, see Nathan Busch, "China's Fissile Mate-

rial Protection, Control, and Accounting: The Case for Renewed Collaboration," *Nonproliferation Review*, Fall/Winter 2002, p. 170.

18. For an excellent summary of China's SSBN development, see Andrew S. Erickson and Michael S. Chase, "China's SSBN Forces: Transitioning to the Next Generation," Jamestown Foundation *China Brief*, Vol. 9, Issue 12, June 12, 2009.

19. At least one potential area of discussion could be the International Atomic Energy Agency (IAEA) initiative regarding "design basis threat." For one discussion on China's physical protection system, see Tang Dan, Yin Xiandong, Fang Ni, Guo Cao, "Physical Protection System and Vulnerability Analysis Program in China," presented to the International Seminar on Disarmament and the Resolution of Conflict (ISODARCO), Beijing, China, October, 2002. The authors are from CAEP's Institute of Electronic Engineering. Also see Busch, "China's Fissile Material Protection, Control, and Accounting"; and Hui Zhang, "Evaluating China's MPC&A System," paper presented at the INMM 44th Annual Meeting, Phoenix, Arizona, July, 13-17 2003.

CHAPTER 4

CONTROLLING SOVIET/RUSSIAN NUCLEAR WEAPONS IN TIMES OF INSTABILITY

Nikolai Sokov

Had someone suggested during the Cold War that the Soviet leadership might lose control of its nuclear arsenal, such an outlandish notion would have been brushed aside in an instant. Even as the Soviet Union was sinking ever deeper into economic crisis and political turmoil in the late-1980s, one undisputable island of stability remained — the Soviet nuclear forces.

This island could not remain immune. As the country was undergoing a complex socio-economic transition and eventually fell apart, at least three situations occurred during a relatively short period from early-1990 to mid-1992, when control over nuclear weapons could slip from the hands of authorities. At the same time, one must admit that the system of control over nuclear weapons and materials was the last to succumb to general chaos, that chaos affected it less than other areas, and that control was restored earlier than in other areas. (By the middle of 1992, the Russian leadership, by and large, had acquired control of all Soviet nuclear assets or was firmly on track toward that goal.) Nonetheless, it was a close call in each of the three instances.

All three occurred under distinctly different circumstances and represented distinctly different types of loss of control. Each case also took a different amount of time: It was barely a few days each in 1990 and 1991, but in 1992 events gradually unfolded over several months. Each case offers important lessons for averting similar situations in the future and might be fungible across different countries.

The chapter will also discuss challenges of controlling weapons-grade nuclear materials and sensitive weapons-related technologies. This problem became a challenge by the mid-1990s, but the first signs had already emerged in 1992. While the demand for materials and technologies, both from state entities and increasingly from nonstate actors, had existed for a long time, supply began to appear only in the early-1990s.

TYPES OF LOSS OF CONTROL AND THE SOVIET/RUSSIAN EXPERIENCE

The possession of nuclear weapons is usually associated with power, security, and influence—although many question exactly how much power, security, and influence nuclear weapons confer onto their possessor and whether the burden is worth the benefits—as well as responsibility. Among the responsibilities is maintaining control of everything associated with nuclear weapons—the weapons themselves, delivery vehicles, fissile and other related materials, technologies, etc. Of all the varieties of potential crisis situations, this chapter will primarily address those that pertain to the "end products"—nuclear weapons and their delivery vehicles. In a separate section, the chapter will also address control of weapons-grade nuclear materials.

The loss of control over nuclear weapons and delivery vehicles can be grouped into two categories.

1. The loss of physical control: risk that nuclear weapons might fall into the wrong hands:
    - The most obvious concern is the capture of nuclear weapons by nongovernmental enti-

ties, such as terrorist groups or political movements; and,
- The breakup of a nuclear state, which happened to the Soviet Union in 1991 and might happen to other nuclear-weapons states (NWS) in the future. In that case, it becomes unclear who has the right to own and control nuclear weapons. Perhaps the most dangerous consequence of a breakup of an NWS is freedom for elements of the military and civilian personnel in physical control of nuclear weapons to choose allegiances.

2. The loss of control over use: risk that elements of the state mechanism with the ultimate right and responsibility to use nuclear weapons (for example, the head of state) might lose these prerogatives:
- The breakdown of the command and control system: officials authorized to make decisions cannot convey the order down the chain. This scenario is dangerous to the extent that it indicates a broader problem; moreover, the authority to give a launch order might pass into the wrong hands;
- The breakdown of the command and control system: officers in direct control of weapons acquire the capability to use them without proper authorization; and,
- The penetration of the command and control system by unauthorized persons.

From January 1990 to May 1992, the Soviet Union/Russia encountered at least four out of five types of loss of control. These happened in three separate crises:

1. January 1990: reported attempts by the "Popular Front" (a type of nongovernmental oppositional and often nationalistic movement that was springing up all around the Soviet Union in the late-1980s) of Azerbaijan to seize tactical nuclear weapons during violent events in Baku. This case belongs to type 1 above.

2. August 1991: the failed *coup d'état* in Moscow. For 3 days it remained unclear who had the three portable launch control consoles with codes; later, it became known that they were in the hands of leaders of the coup (including persons who did not have the right to control them). This case belongs to type 3 above.

3. Fall 1991-Spring 1992: breakup of the Soviet Union. Four out of 15 newly independent states had nuclear weapons in their territories, and it took several months to finalize the decision that Russia would remain the sole inheritor of the Soviet Union's nuclear status. (Ukraine in particular apparently played with the idea of "going nuclear" until May 1992.) This is a type 2 situation above.

During that period of uncertainty, immediate control of nuclear weapons (except for the power to use them) was delegated to the Strategic Forces of the Commonwealth—a rather artificial construct made of part of the Soviet military, which acquired a degree of autonomy (a situation close to type 4 above). Meanwhile, Ukraine sought to inject itself into the command and control chain to prevent the Russian leadership from launching nuclear weapons from its territory (a type 3 situation above).

Moreover, officers in control of some strategic delivery vehicles in Ukraine took an oath of allegiance to Ukraine, which gave the government of that country the capability to use these assets, although reportedly not the capability to arm weapons. That situation could, with some stretching, classify as type 5 above.

In the end, Russia successfully navigated through the Scyllas and the Charybdises of this turbulent time. Control of nuclear weapons was not lost in any of the three cases, and there is no evidence (although there were plenty of rumors) that any nuclear weapons were lost. Yet, most of these cases were close calls, especially the first and the third. Things could have easily turned the other way, and this should remain a lesson to remember. No state that possesses nuclear weapons or has embarked on the path to nuclear status is guaranteed to avoid political and socio-economic turmoil. Hence, appropriate security measures should be put in place to prevent a repetition of similar situations precisely because control of nuclear weapons in each case hung on a very thin thread, and next time we might not be as lucky.

The loss of control over weapons-grade materials can be grouped into two big categories:

    1. Material is stolen by outsiders, whether from facilities in the nuclear weapons complex or during transportation. This threat is ever-present, but the probability of such an event dramatically increased during the last years of the Soviet Union and especially after its collapse because security systems (both physical and human) were weakened, and accounting, which was based exclusively on paper trails, became less reliable.

    2. Material is stolen by an insider(s). This threat also sharply increased during the last years of the Soviet Union and immediately after its collapse because extreme and worsening deprivation (resulting

from the near-collapse of budget funding and record-high inflation rates, which reached an estimated 2,200 percent in 1992) combined with new opportunities to spend money that had not existed before. Since the system had not been designed for the specific political and socio-economic circumstances that emerged in Russia in the early-1990s, the risk associated with insider threats radically increased.

The two categories differ by the type of threat and type of defensive measures that should be taken to prevent loss of control over materials. There can also be a combination of the two scenarios—outsiders working in concert with insiders. The case that developed in 1992 belonged to the second category—an insider stealing material without a specific buyer in mind. That case is particularly important, because the loss of material was found by accident. It served as an early warning about threats that might appear in the future.

BAKU, 1990: RISK OF A NUCLEAR NONGOVERNMENT ORGANIZATION

The Caucasus became a hotbed of tension and violence early into the Perestroika period; that included Azerbaijan, which saw a major outbreak of violence as early as 1988 (pogroms in Sumgait). The next flare-up in Azerbaijan came in January 1990 in Baku, the capital of the republic.[1] The opposition was led by the Popular Front of Azerbaijan; organizations with the same or a similar name were springing up throughout the entire Soviet Union in areas dominated by non-Russian populations. (These included not only the Soviet periphery—the constituent republics—but also autonomous regions of the Russian Federation itself.)

During the 1990s events, the Popular Front of Azerbaijan reportedly attempted to seize control of nuclear weapons stored in the territory of that republic. According to unofficial data, Azerbaijan was home to four "mobile service and technical units" for nuclear weapons, which were assigned to air defense.[2] Reportedly, Azerbaijan was also host to nuclear-armed torpedoes for the Caspian Sea flotilla.[3]

The attempts to seize nuclear weapons were perpetrated by Azeri nationalists commonly referred to as the Popular Front—a broad and rather amorphous organization, many of whose members sought to gain independence for Azerbaijan from the Soviet Union. Many were Islamists. It should be noted that formal leaders of the Popular Front did not have full control of rank-and-file members and subgroups. At the same time, there also was, by all accounts, a well-organized core that performed preparatory work, but largely remained in the shadow.[4] Leslie and Andrew Cockburn specifically point at outspoken nationalist radical Nimet Panakhov, who was close to the Turkish Islamic organization "Grey Wolves"; it became famous for organizing an assassination attempt on Pope John Paul II. According to the Cockburns, speaking at a rally in the second half of January 1990, Panakhov promised the crowd he would take control of Soviet nuclear weapons.[5]

Information about events in Azerbaijan is very sketchy, but apparently there were three incidents, probably at two locations. According to well-known Russian journalist Mikhail Khodarenok, nationalists attacked a "mobile technical unit" in the vicinity of Baku that belonged to Air Defense Forces. According to Khodarenok, the commander of the unit was captured and fire was exchanged, but in the end the attackers failed to capture the facility or the weapons.[6] According to the journalist's account, the unit was able to defend itself only because it had been ordered in advance to dig trenches and take other defensive measures. There is no independent confirmation for that story, and details remain unknown.

Another incident took place at a military airfield in the vicinity of Baku involving an apparent attempt to seize nuclear weapons that were being taken out of Azerbaijan. It is possible that these were the weapons from the facility described above. The account below is based on an interview with an immediate participant; the interview was given on condition of anonymity in the summer of 1991. The general outline of events was additionally confirmed by an independent source that belonged to a different agency in the fall of 1991.

According to the story told in these interviews, several (at least three) *Tupolev Tu-22M3* medium bombers were sent to take weapons on board and relocate them to the territory of Russia (the sources did not disclose the destination). As the aircraft were preparing to leave with the weapons on board, a crowd of civilians (mostly women, children, and old men) penetrated the perimeter of the airfield and positioned themselves on the runway to prevent the takeoff. Shortly after the beginning of the standoff, the military received information that several trucks and/or buses with armed men were driving toward the airfield.[7] According to the source, personnel at the base were certain that an attempt to seize the nuclear weapons was afoot.

Under the circumstances, the captain of the first Tu-22M3, who also commanded the entire group, decided to use an automatic cannon mounted on the bomber to scare the crowd away. According to the witness, the cannon "dug up a trench in solid concrete that was half a meter deep." The operator started to shoot close to the aircraft and gradually lifted the cannon so that the "trench" moved toward the crowd. Civilians assembled at the runway were scared and dispersed. After that, the aircraft immediately took off, one after another.

Finally, the Cockburns report that an attack on a naval base at Zuh, where nuclear-armed torpedoes were stored, took place as well. Fighting ensued and continued for 24 hours, but the attempt failed.

There are several uncertainties about these accounts. First of all, it is not clear whether there were nuclear-armed torpedoes at the Caspian Sea or, at least, at Baku—nuclear weapons were intended to be used by the Soviet Navy against the U.S. Navy, and the Soviets did not face major enemy naval forces in the Caspian Sea that would require reliance on nuclear weapons. The vast majority of sources mention only nuclear weapons assigned to Air Defense Forces or the Air Force.

Assuming that there were nuclear weapons assigned to the Navy, it is unclear whether all the events took place at the same facility (in which case, Khodarenok and the Cockburns described the same incident). Nuclear weapons were in the custody of the personnel of the 12th General Directorate of the Ministry of Defense (Glavnoye Upravleniye Ministerstvo Oborony, GUMO) and were kept at specially designed and constructed storage facilities. Some of these were located at or adjacent to military bases, but some were located at some distance from them. It is possible that weapons for both the Air Defense and the Navy were kept at the same location that came under an attack, but, alternatively, there could have been two separate storage facilities and, in that case, these were two separate incidents.

It is also unclear whether the Tu-22M3s taking nuclear weapons away from Azerbaijan carried all of the nuclear weapons or just those from the air defense base (assuming, again, that there were weapons assigned to the Navy). If the latter is the case, then the way other weapons were taken away and whether there were any incidents is unclear as well.

Given these uncertainties, conclusions from that case appear limited: During the time of broad popular unrest and chaos, when political authority loses control of the situation and when security and military structures get caught in a whirlwind of events, a well-organized group can attempt to seize a nuclear weapon with relative impunity. Such action will be difficult to predict with any acceptable degree of certainty, and normal security protocols are likely to fail. In that case, only personnel on the ground in immediate control of weapons would stand between the group that attempts the seizure and its target. The only sure course of action is to remove weapons in advance when events have not yet gotten out of hand.

The decision to remove nuclear weapons from Azerbaijan was apparently made in haste and under considerable stress, but it also triggered a wholesale withdrawal of nuclear weapons from almost all constituent republics of the Soviet Union. The process continued during the entire year of 1990 and probably into early-1991. It is difficult to ascertain when the task was completed, but there are reasons to believe that by the spring of 1991, tactical nuclear weapons remained only in Russia, Belarus, Kazakhstan, and Ukraine, the republics where strategic weapons were also deployed.

In any event, by the fall of 1991, when the United States proposed a reduction of tactical nuclear weapons[8] to facilitate the consolidation of nuclear weapons in the territory of Russia, the withdrawal had been completed. This was a massive undertaking that was conducted, furthermore, in almost complete secrecy.

The withdrawal led to the consolidation of nuclear weapons at a smaller number of storage sites. The weapons withdrawn from constituent republics were put into existing storage sites and, moreover, sent primarily, if not exclusively, to the so-called Facilities-S—the central storage sites, which were better protected, manned, and fortified than storage sites associated with military units. This certainly helped to ensure the security of nuclear weapons as the Soviet Union entered the last months of its existence and during the turbulent time of the first post-breakup years.

The negative aspect of the hasty withdrawal conducted in 1990, and the additional ones in 1992-96 from Belarus, Kazakhstan, and Ukraine, was a breakdown in the accounting protocols. According to interviews with active-duty and retired military in the first half of the 1990s, bookkeeping was often substandard. This deficiency led to a range of problems in the late-1990s, as will be discussed later in this chapter. Moreover, the choice of destination facilities was often almost random—it was often the ones that were closer to the original site or had spare space. Time and transportation assets were at a premium; thus, planning was sacrificed to the speed of withdrawal. This created safety problems at some facilities, as the number of warheads exceeded the maximum allowed and personnel had trouble maintaining the controlled environment inside. This problem was resolved only about 15 years later when the number of tactical nuclear weapons was reduced by three-fourths, according to public data released by the 12th GUMO.[9]

THE 1991 COUP: ADVENTURES OF A NUCLEAR SUITCASE

The control of nuclear weapons was a decidedly marginal aspect of the attempted *coup d'état* in August 1991—or, rather, it was marginal for the Soviet leaders and population, although it was of primary importance for foreign leaders. The main story, of course, is how an attempt to save the Soviet Union undertaken by a group of key officials—which included the vice-president, the prime minister, the minister of defense, and the chairman of the Soviet Secret Service (KGB)—either doomed it (by preventing the signing of a new Union Treaty), accelerated a disintegration process that could no longer be stopped, or perhaps had no impact at all, and the Soviet Union would have fallen apart by the end of the year anyway. We can never know, and arguments could be found to support any of these interpretations. Some—the leaders of the coup themselves—even claim that there was no coup at all, and that Mikhail Gorbachev gave them, whether implicitly or explicitly, his blessing.

Where control of nuclear weapons is concerned, the story is quite straightforward: The president of the Soviet Union (also the commander in chief of the Soviet Armed Forces) lost control of the country's nuclear weapons for 3 days. That action involved two discreet steps: First, Gorbachev's dacha, where he was spending his vacation, was cut off from all communication with the outside world. Second, the portable console of the Kazbek launch control system was removed. The president regained control only after the defeat of the coup attempt.

The decision to cut off communications was apparently made at a meeting of the State Committee on the State of Emergency (GKChP) leaders on August 17, although preliminary plans had clearly been drawn earlier. Communications systems were switched off when the group sent by the coup leaders arrived at Gorbachev's dacha at Foros. According to KGB Chairman Vladimir Kruychkov, this was done to prevent Gorbachev from contacting Boris Yeltsin—the president of Russia and the main proponent of the devolution of the Soviet Union—or the President of the United States, George H. W. Bush. Communications were cut off, Kruychkov wrote later, minutes before the team sent by the GKChP to Gorbachev reached its destination.[10]

Gorbachev lost access to the Cheget portable console immediately after the GKChP group arrived in Foros, and communications were cut off.[11] Although officers of the "communications group" are supposed to obey only the president's orders, their access to the president is controlled by his security detail,[12] and in this case, the security detail had an order to completely isolate Gorbachev. According to their testimony, communications were cut off at 4:32 pm, and only a few minutes later, the senior member of the team was summoned to Army General Valentin Varennikov, one of the members of the GKChP and Commander of Ground Forces, who told them not to worry about the absence of communications.

The situation continued into the next day. In the morning of August 19, Minister of Defense Dmitri Yazov learned that Gorbachev's Cheget was still in Foros and ordered it to be brought to Moscow. Colonel Viktor Boldyrev, the commander of the unit in charge of the command and control system for nuclear weapons, flew to Foros himself (having first obtained permission from the KGB) and brought both the suitcase and "communications officers" back to Moscow. They arrived in Moscow after 7 p.m. on August 19, and after that the "nuclear suitcase" remained at the Ministry of Defense. Reportedly, all information was deleted from it, and the console became inoperable. According to Gorbachev, he regained control of his "nuclear suitcase" only on August 21, after he returned to Moscow, approximately 73 hours after losing control.

It is difficult to assess fully the implications of the seizure of the "nuclear suitcase" on August 18 because many vital details pertaining to the functioning of the Kazbek launch control system remain classified. Portable consoles known as Chegets (they were introduced into service in 1983) allowed their owners to give an order to launch nuclear weapons. There were three Chegets: During the Soviet time, one belonged to the General Secretary of the Communist Party (later to the president of the Soviet Union), the other to the minister of defense, and the third to the chief of the general staff. According to available information,[13] Cheget No. 1 had priority status: Its owner could enact a heightened level of alert and, after the early warning system registered the launch of U.S. nuclear weapons, give the launch order (transmit codes unblocking the launch command). The other two Chegets had somewhat limited functionality: They allowed their owners to maintain contact with the commander in chief to confer and give advice, but not to give launch orders. The latter became possible only under two conditions: First, a preliminary order had already been given (the system moved to heightened alert status) and second, Cheget No. 1 had remained incommunicado for an extended period. In that case, the power to authorize the launch transferred to the next level in the command and control system.

The removal of the Cheget from Gorbachev (or preventing him from accessing the console) certainly had major symbolic meaning. The Cheget is the most visible, perhaps the ultimate, symbol of political authority; thus, losing it amounted to a de facto forced resignation. Additionally, it could have theoretically prevented Gorbachev from using his authority to introduce a heightened alert level as a bargaining lever vis-à-vis the GKChP. A scenario of Gorbachev resorting to such a step is purely hypothetical, however, and thus was probably not the main motive for the coup leaders.

Finally, and perhaps most importantly, the coup leaders gained full access to the command and control system, enabling them to increase the level of alert and to give the order to launch nuclear weapons under certain circumstances (if the early warning system registers an attack). It is unclear whether they were able to give an order to launch without an attack.

Even though the coup leaders did not physically possess Gorbachev's Cheget and, by implication, the command and control system, until the evening of August 19, the unit had remained incommunicado since 4:30 p.m. of August 18. Since the system registered the chief executive as incommunicado, the other two Cheget consoles, those controlled by the minister of defense and the chief of general staff, acquired full functionality. One of these two officials clearly used their Cheget, as it will be demonstrated below, but it remains unknown who exactly did that, Minister of Defense Dmitri Yazov or Chief of General Staff Mikhail Moiseev.[14]

David Hoffman states that the key military leaders in control of nuclear forces, the Strategic Rocket Forces (SRF), the Air Force (which controlled all air-launched nuclear weapons, both long-range and tactical), and the Navy (strategic and nonstrategic sea-launched nuclear weapons) did not support the coup. He singles out Commander of the Air Force Yevgeni Shaposhnikov, who openly refused to follow the orders of the GKChP.[15]

That, however, left out some other elements of the nuclear capability—for example, short-range, land-based nuclear weapons that belonged to Ground Forces, whose Commander, Valentin Varennikov, was one of the leaders of the coup. Nothing is known about the position of the 12th GUMO, the element of the military structure in direct physical control of nuclear weapons and responsible for releasing them to troops. Bits and pieces of information to be discussed below suggest that at the very least the 12th GUMO did not contest orders from the minister of defense or the chief of general staff.

More importantly, control of the Chegets allowed two top military leaders to bypass commanders of forces (including the SRF, Air Force, and the Navy). In any event, they were able to give the order to enhance the level of alert (not fearing that Gorbachev, the commander in chief, would countermand it) and, in case the early warning system registered a nuclear attack, they could have ordered a retaliatory launch.

The ability to execute these two actions was clearly sufficient for the purposes of these military leaders. Specifically, by enhancing the level of alert, they could send a warning to the United States and the North Atlantic Treaty Organization (NATO) not to interfere with what was going on in the Soviet Union and also perhaps communicate that the new leadership was "tougher" and less prone to make concessions than Gorbachev. In the improbable case the West would have decided to threaten to use force, the system gave the military leaders the power to deter.

The GKChP ordered a higher alert level for nuclear forces in the morning of August 19, when it publicly announced that power had transitioned into the hands of the "Emergency Committee." The state of high alert continued only for several hours and was reduced in the middle of the day on August 19, although not yet returned to the normal, peacetime level. The increase of the alert level was apparently executed through a direct order that bypassed the chain of command. Only bits and pieces of what was happening "on the ground" are available.

For example, Igor Kudrin, a commander of one of the strategic nuclear submarines,[16] disclosed recently that all strategic submarines of the Northern Fleet were put on alert on August 19.[17] In this particular case (the submarines were at their bases), this meant that the submarines, even those moored at the pier, were ready to launch missiles from the surface. Soviet strategic submarines were given the capability to launch missiles on warning about an ongoing attack in order to compensate for the relatively small number of submarines on patrol.[18]

Another source told a story about the first day of the coup at an Air Force base near Khabarovsk. At that time, the source served as a navigator in a Su-24M dual-capable aircraft. At 7 a.m. Moscow time on August 19 — the time when the announcement about the coup was aired on Soviet television — their regiment was put on high alert: Namely, the 12th GUMO personnel loaded nuclear weapons on board the aircraft (for the first time in the memory of the source), and crews were ordered to be ready to take off 1 hour after the order. Crews were also given two envelopes. One envelope had codes necessary to arm nuclear weapons — the first step in the arming process, according to the source, was to be performed prior to takeoff by a team from the weapons storage facility, and the final arming procedure would be executed while in the air on the approach to the target. The second envelope contained information about the target. The high alert status continued for 1 hour and then was reduced to 4-hour readiness for takeoff.[19]

The story from Khabarovsk appears particularly significant. First, it proves that leaders of the coup, indeed, did not need cooperation from commanders of the various forces in control of nuclear weapons. Specifically, Shaposhnikov, the most open and vocal opponent of the coup, was unable to prevent it: The order was sent by higher authorities, and he could not contest it. Obviously, the same could be expected from the other forces, including the tactical nuclear weapons assigned to Ground Forces.

That story also makes clear that not only were the strategic forces put on high alert, but the entire Soviet nuclear arsenal. Most likely, this reflected the extreme paranoia of GKChP leaders, but it clearly represented a very dangerous situation. One could easily anticipate a contingency under which a move by an adversary could be misinterpreted as a provocation and lead to most grave consequences.

What truly draws attention in the story of the "adventures of the nuclear suitcase" is the ease with which the commander in chief was relieved of one of the most important vestiges of his power, and the control of nuclear weapons transitioned to his subordinates, who decided to stage a *coup d'état*. It required the collusion of just three people: the Chairman of the KGB (who was responsible for the security detail and communications of the chief executive), and the minister of defense and the chief of general staff—

who were responsible for the command and control system of nuclear weapons. The KGB could isolate the chief executive and cut him off from all forms of communication; the military, while the commander in chief was incommunicado, could assume control of nuclear forces.

The first and the most obvious remedy was taken almost instantly. In September 1991, the responsibility of providing security for the top leaders was taken away from the KGB and given to a separate service, the FSO,[20] which was directly subordinate to the president (first of the Soviet Union, then of Russia). From the fall of 1991 until the final breakup of the Soviet Union, the president of Russia had his own security service, independent of the one entrusted with the security of Mikhail Gorbachev. The next step was taken on December 24, 1991, only days after the Soviet Union was formally disbanded: Boris Yeltsin created the Federal Agency of Government Communications and Information (FAPSI),[21] a special service in charge of all government communications that also reported directly to the president.

By removing security and communications from the KGB and transforming them into independent governmental agencies, the top leadership could sleep a bit more easily, because their own bodyguards and their communications were no longer controlled by a single person. The command and control system for nuclear weapons, however, remained intact, as far as is known. Yeltsin used his Cheget in 1995 to monitor the launch of a Norwegian research rocket that triggered an alarm of the Russian early warning system.[22]

Moreover, it appears that events in the Soviet Union in 1991 illustrate a much more fundamental problem that is inherent, to a greater or lesser degree, in all nuclear-weapons states—the vulnerability of the nuclear weapons command and control system to an attempted coup. Essentially, the requirements for such a system, dictated by the logic of nuclear deterrence, also make it vulnerable to sabotage. To ensure political control and the ability to strike on warning, the system must be centralized (a single person, the chief executive, must be able to sanction the launch of weapons), but also account for the risk of losing the chief executive by giving the same power to other levels in the command and control system. As a result, the subversion of the system becomes possible, too.

The Soviet system, in which the single civilian leader, the president, was followed in the chain of command by the military, was clearly excessively top-heavy, as events in August 1991 demonstrated. The Russian system inherited the same drawback: Once the president is "taken out," the military assumes full control of nuclear weapons. The fact that the prime minister is supposed to be second-in-command means relatively little to the extent that he does not have the means to execute his rights. One of the leading Russian experts on nuclear policy, Alexei Arbatov, proposed a few years ago to transfer one of the Cheget consoles from the Chief of General Staff to the prime minister,[23] but that proposal went unheeded.

BREAKUP OF THE SOVIET UNION: FINDING A NEW HOME FOR THE NUCLEAR WEAPONS

The breakup of an NWS presents a unique challenge with respect to the control of nuclear weapons. In previous cases we dealt with attempts by unauthorized persons or entities to seize control of weapons or the chain of command; the prevention of such situations is a "normal" threat, which all security services and all protocols are configured to address. The breakup of a country, however, involves the transition of authority: For a period of time it becomes unclear who is a legitimate authority, to whom personnel in direct control of nuclear weapons must report, and whose orders they must follow. The same is true for the chain of command: It becomes unclear whose launch order is legitimate. As a result, we end up in a particularly dangerous situation, when military and civilian personnel are free to choose allegiances. Even worse, competing political authorities seek to gain the trust and loyalty of personnel in the direct control of nuclear weapons and the chains of command, and the latter can dictate their conditions.

The period of relative autonomy can last a significant amount of time. In the case of the Soviet Union, it lasted at least 6 months (from December 1991, when the Soviet Union was formally disbanded, to the signing of the Lisbon Protocol) and perhaps even longer. (One can claim that the period began earlier, in the fall of 1991, and ended in 1994, when all nuclear weapons were transferred to Russia.) It can be hypothesized that the longer the period of uncertainty, the greater the chance that *all* competing political authorities will lose control of nuclear weapons or retain it only formally.

The best and perhaps the only remedy is to consolidate nuclear weapons and, if possible, weapons-grade fissile materials, in one part of the territory of the disintegrating country under control of one of the competing political groups—the future government. At least, in this case, it might become possible to ensure the loyalty of personnel in direct control of nuclear weapons and materials, since there will be a direct transition of authority from one government to another, and the period of uncertainty will be minimal.

This is what happened in Russia: When Gorbachev formally retired as president of the Soviet Union, he ceded his console for control of nuclear weapons to Yeltsin, the president of Russia. Subsequently, Yeltsin's authority to control nuclear weapons was not questioned in Russia except for certain limitations to be noted below (and even then, the situation never reached dangerous proportions). The key challenge was the fate of nuclear weapons and delivery vehicles that remained outside Russia.

The following features of the situation surrounding the breakup of the Soviet Union deserve close attention.

The Soviet Government Began to Lose Control of Nuclear Weapons Months before the Actual Breakup of the Country.

Although the chain of command was restored after the failure of the August 1991 coup, the Soviet government no longer felt sufficiently sure of itself to make some important decisions, in particular with regard to nuclear posture. This limitation was revealed when the Soviet leadership was contemplating a response to the September 1991 initiative of George H. W. Bush.

The primary reason for the U.S. announcement of a unilateral reduction of tactical nuclear weapons and a list of proposals regarding strategic weapons was to help the Soviet leadership consolidate nuclear weapons in the territory of Russia. In particular, the proposal to eliminate multiple independent reentry vehicled (MIRVed) intercontinental ballistic missiles

(ICBMs) with more than one warhead would have resulted in the complete removal of nuclear weapons from Kazakhstan and a very significant reduction of nuclear weapons in Ukraine.[24] The Soviet Union, while responding favorably to the American initiative on tactical nuclear weapons, rejected the proposal to ban MIRVed ICBMs, but for different reasons: The bulk of Soviet strategic forces were on MIRVed ICBMs, and accepting that proposal would have meant a massive (and extremely expensive) restructuring of the force.

Still, the U.S. concern about the increasingly shaky control of Soviet authorities over nuclear weapons was shared by some in the Soviet Union. In early October 1991, two leading Soviet scientists who had been proactive in matters of disarmament, academicians Yevgeni Velikhov and Yuri Ryzhov, sent a letter to Mikhail Gorbachev imploring him to use the opportunity and withdraw nuclear weapons to Russia: "Developments in Ukraine or in Kazakhstan are unpredictable," they wrote. "One cannot rule out that the very fact of presence of [nuclear] weapons in their territories might be used as an instrument of political influence."[25]

Governmental agencies took a second look at the American proposal and still rejected the de-MIRVing proposal, but this time for a different reason: Foreign Ministry experts doubted that even with the "cover" provided by the Americans, the withdrawal of nuclear weapons from other republics would be politically feasible. "The [American] proposal," they wrote, "contradicts the well-known position of Kazakhstan, which insists on proportional reductions of strategic offensive weapons in Russia and Kazakhstan, and even more so the position of Ukraine, which rejects any actions with regard to nuclear weapons in its territory without its agreement."[26]

In contrast to 1990, when the Soviet government was able to withdraw nuclear weapons from problem regions, it now believed it had lost this power. While all other forms of control over nuclear weapons appeared to function properly, one important element of the central government's authority — the power to choose the locations where nuclear weapons are deployed and stored — was probably lost. We will never know this, because withdrawal was never tried. But it is sufficient for our purposes that key agencies of the Soviet government believed that problems would have ensued.

Nuclear Weapons Quickly Became Hostage to a Political Struggle between the Governments of Emerging Independent States and Soviet Leadership.

In October 1991, several months before the breakup of the Soviet Union, a group of experts prepared a lengthy paper outlining the future policy of the Russian Federation with regard to nuclear weapons.[27] That document was approved by Yeltsin and was supposed to become the guidelines for a Russian government still *within* the Soviet Union. It proposed to concentrate all Soviet nuclear weapons in the territory of Russia; withdrawal from Belarus and Ukraine was scheduled for 1993 and from Kazakhstan for 1996. The document also insisted on fully consolidating the production of delivery vehicles in Russia, eliminating dependence on the defense industry in other Soviet republics and even on the parts of Russia with significant levels of separatism:

> Beginning in the middle of 1992, all R&D performed by chief designers outside Russia should be terminated.

> First of all this measure should affect NPO [Nauchno-Proizvodstvennoe Ob'edinenie, or Scientific and Production Association] *Yuzhnoe*, plants in Dnepropetrovsk and Pavlograd, and, in the case disintegration trends in Russia should increase, the Kazan' aircraft complex in Tataria.[28]

Given the realities of the political tug-of-war (influence of the Russian leadership was on the rise and that of the Soviet leadership in rapid decline), these proposals effectively amounted to shifting control of nuclear weapons from the Soviet government into the hands of what was then a regional government.

In contrast to Russia, Ukraine paid scant attention to nuclear weapons during that period. On October 24, Verkhovna Rada, the Ukrainian parliament, adopted a declaration that reaffirmed the 1991 declaration of the future non-nuclear status of the country and said that the presence of nuclear weapons in its territory was "temporary." The declaration proclaimed, however, that Ukraine sought control over nonuse of nuclear weapons from its territory and that all nuclear weapons located in its territory would be eliminated. The latter phrase suggested that the disposition of nuclear weapons required negotiations and would not be left to the discretion of a central authority (at the time, still the Soviet Union).

The Attraction of Nuclear Weapons is Difficult to Resist. Given an Opportunity, Newly Independent States Would Seek to Control as Many Nuclear Weapons as They Can Lay Their Hands on, Even If Originally They Intended to Do Otherwise.

In spite of public rejection of its nuclear status, developments in Ukraine were increasingly complicated. The closer the republic moved toward full independence, the more attractive nuclear weapons seemed. In the fall of 1991, the Center for Operational and Strategic Studies (COSS[29]) of the newly created Main Staff of the Ukrainian Armed Forces[30] conducted an in-depth study looking into two questions: Could nuclear weapons deployed in Ukraine be used to deter Russia, and could Ukraine take control of these weapons? Expert support was provided primarily by the Dniepropetrovsk chapter of the National Institute of Strategic Studies.[31]

The results of the study were not encouraging for proponents of a nuclear status of Ukraine.[32] It was concluded that strategic weapons were too long-range and could not reach closer than the Urals; thus, Moscow and other key political and military targets in the European part of Russia were out of reach. Moreover, even that task would have required retargeting missiles, which was impossible without completely overtaking all command and control systems, as well as obtaining data for new targeting. As things stood in late-1991 and early-1992, all nuclear weapons were targeted at the United States. The use of tactical nuclear weapons was apparently not even seriously considered — and, in fact, at the dissolution of the Soviet Union, Ukraine quickly agreed to transfer them to Russia in a matter of months. The withdrawal was completed in May 1992.[33]

With regard to Ukraine's ability to take over control of nuclear weapons, the study was more optimistic. It reportedly concluded that, in principle, this was possible. The Russian military concurred with that finding: According to Strategic Rocket Forces experts, Ukraine could assume operational control over nuclear weapons in just 9 months.[34] Work was reportedly performed at *Khartron*, a research institute in Kharkiv that specialized in the development of control and guidance systems for space and military programs, and continued probably until the end of 1992.

In spite of these (relatively) optimistic findings,[35] the study recommended that Ukraine should refrain from attempting to acquire a nuclear status. This recommendation was based, according to Grechaninov, on a comprehensive assessment of programs that had to be implemented in support of a nuclear status, including the ability to produce nuclear weapons, maintain weapons and delivery vehicles, etc. All in all, it is clear that even before obtaining formal independence, political leaders in Ukraine seriously contemplated pursuing a nuclear status and were dissuaded by military and technical experts who demonstrated that such a move was impossible for technical and financial reasons.

Companion evidence was supplied by former U.S. Ambassador to Ukraine Steven Pifer, who reported that shortly after Ukraine acquired independence, a group of foreign and defense ministry officials had a meeting with senior officers of the 43d SRF Army deployed in Ukraine. The former wanted to explore whether the country could maintain a nuclear capability if it chose to do so, but the military explained that Ukraine would have needed to build an extensive infrastructure, which was both financially and technologically challenging.[36]

There is also unconfirmed information[37] that in December 1991, the Kharkiv Institute of Physics and Technology, which had been involved in nuclear weapons research from the early days of the Soviet nuclear program, requested and received from Arzamas-16 (currently known as Sarov), one of two primary Soviet nuclear weapons laboratories, the manuals necessary for the maintenance and refurbishment of nuclear weapons. Since Ukraine was not yet formally classified or perceived as another country during the transitional period, the request from Kharkiv was apparently treated in Sarov as routine.

In spite of the recommendations of the study group and the political declarations, the issue of the status of Ukraine was not resolved. It is difficult to tell with sufficient certainty whether the Ukrainian government tried to use nuclear weapons in its territory as leverage or if political leaders continued to entertain the thought of acquiring a nuclear status.

On February 23, 1992, the president of Ukraine, Leonid Kravchuk, ordered the discontinuance of the withdrawal of tactical nuclear weapons from the country, a move that was made public only 2 weeks later, on March 12. The official justification was that, in violation of the Minsk and Almaty Agreements, Ukraine had not been allowed to monitor their elimination. The interpretation in Moscow was different: Ukraine was probing for the reactions of Russia and the United States to the possibility of Ukraine's retaining nuclear weapons; otherwise, consultations could have been held first.

On April 5, Kravchuk issued Decree No. 209, authorizing the minister of defense to take all strategic forces in the territory of Ukraine under his administrative command. This decree contradicted the December 1991 agreements between the heads of newly independent states putting all strategic forces of the Soviet Union under command of the Joint Armed Forces of the Commonwealth (JAFC). In all fairness, this decree could have been a response to the actions of the JAFC High Command: While all JAFC personnel were supposed to take an oath of allegiance to the Commonwealth as a whole, commander in chief of the JAFC Yevgeni Shaposhnikov ordered all troops in the territory of Russia to take an oath of allegiance to Russia, and the cable with that order was sent (supposedly by mistake) to Ukraine.[38] Moreover, General Mikhail Bashkirov, who in 1991-92 commanded a division of heavy bombers in Uzin, said that in February he was ordered to relocate all heavy bombers to Russia; Bashkirov refused.[39]

In the middle of February, about half of the officers of the Uzin division took an oath of allegiance to Ukraine.[40] On April 5, Kravchuk issued Decree No. 209, authorizing the minister of defense to take all the strategic forces in the territory of Ukraine under his administrative command. By the end of April, the officers of all the Strategic Forces units in Ukraine did the same.

The transition of SRF and Strategic Air Force units from Soviet/JAFC structure to the Ukrainian national army gave Kiev direct administrative and operational control over nuclear-capable delivery vehicles, but not over nuclear weapons. The latter remained under control of units subordinated to the 12th GUMO in Moscow, but not for long.

In May 1992, the personnel of two nuclear weapons storage units located at Air Force bases took oaths of allegiance to Ukraine, which gave the latter physical control of some nuclear weapons. In contrast to delivery vehicle personnel, however, the personnel at weapons storage facilities took much longer to switch allegiance to Ukraine, and that process was completed only in 1993. Physical control of nuclear weapons made Ukraine a de facto NWS. The only element of full-scope control it lacked were the codes needed to arm the weapons, but there were persistent rumors that the Ukrainians were working on that, too. Also, air-launched cruise missile (ALCM) warheads reportedly did not have targeting information ("zero flight path," according to Russian military lingo), which had been removed on orders of the 12th GUMO prior to the switchover of personnel to Ukraine.[41]

It is difficult to say definitively whether events in Ukraine could be classified as the loss of control over nuclear weapons, because the weapons ended up in the hands of a recognized state. On the other hand, Ukraine was widely regarded by everyone—and was officially proclaimed by its leadership—as a nonnuclear state where nuclear weapons were located only temporarily. The immediate reason for the awkward situation that emerged by the middle of 1992 was the hasty and poorly conceived process of disbanding the Soviet Union: Leaders concluded only very general and imprecisely worded agreements, and many key issues were not discussed at all.

Other post-Soviet states with nuclear weapons in their territories experienced the same attraction to nuclear weapons, although to a much smaller extent than in Ukraine. For example, Belarus, which at first displayed a determination to get rid of nuclear weapons in its territory as quickly as possible, began showing signs that it might want to reconsider its earlier decision. In April 1992 the new defense minister of Belarus, Pavel Kozlovski, demanded compensation and security guarantees from the West in exchange for the renunciation of nuclear weapons. Simultaneously, at a meeting with commanders of troops deployed in Belarus, President Stanislav Shushkevich made an unprecedented statement about feeling particularly confident about the country's security because of the knowledge that he had nuclear weapons behind him.[42] The change of attitude in Belarus, however, was limited to a handful of political statements and was most likely caused by the example of Ukraine.

Kazakhstan presents yet another story. Even as Russia and Ukraine were increasingly engaged in a bitter fight over the fate of Soviet nuclear weapons, Almaty remained almost completely silent, but it appears that Nursultan Nazarbaev, the first president of Kazakhstan, was simply watching unfolding events. Had Ukraine become nuclear, Kazakhstan could have followed suit; had it failed, Kazakhstan would have ceded nuclear weapons without much argument.

In the end, Kazakhstan could not wait forever. In early-May 1992, apparently influenced by a recent visit of Kravchuk to Washington,[43] Nazarbaev pointed out:

> Our neighbor China has nuclear weapons, our neighbor Russia has nuclear weapons. Some Russian politicians have territorial claims on Kazakhstan. There are Chinese textbooks that claim that parts of Siberia and Kazakhstan belong to China. Under these circumstances, how do you expect Kazakhstan to react?[44]

Shortly afterward, Nazarbaev attempted to retain Soviet strategic missiles in Kazakhstan, but with a status of a Russian military base rather than his own.[45] He even had Yeltsin sign a joint statement to that effect, but Moscow had to rescind the document because of strong U.S. opposition and the fear that such a step would undermine delicate maneuvering around the fate of nuclear weapons in Ukraine.[46] The choice in favor of becoming a basing country instead of a nuclear country was clearly dictated by the absence of any infrastructure whatsoever for the maintenance and production of both weapons and delivery vehicles.

On April 11, 1992, Ukraine, Kazakhstan, and Belarus issued a joint statement declaring that they, along with Russia, were legal heirs to the assets of the Soviet Union, including the ownership of nuclear weapons.[47] This clearly indicated that the three countries were looking for common ground vis-à-vis Russia (and, to some extent, the United States) to at least leverage nuclear weapons that remained in their territories after the breakup of the Soviet Union. The statement certainly did not amount to a claim for control of these weapons, but strengthened the hand of the states (Ukraine, in particular) that toyed with such a prospect.

Even allowing for imperfect and unavoidably incomplete data, *the overall trend* appears quite clear. Nuclear weapons were regarded by at least some of the emerging governments as a valuable asset, and they were prepared to explore the options for laying their hands on them. There were several reasons the "game" did not turn violent and was resolved with a reasonable degree of success and in a reasonable amount of time. The first reason was the firm position of the United States. Very early in the game, the United States made it abundantly clear that the membership of each newly independent state, except Russia, in the Nuclear Non-Proliferation Treaty (NPT) as a non-nuclear state was a critical criterion by which Washington would assess its behavior.

Second, in the run-up to and during the formal dissolution of the Soviet Union, the newly independent states with nuclear weapons in their territories felt they had to maintain a disarmament and nonproliferation decorum. Hence, they quickly concluded a series of agreements on the future of nuclear weapons and, in spite of the many shortcomings of these agreements and attempts to revise them afterward, the agreements helped provide a framework for subsequent negotiations and political games. Moreover, some states (Kazakhstan and Ukraine, in particular) used anti-nuclear sentiment in their countries to consolidate public support for independence and could not revise them easily.

Third, the game was influenced by the availability of the technological and industrial infrastructure. Hence, for Kazakhstan, a nuclear status was simply out of the question. Ukraine had some elements of the infrastructure required for a nuclear state, but completing it would have been so expensive and time-consuming, and Ukraine faced such strong opposition from other countries (the United States, in particular) that the project was not even attempted.

The experience of the Soviet breakup offers several important lessons:

1. Regardless of what leaders of future new states say about nuclear weapons, they are very likely to change their attitudes once independence is achieved and will seek to lay their hands on all the nuclear weapons they can reach. The attraction is very difficult to resist. This is not only about the aura of influence and power nuclear weapons are often believed to carry, but is often simply a habit of an elite and a public that is used to living in a nuclear state. Losing that nuclear status is difficult to accept.

2. Any agreements newly independent states conclude to ensure orderly transition from one state to several will likely be of poor quality and remain short-lived. Any final resolution of the nuclear inheritance will require new negotiations that will be time-consuming and difficult. Chances are, before such negotiations even begin, there will be a high risk of open conflict.

3. New states are likely to seek legitimacy in the eyes of the international community and comply, at

least outwardly, with disarmament and nuclear non-proliferation regimes. While these regimes cannot, in and of themselves, prevent conflicts or the division of nuclear weapons among newly independent states, they can considerably reduce freedom of action and serve as criteria for legitimacy. These regimes also can justify and facilitate outside interference in the process of settlement on the issue of nuclear inheritance.

4. The United States, which clearly and completely dominated the international scene in the early-1990s, played a pivotal role in the successful outcome of events in the former Soviet Union. It is unclear whether it can play the same role in the future, in case a nuclear state breaks up, or will need to cooperate more closely with other great powers.

The Breakup of the Soviet Union Resulted in the Weakening of Political Authority, (Almost) Decapitated the Nuclear Command and Control Chain, and Gave the Military an Opportunity to Choose Its Allegiance.

The disintegration of central authority in the Soviet Union—the emergence of several independent states in the place of a single country and the inevitable competition of these states for legitimacy, allegiance of the population, and the attributes of statehood—created a legal and psychological vacuum for the Soviet military. In an attempt to smooth the transition, new states created an artificial structure called the Joint Armed Forces of the Commonwealth (JAFC). The JAFC included all the parts of the Soviet Armed Forces that were not immediately "privatized" as in Ukraine, and the Strategic Forces of the Commonwealth—a part of the JAFC, which was responsible for nuclear weapons. Some states (Ukraine, in particular), however, sought to control all the military structures in their territory rather than yield to a nonstate authority that was widely (and justifiably) suspected to be primarily loyal to Moscow.

An immediate consequence of that transition was the uncertainty of the chain of command and control of nuclear weapons. The ultimate power to use nuclear weapons was entrusted to President of Russia Yeltsin, who controlled Gorbachev's portable control unit and was supposed to coordinate the use of nuclear weapons with heads of three other post-Soviet states that had nuclear weapons in their territories through a special conference phone.[48] These three leaders, however, could not prevent Yeltsin from launching a nuclear strike, whether using nuclear weapons deployed in Russia itself or those deployed in their territories. Consequently, Ukraine, which sought full statehood, talked about cutting into the chain of command and installing systems that would deny Yeltsin the ability to send launch orders to nuclear assets in the Ukrainian territory.

Beyond the ultimate decision authority, the system that emerged from the breakup of the Soviet Union was unique, unworkable, and ultimately dangerous, as there was no political authority above the military leaders. The JAFC became a semi-autonomous organization that reported to all heads of state (governments) of the Commonwealth of Independent States (CIS) simultaneously — and where nuclear weapons were concerned, to four heads of state — which, in practice, meant they reported to no one. It is worth bearing in mind that Yevgeni Shaposhnikov, the commander in chief of the JAFC, and his chief of staff inherited the two portable control units that previously had belonged to Soviet military leaders. Under certain circumstances (the incapacitation of Yeltsin's unit), they could acquire full control of nuclear weapons.

The close association between the Russian government and the JAFC High Command was strongly resented by other newly independent states, Ukraine in particular, but the Russian leadership was uncomfortable with it as well. Even though Shaposhnikov demonstrated his loyalty to Yeltsin at every turn and acted, especially in the first months following the breakup of the Soviet Union, as a de facto minister of defense of Russia, the JAFC actively interfered in CIS politics and decisionmaking. For example, it effectively monopolized the process of drafting agreements on all military matters within the CIS; governments would only receive drafts of new agreements days prior to their meetings and did not have time to properly examine these drafts. Political leaders rarely went into the finer details, so the High Command had broad discretion over military policy.

Increasingly often, the drafts included Shaposhnikov as a co-signer along with the heads of state. For example, a High Command draft of an agreement between Russia and Ukraine on Strategic Forces was titled "Agreement between the Russian Federation, Ukraine, and the High Command of the Joint Armed Forces of the Commonwealth on the Division of Functions of Operational and Administrative Control over Strategic Forces Located in the Territory of Ukraine." The agreement was supposed to be signed by Yeltsin, Kravchuk, and Shaposhnikov.

In the summer of 1992, Shaposhnikov tried to become a voting member of the Collective Security Council (a body that consisted only of heads of state or government). That could have completed the process of transforming the military into a nearly sovereign entity not subject to any political authority whatsoever.

Another area in which civilian authorities were losing control over the military was the power of the purse. Even Russia, which shouldered the bulk of defense spending in the CIS—the other state that spent money on the military was Ukraine—virtually lost that power. A member of the Supreme Soviet (the Russian parliament prior to the adoption of the new Constitution in 1993) Committee on Defense, Valeri Shimko, complained that the JAFC High Command denied the parliament control over spending and expected blind approval of all requests. As a result, in the first quarter of 1992, the actual spending on armed forces was 60 to 65 percent higher than the budget allocation[49] — the only category of the budget in which this happened.[50]

In early-1992, one could see even more ominous signs: The military was quickly asserting a political role of its own. The last months of the Soviet Union saw the emergence of officer assemblies in individual units and an umbrella organization, the "All-Army Conference" — an independent organization that positioned itself initially as a military trade union, but which quickly assumed a political role. The organization was dominated by the top level of the military elite (generals and senior officers). Even more troubling was the Conference's close association with the JAFC: Officers' assemblies and the All-Army Conference were supervised by a JAFC official, Major General N. Stoliarov, a former KGB officer. His deputy, Alexander Zyuskevich, said that politicians should be aware that they "cannot make decisions that affect the lives of [servicemen] without regard to their opinion."[51] The executive arm of the assembly, the Coordination Committee, was funded from the JAFC budget.[52]

A stark reminder of the risks was the All-Army Conference in January 1992, which demanded that all newly independent state leaders appear before the delegates (a meeting of 11 heads of state of the CIS was under way in Moscow at that time). Only Yeltsin and Nazarbaev showed up, though, and the conference almost went out of control. Shaposhnikov managed to calm it down, but only at the expense of vowing to fight for the preservation of unified Soviet Armed Forces.[53] Just prior to the Minsk summit in February 1992, a spokesman for the Coordination Committee declared that the military would take matters into their own hands if CIS leaders did not adhere to their demands.[54] In February 1992, Shaposhnikov agreed to make the commanding officers of units chairmen of officers' assemblies. This finalized the transformation of an erstwhile military trade union into an independent political force, with assemblies providing an alternative command and control structure.

The situation was clearly untenable even for Russian leaders. Yeltsin was prepared to tolerate it only as long as he hoped to retain control over all Soviet Armed Forces or at least over all nuclear weapons. When it became clear that the JAFC could not perform that role, he followed the example of Ukraine and established Russia's own Armed Forces in March 1992[55] and the Ministry of Defense (MOD) in May.[56] More importantly, in March 1992, all nuclear weapons mobile control units were already secured in the hands of Russian officials reporting solely to the president of Russia. But it was only by the end of 1992 that the Russian MOD succeeded in curtailing the political activism of the military.

The experience of the breakup of the Soviet Union suggests that governments, whether those of new states or established powers, do not make the final decisions. The conditions of uncertain political authority give the military the de facto power to choose loyalty and could, in an extreme case, make it an independent political player. Nuclear weapons can play the role of the ultimate prize the military could hand to one or the other government in exchange for various favors. This power could be wielded not only by the top levels of military command, but even at the unit level; the only limitation the latter had was lack of access to permissive action links.

Large-scale Relocation of Nuclear Weapons under Conditions of Political Uncertainty, Relative Independence of the Military, and Competition among New Governments Can Result in the Loss of Nuclear Weapons.

The above-referenced massive relocation of tactical nuclear weapons in 1990-91 proceeded in an orderly fashion, even if in considerable haste. The system of control and accounting still functioned reasonably well: Even as the country as a whole was sinking into disorder and sometimes utter chaos, the military machine, particularly elements associated with nuclear weapons, continued to operate in reasonable order. The situation was different in 1992. The withdrawal was hasty, sometimes poorly organized, and badly managed; the physical control of nuclear weapons was, at times, in different hands, and accounting was poor as well. As a result, there was considerable risk that some nuclear weapons would be lost in the withdrawal.

The "suitcase nukes saga" began in the fall of 1997, when General (Retired) Alexander Lebed alleged that, during his short tenure as the Secretary of the Security Council in 1996, he received information that the separatist government in Chechnya possessed small nuclear devices.[57] In an attempt to clarify the situation, he created a special commission led by his assistant, Vladimir Denisov. According to Lebed, the commission was able to locate only 48 such munitions out of a total of 132. (Subsequently, Lebed changed the total number of suitcase nukes several times, stating in the end that the number was between 100 and 500, but probably closer to 100.)[58] Lebed specifically referred to weapons that had been withdrawn to Russia after the breakup of the Soviet Union. According to Vladimir Denisov, his commission was able to find portable nuclear devices that had been in the Russian territory in 1991 or earlier, but not the ones that were supposed to be transported in 1992.[59]

When exploring the hypothesis about the loss of some portable nuclear devices in 1992, authors of a Center for Nonproliferation Studies (CNS) study, performed in 2002 and 2004,[60] noted that Soviet nuclear weapons in Belarus and Kazakhstan were under full control of the 12th GUMO in Moscow. Ukraine could have been a different case, but after the interruption of the withdrawal in the end of February 1992, the removal followed a special procedure codified in a Russian-Ukrainian agreement signed in March 1992. This procedure included the thorough authentication of each warhead by representatives of both sides, including the verification of serial numbers against the logs kept at the 12th GUMO in Moscow. Paradoxically, the tense relations between Russia and Ukraine in the spring of 1992 resulted in a more reliable and verifiable accounting procedure than was the case with other newly independent states.

In any event, the person who was supposed to be the best-informed, the chief of the 12th GUMO, Igor Valynkin, disclosed in 2001 that all portable nuclear devices had been eliminated.[61] This sounds credible, if only because these weapons have a short shelf life and should have been either refurbished or dismantled. In 2004, Vladimir Denisov, the head of the commission established by Lebed, announced that they had completed the inventory and succeeding in matching records to actual weapons.[62] Denisov did not mention how the commission dealt with the dismantled warheads. Most likely, it matched 12th GUMO records with the records at dismantlement facilities, which belong to a different agency—during that time it was the Russian Federation Ministry of Atomic Energy (MinAtom); now it is the Rosatom Nuclear Energy State Corporation (RosAtom). The apparent discrepancy between the actual inventory and records, which was the reason for Lebed's (premature) statement, probably meant that weapons withdrawn from Belarus and Kazakhstan, as well as from Ukraine, prior to the Russian-Ukrainian agreement were moved to the first available facility without taking proper care of the "bean-counting."

There is no reason to question Denisov's statement. In spite of numerous reports, no credible evidence has emerged that any warheads have been lost. Yet, two important points should be made. First, apparently, there was no attempt to match records to actual weapons until Lebed ordered the establishment of a special commission in 1996. Lebed deserves credit at least for doing that. Second, the chance of losing weapons during a hasty and poorly organized (for obvious reasons) withdrawal to Russia was uncomfortably high. If the situation repeats in a different case, nuclear weapons could well be lost.

FROM THE FRYING PAN INTO THE FIRE: CONTROL OF NUCLEAR MATERIALS AFTER THE BREAKUP OF THE SOVIET UNION

The control of nuclear weapons was, by and large, restored by the end of 1992. Physical control was solidified in the hands of Russian political leaders and the Russian military; the transfer of remaining warheads from Ukraine was no longer in serious doubt. Command and control systems were firmly in the hands of the Russian leadership as well. The time of trouble was not over yet, however; 1992 saw the emergence of a different problem that came to haunt Russia, the former Soviet Union, and the world for years—control of weapons-grade fissile materials.

The reasons for the breakdown of the fissile material control and accounting system were different from those that caused perturbations with control of nuclear weapons. The Soviet system for nuclear weapons-grade materials was intended primarily to defend against activities of hostile states, such as espionage, including the recruitment of personnel, infiltration by special forces in times of conflict, etc. The Soviet political and economic system provided sufficient protection from other kinds of threats. In the final analysis, criminals would not have any use for weapons-grade material even if they managed to steal it. There were no potential customers inside the Soviet Union, and material could not be taken outside the country, because travel was restricted and foreign trade controlled by the government. Consequently, fissile materials had military value but almost no financial value.

The introduction of a rudimentary market system in 1992, an almost unlimited right to travel abroad, and the weak ability of the government to monitor income radically changed the structure of incentives. For the first time in Soviet history, fissile materials became attractive for their potential monetary value, and the control and accounting system was not designed to address new threats, including those from insiders. The risks were further exacerbated by extreme deprivation caused by the socio-economic transition, which literally wiped out the salaries and savings of the previously privileged employees of defense enterprises.

These challenges developed against the backdrop of a general weakening of the government and the law-enforcement machine. Simply speaking, governmental agencies—including those in charge of the nuclear industry, the military, security services of all kinds, oversight bodies, and everyone else—functioned only with great difficulty because their rank-and-file personnel were even less committed to their work, interagency coordination was almost nonexistent, etc. Thus, the system had difficulty coping with even standard tasks, to say nothing about new, unconventional challenges.

The first known case of the loss of weapons-grade material took place in 1992.[63] The perpetrator was arrested in October, but had begun to steal material 5 months earlier, in the spring of 1992—only a few months after a radical economic reform was launched by the Russian government following the collapse of the Soviet Union. Leonid Smirnov, an employee of a Luch NPO (Nauchno-Proizvodstvennoe Ob'edinenie, or Scientific and Production Association) in Podolsk, a town southwest of Moscow, was detained with 1.5 kg of weapons-grade highly enriched uranium (HEU). Smirnov's last position at that fuel-production facility provided him with direct access to HEU. He had read in the mass media that weapons-grade materials could be sold for significant amounts of money, and when inflation turned his salary into almost nothing, he decided to use his access to such material to get rich quickly.

Smirnov used his knowledge of the fine details of the production process and the nuances of the accounting system as well as inadequate security protocols. He skimmed small amounts of material (50-70 grams at a time). Thefts went unnoticed because each time the amount of stolen material was within the margin of "natural" loss in the process of production allowed by the accounting system. He was often left alone with material while his co-workers had a smoking break. Guards never detected him taking material out because the gates did not have radiation-monitoring equipment, and there was no procedure for searching employees. The stolen material was kept in a jar on the balcony of Smirnov's apartment.

After 5 months, Smirnov decided that he had enough material to attempt a sale and began looking for a customer, though he had only a very vague idea gleaned from newspapers who such a customer might be. As he was traveling to Moscow to begin the search, he accidentally met with three friends at the rail station in Podolsk. At that moment, his friends were arrested by police on unrelated charges. The uranium was discovered when Smirnov was searched along with the others.

The Podolsk case represents what appears to be a typical pattern for the 1990s.[64] The theft of nuclear materials was carried out by an opportunistic insider with access to material and sufficient knowledge of security and accounting protocols to avoid detection. Perpetrators had only a vague idea of the monetary value of the material, however, and did not procure it for specific customers. Instead, they used the window of opportunity to steal and then began to look for a customer. The latter aspect is not a reason for complacency, however: There is reason to believe the material that surfaced in at least one interception in Georgia in 2006 was a sample from a much larger batch that was likely stolen years earlier and stashed to wait for a customer.[65]

CONCLUSION

The elaborate systems NWS create to control their nuclear weapons have one major vulnerability — internal upheaval that undermines the systems' key building blocks. In the span of just 2 1/2 years, the former Soviet Union encountered almost all the possible situations that could have led to a loss of physical control of nuclear weapons, control of their use, or both. It appears that no NWS is immune to similar challenges in times of political distress. The Soviet case suggests several reasons why this happens:
- Political instability grows quickly, and state machinery and the political system are usually too slow to react. The short period when political opposition has already institutionalized to the point of having paramilitary forces, while the government is still on peacetime footing, is particularly dangerous.
- Separatist forces organize very quickly and are usually more proactive and violence prone than the central government. While nuclear weapons might not be the highest priority of separatists at an early stage, the loss of political control over some regions of the country could result, among other things, in a partial loss of control over nuclear weapons as well.

- When the country finally breaks apart, new states inevitably begin competing for control over pieces of the nuclear legacy. Whether new governments make special arrangements for the orderly transition of the nuclear legacy or enter this competition overtly has little relevance. Almost inevitably, they will seek nuclear status or at least seriously contemplate it. Preventing the division of the nuclear arsenal is difficult and can succeed only under certain types of international systems, which allow control from the outside (for example, unipolar, bipolar, or any type of a hegemonic system); under a multipolar international system, the chances that several nuclear states will emerge in the place of one appear very high.
- The strongest defense against the loss of control of nuclear weapons in times of political upheaval is the motivation of military personnel. They are usually less susceptible to shifting political winds and will safeguard nuclear weapons until the situation stabilizes. The greatest danger here is the disappearance of the state to which they had pledged allegiance. Then the military effectively becomes free to grant control of nuclear weapons to whomever it chooses; in principle, it can even grant it to nonstate actors or take it into its own hands, creating a foundation for a military dictatorship.

Paradoxically, the control of weapons-grade fissile materials is significantly less prone to collapse or, rather, it is likely to collapse only in a small number of states. In Russia, this collapse resulted not from political turmoil, but from economic transition. It created conditions toward which the old system was not sufficiently well adapted. The new control systems were eventually built—with significant financial and technical assistance from other states—but the task took many years to complete, and during that period weapons-grade materials remained vulnerable to theft. One state that immediately comes to mind as far as similar future threats are concerned is North Korea. In case of a collapse of the political system and a transition to a market economy, it will likely experience the full range of pressures and risks that we saw in the Soviet Union; all other NWS will be vulnerable to the loss of control of weapons as a result of political upheaval, but not necessarily to a vulnerability of materials.

As we look into the future, political upheaval in one or more nuclear states does not appear impossible. It is also worth bearing in mind that no one could have predicted the depth and the speed of the crisis in the Soviet Union, much less its breakup. The conclusion one could draw from the Soviet case is rather pessimistic: The collapse of an NWS can happen unexpectedly, and the international system, at least in the short term, is not sufficiently equipped to manage the consequences.

The Soviet Union was breaking apart under a system that could, for all intents and purposes, be defined as unipolar: The United States and its allies exercised significant (if not almost complete) control over the outcomes. Both the outgoing Soviet government and the incoming governments of new states felt pressure to conform to U.S. preferences. This significantly limited their freedom of action. Competition for a piece of the nuclear legacy was reduced to cautious maneuvers and testing grounds for the possible acquiescence of Washington to the emergence of more than one nuclear state in place of the Soviet Union; at a later stage, newly independent states bargained for more advantageous conditions for surrendering nuclear weapons. The United States also possessed almost unlimited financial resources (at least, compared with the needs of new states) and could freely offer economic and other forms of assistance. This assistance proved critical in the case of Ukraine, and also helped facilitate safer, faster, and more orderly withdrawals of nuclear weapons to the territory of Russia.

These conditions are not present today and might not re-emerge in the near future. If a situation even remotely similar to what we saw in the Soviet Union emerges, there will likely be more than one player in the game. Consequently, opposition and/or separatist forces within the NWS undergoing political upheaval could draw external support from sources other than the United States, and it is far from obvious that the interests and decisions of these alternative international players would be identical to those of Washington. At the very least, the situation might require coordination that would be time-consuming and could involve bargaining and concessions on the part of the United States.

Similarly, in the foreseeable future, the United States and its allies might find it difficult to provide financial and economic assistance at the level needed to support their preferred outcome. International assistance would require the pooling of resources of multiple players and, the same as with political decisions, of time and concessions.

Finally, not all players will be state actors and, moreover, some of these nonstate players can have sufficient ideological, financial, and human resources to become attractive patrons for one or more oppositional groups in the troubled NWS. Nonstate actors are particularly difficult to control and to negotiate with, and there is a high probability they will have goals opposite to those of the United States. This is bound to make the situation even more dangerous and unpredictable.

As we draw lessons from the Soviet case and engage in contingency planning to ensure a smooth and safe transition of control over nuclear weapons if (or, rather, when) a nuclear state undergoes a period of political upheaval, we must also be aware of the limitations of these lessons. Hence, we might need another line of contingency planning to address the scenario when the nuclear transition is not orderly and when nuclear weapons fall into the wrong hands.

ENDNOTES - CHAPTER 4

1. For a description and analysis of these events and their context, see Thomas de Waal, *Black Garden: Armenia and Azerbaijan Through Peace and War*, New York: New York Press, 2004; and Michael Croissant, *The Armenia-Azerbaijan Conflict: Causes and Implications*, Santa Barbara, CA: Praeger, 1998, especially Chap. 2.

2. "12th Main Directorate of the Ministry of Defense of Russia," *Wikipedia*, available from *ru/wikipedia.org/wiki/12_ГУ_МО*.

3. Leslie Cockburn and Andrew Cockburn, *One Point Safe*, New York: Doubleday, 1997, p. 11.

4. See Dmitri Furman and Ali Abasov, "Azerbaijanskaya Revoluytsiya" ("An Azeri Revolution"), in *Azerbaijan i Rossiya: Obshchestva i Gosudarstva* (*Azerbaijan and Russia: Societies and States*), Moscow, Russia: Sakharov Fund, 2001, available from *www.sakharov-center.ru/publications/azrus/default.htm*.

5. *Ibid.*, p. 10-11.

6. Mikhail Khodarenok, "Yadernoe Oruzhie za Sem'uy Zamkami" ("Nuclear Weapons—Seven Locks"), *Voenno-Promyshlennyi Kurier* (*Military-Industrial Courier*), August 11, 2004.

7. The source did not disclose the origin of that information. It could have been, in theory, military counterintelligence, the KGB, or the local police. The KGB seems the most likely source.

8. Together with the Soviet response, that initiative came to be known as Presidential Nuclear Initiatives (PNIs).

9. See "Rossiya Perevypolnila Plany po Sokrashcheniyu Yadernogo Oruzhiya" ("Russia Has Exceeded the Plan for Reduction of Nuclear Weapons"), *RIA-Novosti*, June 22, 2005, available from *rian.ru/politics/20050622/40566772.html*; and Nikolai Poroskov, "Takticheskii Yadernyi Kozyr" ("A Tactical Nuclear Ace"), *Vremya Novostei* (*News Time*), September 7, 2007.

10. Vladimir Kruychkov, *Lichnoe Delo* ("Personal File"), Vol. 2, Moscow, Russia: ACT, 1996, pp. 158-159.

11. The account is based on Valentin Stepankov, *GKChP: 73 Chasa, Kotorye Izmenili Mir* (*GKChP: 73 Hours That Changed the World*), Moscow, Russia: Vremya, 2011. Valantin Stepankov was Chief Prosecutor of Russia and oversaw investigations into GKChP activities. His account can be considered the most complete and credible of all available ones. Other accounts have small variations. See, for example: Mikhail Gorbachev's interview on *Ekho Moskvy* (*Echo of Moscow*) radio station on August 18, 2011; Andrey Grachev, *Gorbachev*, Moscow, Russia: Vagrius, 2011; Anatoli Chernyaev, *Shest Let s Gorbachevym* (*Six Years with Gorbachev*), Moscow, Russia: Progress, 1993; David Hoffman, *The Dead Hand*, Garden City, NY: Doubleday, 2009, p. 373. Hoffman's story is the closest to what Stepankov wrote, but contains fewer details.

12. The three-person communications team was located in a guest house about 100 meters from Gorbachev's residence; alternate members lived outside the compound.

13. Pavel Podvig, ed., *Strategicheskoe Yadernoe Vooruzhenie Rossii* (*Russian Strategic Nuclear Forces*), Moscow, Russia: IzdAT, 1998, pp. 48-54.

14. Moiseev claimed in an interview to Corriere della Sera in August 1991 that he was the only one with access to the Kazbek system (Yazov was cut off, he claimed), but that he never used it and, instead, put the "nuclear suitcase" into a "safe place." This is hardly true for two reasons. First, one can believe that the Cheget brought from Foros was put into a "safe place," but there were also two others about which Moiseev remained silent. Second, Soviet nuclear forces were put on heightened alert, which probably involved the use of the Kazbek system.

15. The author can vouch for the accuracy of that information: throughout the entire period of the coup he was in direct contact with one of Air Force staff officers.

16. Available text does not specify whether this was *Delta III* or *Delta IV*, only that the submarine carried 16 strategic missiles.

17. "Veteran-Podvodnik: Vo Vremya Putcha GKChP Severnyi Flot Byl Gotov k Zapusku Yadernykh Raket" ("Veteran Submariner: During the GKChP Coup the Northern Fleet Was Ready to Launch Nuclear Missiles"), *Novaya Politika* (*New Policy*), August 19, 2011, available from *www.novopol.ru/-veteran-podvodnik-vo-vremya-putcha-gkchp-severnyiy-fl-text107335.html*.

18. The Soviet Union was never able to maintain the same share of submarines on patrol as the United States; this deficiency was one of the reasons the Soviet Union built so many submarines, and its submarines were given the capability to launch missiles from the surface. In case of a nuclear attack on a Soviet submarine base, which would have resulted in the loss of all the submarines in port, the Soviets were able to launch the missiles before losing them.

19. "Yadernoe Oruzhie v Den GKChP" ("Nuclear Weapons in the Days of the GKchP"), a blog entry uploaded on September 1, 2011, available from *so-l.ru/news/show/1630176*.

20. FSO—Federal'naya Sluzhba Okhrany (Federal Security Service).

21. FAPSI—Federal'noe Agentstvo Pravitelstvennow Svyazi i Informatsii (Federal Agency for Government Communications

and Information). An employee of FAPSI confided to the author a few years later that splitting off FAPSI from the KGB adversely affected the intelligence and counterintelligence capabilities of Russia. Although the majority of FAPSI personnel were former KGB employees, interaction between the two services was not completely smooth, he disclosed, and often the FSB (Federal'naya Sluzhba Bezopasnosti, or Federal Security Service, the remnant of the KGB minus several services, including Foreign Intelligence) would not receive some data, or received it after a significant delay. In 2003, Vladimir Putin returned FAPSI into the FSB.

22. See Nikolai Sokov, "Could Norway Trigger a Nuclear War?" Policy memo No. 24, *Program on New Approaches to Russian Security (PONARS)*, October 1997.

23. "V Rossiiskoi Sisteme Yadernykh Chemodanchikov Obnaruzhen Iz'yan: Krasnoi Knopki Net u Putina" ("In the Russian System of Nuclear Suitcases a Flaw is Discovered: Putin Has No Red Button"), *News.Ru*, May 28, 2010, available from *www.newsru.com/russia/28may2010/putin.html*.

24. The American proposal would not have affected heavy bombers and weapons for heavy bombers (including long-range cruise missiles); even so, reductions would have been significant. The proposal would not have affected Belarus at all: It only had single-warhead Topol (SS-25) ICBMs in its territory.

25. Velikhov and Ryzhov to Gorbachev, undated. (The contents indicate that the letter was written in early-October soon after Gorbachev's response to the initiatives of George Bush).

26. Karpov to Shevardnadze, November 25, 1991, p. 1.

27. Yuri Petrov, Yuri Skokov, and Yuri Ryzhov, *O predlozheniyakh Presidentov SSSR i SShA i Vozmozhnosti Bolee Radikalnykh Sokraschenii Strategicheskikh Nastupatelnykh Vooruzhenii* (*On the Proposals of the Presidents of the USSR and the USA and the Possibilities of a More Radical Reduction of Strategic Offensive Arms*), October 27, 1991.

28. *Ibid.*

29. *Tsentr Operativno-Strategicheskikh Issledovanii* (TsOSI).

30. The Main Staff was created in the fall of 1991, but did not actually control armed forces in the territory of Ukraine; all troops were still under the control of the USSR Ministry of Defense and its General Staff. At first military commanders pretended they did not even notice the newly appointed minister of defense of Ukraine. The gradual and often painful process of transformation of the Soviet Armed Forces into the Ukrainian Armed Forces began in December 1991.

31. Dniepropetrovsk was home to the largest missile producing company in the Soviet Union and perhaps the entire world. It was known in the Soviet Union as *Yuzhmash* ("Southern Machine-Building Factory"); afterward, that name was translated into Ukrainian (*Pivdenmash*). *Yuzhmash* included a major design bureau (R&D institute) that designed more than half of Soviet ICBMs (including, for example, the "heavy" SS-18, the solid-fuel railroad-mobile SS-24 and others). The National Institute of Strategic Studies was created at the initiative of the *Yuzhmash* design bureau and, although its headquarters were in Kiev, the majority of experts and the bulk of work were concentrated in Dniepropetrovsk.

32. Interview with high-level employees of *Pivdenmash* (Yuzhmash) missile production plant, March 1992; see also Vadim Grechaninov, "*Ukraina i eyo Yadernye Vozmozhnosti*" ("Ukraine and its Nuclear Potential"), April 20, 2010, available from *www.ua-nato.org.ua/2010-10-09-11-32-11/expert/43-2010-03-29-13-38-19/122--q-q?tmpl=component&print=1&page=*. Vadim Grechaninov is the president of the Atlantic Council of Ukraine; in 1991-92 he was the head of Center for Operational and Strategic Analysis referenced above.

33. One wonders whether the fact that key authors worked at Pivdenmash played a role; at least until the end of spring 1992 that factory remained a staunch supporter of preserving Soviet-time production cooperation, which was vital to retaining contracts and thus ensuring the company's survival. Strategic Rocket Forces were also ardent supporters of that scheme, which failed only because of the quickly worsening political relations between the two newly independent states.

34. Mitchell Reiss, *Bridled Ambitions: Why Countries Constrain Their Nuclear Capabilities*, Washington DC: Woodrow Wilson Center Press, 1995, p. 105.

35. Some suggest that Ukrainian experts could have encountered problems trying to override the system that gave Moscow direct control not only to launch strategic missiles, but also to disable them to prevent their unauthorized launches. See Sergey Goncharov, "*Yadernyi (Psevdo)Schit*" ("Nuclear [Pseudo] Shield"), April 6, 2012, available from *www.nuclearno.ru/text.asp?16170*.

36. Steven Pifer, *The Trilateral Process: The United States, Ukraine, Russia, and Nuclear Weapons*, New York: Brookings Institution, 2011, p. 7, available from *www.brookings.edu/~/media/Files/rc/papers/2011/05_trilateral_process_pifer/05_trilateral_process_pifer.pdf*.

37. Same interview with employees of Pivdenmash, March 1992. This information was also used by the author in Nikolai Sokov, "Ukraine: A Postnuclear Country," William C. Potter and Gaukhar Mukhatzhanova, eds., *Forecasting Nuclear Proliferation in the 21st Century*, Vol. II, Stanford CA: Stanford University Press, 2010.

38. See *Foreign Broadcast Information Service* (FBIS)-SOV-92-010, January 15, 1992, p. 58.

39. "Gonka Razoruzheniya" ("Disarmament Race"), *Argumenty i Fakty* (*Arguments and Facts*) in Ukraine, December 9, 2009, available from *www.ukr.aif.ru/society/article/18131*.

40. *Izvestiya*, February 17, 1992, p. 3.

41. For a published account, see Yevgeni Maslin, "Yadernoe Oruzhie i Kontrol za Eto Nerasprostraneniem" ("The Nuclear Weapon and Control over Its Nonproliferation"), *Obozrevatel-Observer*, No. 3-4, 1994, available from *www.rau.su/observer/N03-4_94/3-4_06.HTM*.

42. See *Nezavisimaya Gazeta*, April 24, 1992, cited in FBIS-SOV-92-082, April 28, 1992, p. 3.

43. During that visit, the United States, while adhering firmly to its earlier position that among all newly independent states only Russia was to retain the status of an NWS, also displayed sympathy toward some Ukrainian demands. For details, see Nikolai Sokov, *Russian Strategic Modernization: The Past and Future*, Lanham, MD: Rowman & Littlefield, 2000, pp. 106-107.

44. "Kazakh Sets Conditions on Nuclear Arms; Nazarbaev Seeks Powers' Guarantees," *The Washington Post*, May 6, 1992, p. A1.

45. James Baker quoted in his memoirs a statement of Nazarbaev: "The question of giving Kazakh territory for our common defense and for deployment of nuclear missiles will be decided on mutually advantageous ground" with Russia. James Baker, *The Politics of Diplomacy: Revolution, War, and Peace, 1989-1992*, New York: G. P. Putnam and Sons, 1995, p. 664.

46. The story was extremely complicated. Nazarbaev discussed that joint statement during a face-to-face meeting, and Yeltsin signed it without informing anyone else, including his own staff. As a result, the Russian government remained in the dark and was very surprised to hear protests from Washington about a document that it did not know existed. For details, see Sokov, *Russian Strategic Modernization*, pp. 108-109.

47. See Reiss, *Bridled Ambitions*, p. 157, fn.

48. Stanislav Shushkevich, the chairman of the Supreme Soviet of Belarus, disclosed later that the four heads of state took this special phone very seriously and used it only once to check if it was working; even this was done secretly, without informing relevant services. The four agreed not to use it for any other conversations. See Stanislav Shushkevich, "Monolog o pushche" ("A Monologue about the Forest"), *Ogonyok*, Vol. 49, December 2, 1996.

49. Cited in FBIS-SOV-92-063, April 1, 1992, p. 42.

50. *Izvestiya*, April 11, 1992.

51. *Krasnaia Zvezda,* January 15, 1992, cited in FBIS-SOV-92-011, January 16, 1992, p. 17.

52. *Rossiiskaia Gazeta,* March 4, 1992, cited in FBIS-SOV-92-044, March 5, 1992, p. 17.

53. *Izvestiya,* January 17 and 18, 1992.

54. *Ostankino TV,* February 14, 1992, cited in FBIS-SOV-92-032, February 18, 1992, p. 11.

55. *Vedomosti Verkhovnogo Soveta Rossiiskoi Federatsii* (*The Digest of the Supreme Soviet of the Russian Federation*), No. 13, 1992, pp. 925-926 document 678. As the story was told by an official of the Defense and Security Committee of the Supreme Soviet, the initial draft of the decree was prepared jointly by that committee and the State-Legal Department of the Administration of the president. The text was to be signed on March 16 upon Yeltsin's return from a brief vacation in Pitsunda. However, the chief of the State-Legal Department of the Administration, Sergei Shakhrai, went to Pitsunda and persuaded Yeltsin to sign the draft right away, only hours before his departure. Immediately upon his return to Moscow, Shakhrai made the decree public. The whole story reflected competition between the executive and the legislature, but the intrigues did not prevent collaboration.

56. *On the Establishment of the Armed Forces of the Russian Federation,* Decree of the President of the Russian Federation No. 466, *Vedomosti Verkhovnogo Soveta* (*Digest of the Supreme Soviet*), No. 19, 1992, pp. 1401-2, document 1077.

57. Konstantin Eggert, "General Lebed Nameren Naiti 'Yadernye Chemodanchiki'" ("General Lebed is Determined to Find 'Nuclear Briefcases'"), *Izvestiya,* October 7, 1997.

58. Press conference of Alexander Lebed, *Interfax News Agency,* November 29, 1997; Jeffrey Smith and David Hoffman, "No Support Found for Report of Lost Russian Suitcase-Sized Nuclear Weapons," *The Washington Post,* September 5, 1997, p. 19; and "Is Lebed Russia's Loosest Cannon? An Exclusive NBC interview with Alexander Lebed," October 2, 1997, available from *www.msnbc.com.*

59. David Hoffman, "Suitcase Nuclear Weapons Safely Kept, Russia Says," *The Washington Post*, September 14, 1997, p. A23.

60. "'Suitcase Nukes': A Reassessment," *CNS Research Story*, September 23, 2002, available from *cns.miis.edu/stories/020923.htm*.

61. Dmitri Safonov, "Individualnaya Planirovka" (*Individual Scheme*), *Izvestiya*, October 27, 2001.

62. Yuri Gavrilov, "A Nu-Ka Uberi Svoi Chemodanchik" ("Put Your Suitcase Away"), *Moskovskii Komsomolets*, February 10, 2004.

63. Description of the case taken from an interview with Elena Sokova, available from the Frontline database at *www.pbs.org/wgbh/pages/frontline/shows/nukes/timeline/tl01.html*; Alexander Mytsykov, "Atomic Theft and Atomic Security: What the General Prosecutor's Documents Say," *Yadernyi Kontrol*, September 1995, (the author was an aide to the Prosecutor General of Russia); and Potter, "Before The Deluge? Assessing the Threat of Nuclear Leakage from the Post-Soviet States," *Arms Control Today*, October 1995.

64. For analysis of the patterns in illicit trafficking in nuclear materials, see Potter and Elena Sokova, "Illicit Nuclear Trafficking in the NIS: What's New? What's True?" *The Nonproliferation Review*, Vol. 9, No. 2, Summer 2002.

65. See Potter and Sokova, "The 2003 and 2006 High Enriched Uranium Seizures in Georgia," in *Illicit Nuclear Trafficking: Collective Experience and the Way Forward, Proceedings of an International Conference* Vienna, Austria: International Atomic Energy Agency, 2008, p. 414.

CHAPTER 5

POLITICAL TRANSITIONS AND NUCLEAR MANAGEMENT IN PAKISTAN

Feroz Hassan Khan

Pakistan's independent political history has experienced dramatic changes since the death of its founder, Mohammad Ali Jinnah, who died 13 months after the country gained independence from British India. Jinnah's death led to a succession of political leaders who have been assassinated, overthrown, or exiled. Pakistan's political history is further checkered, with the dismissals of six prime ministers in the 1950s,[1] four military coups,[2] and four dissolutions of the parliamentary government using presidential constitutional powers.[3]

Given this history of tumultuous political changes in Pakistan and with simultaneous progress occurring in its nuclear program for the past 40 years, scholars and policymakers have often questioned the impact of leadership transitions on authority, decisionmaking, the consistency of nuclear management, and the ultimate control of nuclear arsenals in various periods of the country's nuclear history.

Since Pakistan embarked upon its nuclear program, three key political transitions, which are analyzed in this chapter, have affected the nature of Pakistani nuclear management. The military coup in July 1977 brought down the government of Prime Minister Zulfiqar Ali Bhutto, who transformed the peaceful nuclear program into a weapons program. At the time, however, the nuclear weapons program was in its incipient stages. The next transition occurred 11 years later when President Zia-ul-Haq's plane, which also carried the bulk of the ruling military leadership, crashed in August 1988. Pakistan had by then developed a nascent nuclear capability, putting together a nuclear device that could be delivered through a bomber or transport aircraft. Finally, in October 1999, the military once again took over power after a dramatic military coup. This transition happened 1-1/2 years after Pakistan conducted its nuclear tests and while it was in the process of establishing a National Command Authority, under which a robust command and control system would evolve.

The last political transitions were in 2008 and 2013. General Musharraf handed over political power to the elected civilians in 2008. Recently, Pakistan saw its first civilian-to-civilian democratic transition. Both power transitions were orderly, but preceded a period of unprecedented violence in the country that included a civil society movement as well as a spate of violence from extremists and suicide attacks from radicalized forces within Pakistan; this violence continues to date with varying intensities. However, it took a decade for Pakistan to transform its demonstrated nuclear weapons capability into an operational deterrent force. Now it is about to complete building a triad of strategic forces that are integrated under a robust command and control system. In general, Pakistan has experienced 40 years of managing a nuclear program during a tense period of its history.

Within the broad spectrum of Pakistani politics and the strategic community, there is a strong consensus on the rationale and role of nuclear weapons in Pakistan's national security as well as on the current organizational structure that manages both its civil and military nuclear program. Each successive ruler since Zulfiqar Ali Bhutto initiated the program has advanced the nuclear program from where his or her predecessor left it. This pattern has continued regardless of any bitterness between successors and predecessors.[4] While there is national consensus on the question of Pakistan's nuclear deterrent and, more broadly, its management structure, there is a lack of consensus on the system of governance in the country.

At the heart of the controversy regarding the Pakistani political system is a lack of consensus regarding the system of political governance. Pakistan has vacillated between presidential and parliamentary forms of government. Generally, military rulers prefer a presidential form of governance, believing in strong centralized control of the federal government and devolution of power at the local (district) level. By keeping provincial (state) government in check, the military believes it can prevent ethnic polarization and/or secessionism. Political leaders, on the other hand, support a parliamentary form of governance and prefer a federation with restricted powers for the central government but strong provincial governments.

The former school of thought fears provincialism perpetuates ethnic politics, feudalism, and tribalism, and creates conditions for corruption and nepotism. The latter school rejects such a basis and asserts that the presidential system failed to keep the state united and caused the dismemberment in 1971. Devolution at the local level could be manipulated to promote authoritarianism and perpetuate military dominance.[5] The 1956 and 1973 constitutions are thus manifestations of national political will and a consensus about the parliamentary system of governance, the hallmark of which is the devolution of powers to the federating provinces.

The dialectic between these two schools has resulted in the vacillation of political authority between the president and the prime minister.[6] Given the history of military rule in the country, the office of the Chief of the Army Staff (COAS) has developed significant clout in the country's political system. Against this backdrop, the power struggle between the president and prime minister only strengthens the army chief, who then becomes the arbitrator of national politics in extremis and in particular is the custodian of national security policy.[7] On nuclear matters specifically, the COAS became the most powerful sponsor on behalf of the military-scientific community until the National Command Authority was formally announced in February 2000.[8]

After the return of full democracy in 2008, the Pakistani Parliament approved the nuclear management system in 2010, which is an endorsement of the military-dominated nuclear management system that evolved under the dictatorship of President General Pervez Musharraf.[9] Because of an overwhelming national consensus regarding the nuclear program, Pakistan's nuclear management remains unaffected by the turbulence of national political change, as this chapter will show.

Not withstanding this fact, the international community continues to worry about the security of the Pakistani nuclear program. Three interconnected factors are at the roots of this oscillation in national politics. First is the debate between the presidential versus parliamentary system, as highlighted above. Second are poor civil-military relations, which have bedeviled the evolution of stable democratic governance in the state. Last is the dominance of bureaucratic power over the representative government or elected leaders. The civil bureaucracy is believed to be heavily under the influence of the military and intelligence agencies, which are euphemistically referred as the "establishment." Other factors that undermine Pakistani state efforts toward securing arsenals are the proliferation track record under the infamous A. Q. Khan nuclear network and the rise of radicalism in some sections of the society, which has seen bouts of violent attacks on security forces and the establishment in the past 5 years. At the time of this writing, the deterioration of relations with its key ally, the United States, and continued security problems with two key neighbors, India and Afghanistan, has compounded Pakistan's image problem. Thus, organizational efforts and best practices to manage the security of arsenals and sensitive materials developed during the last decade remain inadequate to quash the perceptions of insecurity in the Pakistani nuclear program.

This chapter analyzes Pakistan's political transitions in relation to their impact on the national nuclear program, the security of nuclear arsenals, and the evolution of a nuclear command and control system. The first section gives the background of Pakistani political transitions and nuclear management from the nation's birth through its dismemberment as a unified country in 1971. The second section examines the period under the leadership of Zulfiqar Ali Bhutto, when the nuclear weapons program commenced; it ends in his ouster from power after a military coup, which marked the end of the civilian-controlled nuclear weapons program. The third section studies the military-dominated command system under which Pakistan attained a nascent nuclear weapons capability. It ends with the sudden transformation from a military system to a cycle of democratic regimes as a result of the plane crash in which the bulk of the military leadership perished. The fourth section explains the two-phased transition back to military control.

From 1993 to 1999, the nuclear program remained under quasi-military control while the president and prime minister jockeyed for political power. For over a decade, the president, prime minister, and COAS (the troika) shared political power, while the nuclear program advanced covertly, under the guidance and support of the military. This quasi-control finally transited into a fully military-dominated system after the coup of 1999. The fifth section examines the Pakistani force posture that evolved under a command and control system during the Musharraf era. The next political transition occurred with the return to civilian democratic rule in 2008. Nevertheless, even as General Pervez Musharraf departed from the scene into exile, the nuclear command authority remained unscathed, and the new government adopted the system, ensuring a smooth transition. The sixth section analyzes concerns about Pakistani nuclear management against organizational efforts and best practices by the state to nurture nuclear security culture and a regime to keep arsenals and sensitive material secure, especially due to the deteriorating political climate, disturbing internal security threats, and tense relations with the United States after the events of 2011.

The chapter concludes that despite the domestic instabilities and rough political transitions, control of the nuclear program has remained unaffected. The main reason for this is the general national consensus over the state's nuclear policies: the decisionmaking system under the National Command Authority, its employment and development goals, and the status of the program. Notwithstanding this conclusion, internal security challenges and domestic instabilities in Pakistan are real; therefore, Pakistan has to work hard continuously to meet these challenges as well as redress the perceptions of the world.

POLITICAL TRANSITIONS AND NUCLEAR MANAGEMENT, 1947-71

When the British left Pakistan in 1947, the birth of a new nation took place in a massive vacuum, caused by factors such as a leadership crisis, weak political institutions, a nonexistent constitutional direction, and economic challenges. At the time of partition in 1947, Pakistan was distressed on three counts: It was recovering from the trauma of a bloody partition that involved millions of deaths, migrations, and internal displacements that crossed hurriedly demarcated borders; an unfair distribution of assets was compounded by India's refusal to deliver Pakistan's due share; and finally, the fate of the princely state of Jammu and Kashmir—over which India and Pakistan fought an immediate war, and which to date remains a bone of contention even after 6 decades—was uncertain. As one author described the Pakistani situation, "Pakistan inherited a paper army and skeleton navy and air force."[10] Though a professional military structure developed over time, in contrast, social institutions remained weak or nonexistent, feudal lords and tribal leaders wielded power, much of the population was uneducated, and ethnic groups were polarized. This structural imbalance has plagued Pakistan throughout its history.[11] The failure to establish a viable political system in the first decade of its existence led to the military coup in 1958, which set the pattern for all future military takeovers. The military institution quickly became a vital stakeholder in Pakistan's governance system and security policy.[12]

Atomic science in the 1950s was a low priority for the policymakers in Pakistan. Consolidating the nation-state was a monumental task, as the country was veritably beginning nation-building from scratch in the absence of strong leadership because of the death of the nation's founder in 1948. Facing multitudinous domestic political instabilities, regional crises with neighbors, and lacking adequate infrastructure, Pakistan readily accepted a U.S. military alliance (Southeast Asia Treaty Organization [SEATO] and Central Treaty Organization [CENTO]) that, coupled with military leadership, gave the nation a semblance of stability and a new direction toward national development. By the mid-1960s, the nation was stable and prospering economically; its political structures remained weak, however, and ethnic resentment and polarization between West Pakistan and East Pakistan began to grow, ultimately coming to a head by 1971.

Under these disturbing political conditions, Pakistan's nuclear program was founded in the mid-1950s. President Dwight Eisenhower's Atoms for Peace initiative generated interest in nuclear energy, and soon after, the Pakistan Atomic Energy Commission began to study the feasibility of atomic science and prepare blueprints for peaceful uses of atomic energy.[13]

It was not until a young Zulfiqar Ali Bhutto became Minister of Fuel, Power, and Natural Resources in 1959 that political interest and insight in the Pakistani atomic energy program emerged. Bhutto later wrote: "When I took charge of Pakistan's Atomic Energy Commission, it was no more than a signboard of office." He explained how under his stewardship, he "put his entire vitality behind the task of acquiring nuclear capability for [his] country."[14] The combined efforts of Zulfiqar Ali Bhutto; Dr. Abdus Salam, an eminent physicist, Nobel Laureate, and Advisor to the President on Science and Technology; and Dr. Ishrat Hussain Usmani, the Chairman of the Pakistan Atomic Energy Commission (PAEC, 1960-72), enabled Pakistan to send hundreds of young men to top Western universities to train in the new atomic sciences.[15]

Around the mid-1960s, a bomb advocacy lobby emerged under the leadership of Zulfiqar Ali Bhutto, who as Foreign Minister (1963-66) urged President Ayub Khan to purchase nuclear power reactors and a reprocessing plant from France. Bhutto argued that India was proceeding ahead with nuclear weapons development after China's test in 1964, and the window of technological availability was becoming short as deliberations on the Nuclear Non-Proliferation Treaty (NPT) drew to a close.

Ayub disappointed the bomb enthusiasts, however.[16] His concern was that any move toward obtaining such technologies would jeopardize the country's Western alliance, military aid, and economic progress. Ayub's focus on national development was disastrously affected by his decision to up the ante in Kashmir, which resulted in the 1965 war with India and the subsequent downward slide of the nation. Ayub was reluctant to put Pakistan on the path toward nuclear weapons. As revealed in his dairies, he was never convinced nuclear weapons were good for mankind.[17]

Ayub was forced out of office after his protégé, Zulfiqar Ali Bhutto—who founded Pakistan's People's Party in 1967—led a movement in late-1968. Ayub's failing health and street protests forced him to hand over power to the army chief, General Yahya Khan, who declared martial law and became president. In essence, this political transition was rather orderly, but did not occur until after months of violent protests. Bhutto in West Pakistan and Sheikh Mujib Rahman in East Pakistan led political movements that rocked the foundations of a united Pakistan. Yahya Khan's military regime allowed fair elections, but was unable to cope with the results—to hand over power to majority East Pakistanis. His poor handling of the situation resulted in violent protests, leading to civil war. India exploited Pakistani miseries, invading East Pakistan and dismembering the once united country.

Throughout his term as president, General Yahya Khan was too consumed with domestic crises to focus on any other aspect at the time. The so-called "bomb lobby" blamed the military leadership for its failure to grasp the changing regional strategic environment and remained critical of the faith in American-led security alliances (SEATO, CENTO),[18] which had given a false sense of confidence in Pakistan's national defense capabilities against India's intentions and conventional force capability.[19]

BHUTTO'S NUCLEAR PROGRAM AND THE ZIA COUP, 1971-77

Zulfiqar Ali Bhutto was undoubtedly the political father of the Pakistani bomb. Within a month of assuming power, President Bhutto summoned a meeting of all the scientists in Multan on January 20, 1972. He removed the incumbent Chairman PAEC, Ishrat Usmani, who, Bhutto believed, had little interest in pursuing the nuclear weapons program, and replaced him with his friend and confidante, Munir Ahmad Khan. Formerly the Director of the International Atomic Energy Commission (IAEA), Khan had worked on plutonium reactors.[20] Bhutto's objective was to indicate the shift in the nature of the nuclear program. Bhutto was aware that the wherewithal needed for nuclear capability would take time. He simply wanted to boost the morale of the scientists and let it be known that the new government meant serious business.

It was in 1974, however, after India's nuclear test, that Bhutto's strategy of a slow-and-subtle acquisition of nuclear capability transformed into a crash nuclear weapons program. Bhutto brought the entire civil and military leadership into his confidence and galvanized the nuclear program to become the highest national priority. He made a vow to the nation: "I give a solemn pledge to all our countrymen that we will never let Pakistan be a victim of nuclear blackmail."[21]

Bhutto tightly controlled the nuclear program for secrecy. He had little time to devote to the program, however, since he was focused on many national issues. Bhutto constituted an interministerial committee of senior ministers, bureaucrats, and scientists. The main purpose of the committee was to ensure the continued progress of the nuclear program and remove any bureaucratic obstacles or snags, particularly in finances and the procurement of technologies.

Prime Minister Bhutto later convinced Dr. Abdul Qadeer Khan, a Pakistani scientist, to return from Holland to run the centrifuge program. In the summer of 1976, Bhutto directed the separation of the centrifuge project from the PAEC and gave A. Q. Khan independent responsibility to run it, free from any outside pressures. Bhutto promised open-ended funding to A. Q. Khan to complete the task as well as direct access to the prime minister, a privilege until then employed only by the Chairman of the PAEC.

Throughout the Bhutto era, decisionmaking on the nuclear program did not involve the military leadership. Bhutto kept the military hierarchy away as a means to maintain civilian control of national security, particularly with regard to the nuclear program. The military as an institution, however, provided the resources and assistance that the PAEC needed. Later, when the construction of the Engineering Research Laboratories commenced, the military provided manpower and equipment from its technical branches and played supporting roles in helping select sites for future tests. The military also provided barracks and ammunition depots for housing centrifuge facilities and supplied knowledge for explosives training. The military was well aware of the nature of the classified project but remained aloof from the technical details, blueprints, or goals of the program.[22]

In the spring of 1977, Prime Minister Bhutto held elections. His party won the elections, but allegations of rigged ballots triggered massive protests from the opposition. A coalition of nine right-wing political parties mounted a massive campaign to oust Bhutto from power in the summer of 1977. Bhutto summoned the military to control the protest, resulting in a temporary martial law in Lahore and foreshadowing the military takeover on July 5, 1977.[23]

After the bloodless military takeover, General Zia-ul-Haq became the Chief Martial Law Administrator (CMLA). Prime Minister Bhutto and his family were taken into protective custody at the nearby hill station in Murree. A few days later, the new military leader visited his former prime minister and discussed the future course of action, which included holding elections within 90 days as stipulated in the constitution. But Zia reneged on the promise to hold elections in 3 months' time. Instead, he decided to become president and formed an interim government, bringing in several ministers who were members of Jamaat-i-Islami, a religious political party that was in the forefront of the opposition against Bhutto throughout the summer of 1977. Meanwhile, Bhutto faced trial for abetting the murder of a political opponent.

Bhutto was concerned that the nuclear weapons program was adversely affected by Zia-ul-Haq's coup. He doubted Zia had the ability, much less the vision, to see it through. Given his experience with Ayub and Yahya Khan, it was possible Bhutto did not trust that the military was even interested in pursuing the nuclear weapons program. He feared that Zia might barter away the nuclear weapons with conventional weapons to expand the army or simply get some financial aid to support the ailing economy.[24]

Bhutto was convinced that had he remained prime minister, France would not have backed out of the reprocessing plant agreement that he had negotiated with it, a deal he believed was struck because he had personal rapport with President Giscard d'Estaing and because he had satisfied the international community by agreeing to have an IAEA safeguard agreement over the French reprocessing plant. On August 23, 1978, when President Zia-ul-Haq admitted that France had defaulted on the reprocessing plant, Bhutto held the military regime responsible for this failure and responded that:

> The French had concluded the agreement with a civilian and constitutional government, not with a military and dictatorial regime . . . what does the [Zia-ul-Haq]

regime propose to meet the threat of this qualitative change? More Foreign Aid? Now that it is officially admitted that nuclear reprocessing plant is lost, with or without foreign aid, Pakistan would have to unquestionably move towards steeper dependence and alien-reliance . . . it will be more at the mercy of those who are professionals in the art of nuclear blackmail . . . what a fall, my countrymen! What a shattering blow to the dream of a lifetime.[25]

NUCLEAR MANAGAEMENT UNDER ZIA-UL-HAQ, 1977-88

When General Zia-ul-Haq overthrew the government of Zulfiqar Ali Bhutto in 1977, the nuclear weapons program (highly enriched uranium) was in its nascent stages. The PAEC, however, continued building the infrastructure needed to complete the nuclear fuel cycle. The military takeover in 1977 marked the first transition from civilian-dominated control of the nuclear program to a military-dominated one, which lasted over a decade. Under General Zia-ul-Haq, a unified command system evolved because he held the office of both president and COAS.

Like Bhutto, Zia-ul-Haq took personal charge of the nuclear program. Zia, however, retained the same core senior civil servants in the coordination committee and brought the military and scientific communities together, further shrouding the program in secrecy. Zia-ul-Haq received briefings from the two main scientists in the program, Munir Ahmad Khan and A. Q. Khan, and he retained the two most important people in the interministerial committee, Defense Secretary Ghulam Ishaq Khan and Foreign Secretary Agha Shahi.

Zia appointed Lieutenant General Khalid Mahmood Arif as his Chief of Staff, an office that became the focal point of all coordinating activities; all nuclear matters were transferred to Arif's office from what had been the prime minister's office. The office was closely connected with his Military Secretary, Major General Imtiaz Ali, who was removed from the office and posted back to the army.[26]

General Zia-ul-Haq made all decisions and issued personal directives in close consultation with his team of Ghulam Ishaq Khan, Agha Shahi, and General Arif, who ensured the continuity of the nuclear program. Initially, Zia had some doubts about the loyalty of PAEC Chairman Munir Khan, who he considered a protégé of Bhutto, and even suspected many in the nuclear program to be from a minority sect.[27] Zia also feared the infiltration of Western spies into the nuclear program. He directed scientific organizations and intelligence agencies to keep a close eye on the "insider threat," which could have been a mole in the program who would sabotage it from within or perhaps facilitate an attack from the outside. Zia directed the army to undertake the defense of the Kahuta centrifuge plant and the Karachi Nuclear Power Plant (KANUPP) installations. Such fears about threats to Pakistan's program began in late-1979 after reports surfaced that the United States was contemplating a preventive strike against Pakistani nuclear installations. These fears gained more credence in 1981, after Israeli planes attacked and destroyed an Iraqi power plant at Osiraq.

Throughout the 1980s, the Pakistani nuclear program steadily progressed, though Zia-ul-Haq downplayed the nuclear card by insisting on its peaceful nature. Zia had made a secret agreement with President Ronald Reagan that he would not embarrass Reagan by pursuing any nuclear activities. The United States had given four nuclear restraint requirements to Pakistan: not to conduct hot tests; not to enrich low-enriched to high-enriched uranium; not to machine existing stocks into core; and not to transfer any know-how or material to any entity or state.

ZIA'S PLANE CRASH

On a bright sunny afternoon on August 17, 1988, President Zia and some of Pakistan's top military leadership were returning from Bahawalpur, a city in southern Punjab, after witnessing the trial of a U.S armored tank. Within minutes of takeoff, Zia's plane lost contact and mysteriously crashed. Zia was killed, along with the U.S. Ambassador to Pakistan—Arnold Raphel—and Defense Attaché, as well as senior Pakistani military leaders, most prominently the Chairman of the Joint Chiefs of Staff, General Akhtar Abdul Rehman, and Lieutenant General Mian Muhammad Afzal.

This event was really dramatic and left a huge leadership void. From 1985 till 1988, Pakistan functioned under a hybrid system of governance, with an active duty army chief as president and an elected prime minister who headed the government with a functioning elected parliament. On May 29, 1988, General Zia-ul-Haq, in exercise of his presidential powers, dismissed Prime Minister Muhammad Khan Junejo and Parliament. When Zia's plane crashed, there was no political government, except for the Senate, that had not been dissolved. With the bulk of the military leadership now deceased, the leadership transferred to the Vice Chief of Army Staff, General Mirza Aslam Beg, who, after witnessing the same tank demonstration, had flown in a separate plane on that fateful day. Under military rules of succession, General Mirza Aslam Beg automatically assumed the responsibility as acting Chief of Army Staff.

Under the country's constitution, the Chairman of the Senate becomes the acting president, which in this case was Ghulam Ishaq Khan. General Beg had the option of declaring martial law and overruling the constitutional succession of the president. To his credit, General Beg allowed the constitutional process to proceed. Thus, Chairman of the Senate Ghulam Ishaq Khan became the acting president of Pakistan. President Khan then formally named General Mirza Aslam Beg to become the Chief of the Army Staff. He also appointed the Chief of Naval Staff, Admiral Iftikhar Sirohi, as the new Chairman of the Joint Chiefs of Staff to replace General Akhtar Abdul Rehman, who had also died in Zia's plane crash.

This was the second major change in the system after the nuclear weapons program had commenced. By this time, Pakistan had developed enough fissile material to put together a few devices on short notice. Though Zia had agreed on nuclear restraint with President Reagan, there was no agreed-upon mechanism to verify its implementation. Zia prohibited nuclear explosion tests (hot tests), but he allowed scientists to carry out cold tests and continued research and development on bomb designs and delivery means. Like his predecessor, Bhutto, Zia tightly controlled the nuclear program, personally making all related decisions.

After Zia's death, the nuclear responsibility naturally acceded to the most knowledgeable and experienced man in the country. President Ghulam Ishaq Khan had significant institutional memory and had held a role in the nuclear program since it began in the 1970s.[28]

Together, President Ishaq Khan and COAS General Aslam Beg guided the nuclear program. Army Chief General Beg coordinated the nuclear program on behalf of the president and provided the defense of key atomic institutions as well as support from the army to facilitate the goals of the strategic organizations.[29] The interministerial committee disappeared, as the offices of the president and the COAS managed decisions until the election of the prime minister, who then became the third pillar of decisionmaking.

Elections were held in November 1988 and, as expected, Benazir Bhutto won a plurality to form a government. In the aftermath of the 1988 election, President Ghulam Ishaq Khan and Army Chief General Mirza Aslam Beg emerged as the guarantors of the policies of the Zia era, and gradually allowed Benazir Bhutto to share power in a limited manner.

THE DECADE OF DEMOCRACY AND THE POWER TROIKA

The Pakistan People's Party had barely ended the electoral victory celebration when COAS General Mirza Aslam Beg invited Ms. Benazir Bhutto to discuss the modalities of the power transition. General Beg explained his role in ensuring fair and free elections and the return of democracy after years of autocratic rule. Beg assured Ms. Bhutto of full cooperation from the Army and, in a detailed exposé, explained the precarious regional and internal security situation. The Soviet withdrawal from Afghanistan was proceeding apace to meet the February 1989 deadline; tension between the United States and Ayatollah Khomeini was continuing despite the end of the Iran-Iraq War; and most importantly for the nuclear program, an unprecedented India-backed uprising in Kashmir had begun, which had severe implications for Pakistan. With the end of the Cold War in sight, the alliance with the United States was unclear.

Pakistan's overall domestic situation was tense and fragile. In order to prevent further domestic turbulence, General Beg suggested a continuity of policy and the retention of key personalities in the government once power was handed over. The army would fully back the prime minister if she agreed to four major points: 1) continue to support and elect President Ghulam Ishaq Khan; 2) pledge not to seek revenge for her father's death from General Zia-ul-Haq's family; 3) continue the services of foreign minister Sahabzada Yaqub-Khan; and, 4) not to meddle in the internal matters of the armed forces.

Beg emphasized that Benazir Bhutto was extremely intelligent but young and inexperienced, and therefore she needed the wisdom and guidance of President Ghulam Ishaq Khan, who had a long, distinguished career and, more importantly, had been a constant in the evolution of the nuclear program ever since her father's time in office. The vast experience of veteran foreign minister Sahabzada Yaqub-Khan would allow continuity of the country's foreign policy, especially given the regional uncertainty. Finally, Ms. Bhutto needed to consolidate her position and would need constant help from the army. Bhutto agreed to these conditions and was sworn in as prime minister.[30]

Benazir Bhutto was charismatic and an international icon for her struggle against the conservative military dictator who had hanged her father. As the first female prime minister in a Muslim country with a nuclear program, she had extraordinary celebrity appeal. She emerged as a leader from the shadows of war and instability, but did not realize that the office she assumed was not as powerful as it had been during her father's time in the 1970s. Ms. Bhutto was actually sharing power with the president and army chief on the terms she had agreed to in exchange for a smooth power transfer. In essence, it meant she could operate within the agreed framework with the president and the army.

Benazir Bhutto was new to the vicissitudes of statecraft and the role of the state bureaucracy and a powerful military in national policy. The president represented the bureaucracy and had the ultimate power under the constitution to dismiss the prime minister as well as the parliament. Additionally, the Army held the key to national security policy and was the backbone of presidential power.

The diffusion of power at the apex of national governance resulted in a troika of leaders: president, prime minister, and COAS. This governance structure in the political system of Pakistan was not formal, but the execution of policy was based on the consensus of the three. In reality, it was the president and COAS who wielded decisive power over the most critical security policies of the state, which included the nuclear policy.[31] For the next decade, the Pakistani governance system functioned under this diffuse structure, which saw three dismissals of governments (1990, 1993, and 1997), successively recycling the governments of Benazir Bhutto and Nawaz Sharif before the military coup in 1999.

In the context of nuclear management, the decade of democracy (1988-99) was divided into two periods. The first half was during the tenure of President Ghulam Ishaq Khan (August 1988-July 1993), during which he was the ultimate authority on all decisions and financial approvals on all civil and classified projects. The president had the final say on all nuclear matters, and the Army Chief supported and coordinated the nuclear program on his behalf.

Benazir Bhutto maintained that she was never kept fully in the loop on nuclear matters and claimed the president and Army did not trust her.[32] COAS General Aslam Beg denies Benazir Bhutto's assertion that she was not informed or that she was intentionally kept out of the loop regarding the nuclear program. In an interview with the author, General Beg said that both Chairman of the PAEC Munir Ahmad Khan, as well as A. Q. Khan, Director of the Khan Research Laboratory (KRL), briefed the prime minister in complete detail on the status of the nuclear weapons program soon after she took office and that she was regularly updated on all nuclear developments.[33] General Beg insists that the ruling troika (which Beg dubbed as the national command authority of the time) collectively agreed to a nuclear restraint policy in 1989, in which Benazir Bhutto's consent was primary.[34] This so-called restraint policy involved capping the production of weapons-grade uranium and permitting only the KRL to enrich up to low-enriched uranium (LEU) levels; prohibiting turning the existing stock of highly enriched uranium (HEU) into bomb cores; not conducting hot tests; and not transferring any technical expertise or technology to a third party or country.[35] In substance, this restraint policy was no different from the pledge General Zia-ul-Haq had secretly made to the Reagan administration in 1981.[36] In reality, the fissile production continued apace; the only real restraint was on refraining from conducting hot tests.

Prime Minister Benazir Bhutto made a public commitment to the U.S. Congress during her state visit to Washington, DC, in June 1989.[37] During that visit she also agreed to receive a detailed briefing from U.S. Central Intelligence Agency Director William H. Webster on the progress of Pakistan's nuclear program. This event finally broke the trust of the troika. The president and COAS were miffed about Prime Minister Bhutto's distrust of her own country's system, symbolized by her bid to seek an outside briefing from the United States—a country that was fundamentally opposed to the Pakistani nuclear program. From then on, the president and Army Chief never trusted the prime minister. Thus, a cloud of suspicion loomed over the office of the prime minister. Subsequently, the president and COAS were reluctant to share classified details of the strategic development program with Bhutto.

Benazir Bhutto's government was dissolved in August 1990 after months of tension between the president and prime minister. After a brief interim government, Nawaz Sharif was elected prime minister. Sharif was a protégé of President Zia-ul-Haq and was expected to have a harmonious relationship with the military. But he, too, was soon involved in tension with both the president and successive army chiefs until he was removed from office in 1993.

FROM THE PRESIDENCY TO THE GENERAL HEADQUARTERS

The political transition in July 1993 was a significant development in the history of Pakistani nuclear management. In early-1993, after several months of a bitter power struggle between President Ghulam Ishaq Khan and Prime Minister Nawaz Sharif, the Chief of Army Staff, General Abdul Waheed, intervened and pressured both to resign from the office.[38]

The resignation of both the president and prime minister created a power vacuum at both the state level (the president) and the government level (the prime minister). Under the constitution, the Chairman of the Senate, Waseem Sajjad, became the acting president, and Moeen Qureshi, a former vice president of the World Bank who was living in Washington, DC, at the time, was made the interim prime minister for 3 months. The task of the interim government was to hold free and fair parliamentary elections in October 1993 and hand over power to the newly elected government.

After a brief interim government, Benazir Bhutto returned to power by the end of the year. She ruled for about 3 years until President Farooq Leghari dismissed her government in 1996, only for her rival, Sharif, to return in 1997. Sharif made constitutional amendments to make it impossible for the president to dismiss the parliament. After 3 years, the military removed Sharif from power, completing a full circle.

President Ghulam Ishaq Khan, who had been custodian of the nuclear program until then, could not trust the interim arrangement, and the political future of the country was uncertain at the time. He handed over the responsibility of the classified nuclear weapons program, including all documents, to COAS General Abdul Waheed.[39] For the first time, the nuclear responsibility and records were transferred from the office of the president to Pakistan's Army General Headquarters (GHQ). General Abdul Waheed tasked Major General Ziauddin, Director General of the Combat Development Directorate (CD Directorate) in the GHQ, to take charge of the documents and coordinate the nuclear program on his behalf. All nuclear issues were coordinated at the CD Directorate in the GHQ from July 1993 until December 1998, when the Strategic Plans Division (SPD) was established. The SPD later became the secretariat of the National Command

Authority (NCA) and functions as such to date.[40] From 1993 through 1999, until the military formally took political power, the GHQ was the custodian of sensitive documents and coordinator of the nuclear program even though political power continued to vacillate between the president and prime minister.

Under such circumstances, and given their previous dismissals, Prime Ministers Benazir Bhutto and Nawaz Sharif preferred not to ruffle feathers with the military-civil bureaucratic-scientific nexus that was managing the nuclear program, an arrangement that by and large became politically acceptable to all. It suited both the president and prime minister to let the GHQ be the locus of coordination and resources. But despite this tacit understanding, the military did not have the legal authority to intervene in the autonomy of the scientists, who had direct access to any of three power centers. This diffusion is what prevented one single authority from having final oversight until after General Musharraf's coup, when the institutional control of scientific organizations were made effective through both de jure and de facto measures.

Under the leadership of General Jehangir Karamat, Chief of the Army Staff from January 1996 till October 1998, the army steered away from the political feud in Islamabad in 1997. Once the 13th Constitutional Amendment became law in 1997, presidential powers were clipped, and maximum political power rested with the prime minister.[41] In 1998, the nuclear decisionmaking authority rested with the prime minister, but the nuclear coordination continued to be with the GHQ (CD Directorate).

By October 1998, after a tense summer that involved nuclear tests and resulted in nuclear sanctions, Prime Minister Sharif attempted to gain absolute control when he asked COAS General Karamat to resign from office. Sharif replaced Karamat with General Musharraf in October 1998. Within a few months, civil-military relations went sour, especially after the Kargil crisis with India—resulting in much bloodshed and regional tensions less than a year after Pakistan's nuclear test—and eventually lead to a military coup. This brought an end to the era of democracy and domestic instability.

Despite political instability and jockeying for political power among the leadership, the nuclear weapons development continued apace. In the process, the nexus between the military, scientific, and civil bureaucratic communities was strengthened. The three communities developed a synergy of thoughts and action over nuclear policy and provided considerable autonomy to the scientific organizations to achieve national goals.[42]

ESTABLISHING ACCOUNTABILITY AND ROBUST COMMAND AND CONTROL, 1999-2008

General Pervez Musharraf led the last military coup in October 1999. This was the first power transition after Pakistan had declared itself an overt nuclear power and returned the unity of command that had existed in the Zia era when the president served in the role of both the president and the COAS.

After taking over as the army chief, one of the first organizational changes Musharraf made was to create a dedicated organization—the Strategic Plans Division (SPD)—that would exclusively deal with the nuclear issues. He returned the conventional operations and acquisitions in GHQ to the Military Operations (MO) directorate. Musharraf merged the nuclear components of the CD Directorate with the SPD and moved it to the Joint Services Headquarters (JSHQ), where the nuclear operations and assets of Pakistan's Air Force and Navy were merged into one coherent command system under whose control all scientific organizations were brought. The head of the SPD was Lieutenant General Khalid Ahmad Kidwai, who has retained this position since December 1998; he serves in this role as a civilian now, after his retirement from active military duty in 2007.

In April 1999, some 6 months after becoming the Chief of Army Staff, General Pervez Musharraf presented a new plan to Prime Minister Nawaz Sharif for the establishment of a National Command Authority (NCA). The plan was presented in a detailed briefing in the GHQ, which included key cabinet ministers, senior bureaucracy, and service chiefs. The proposal envisaged a three-tier institutional structure over the country's nuclear weapons. The first tier constituted an Employment Control Committee (ECC), the apex body of decisionmaking under the prime minister, comprised of five key cabinet ministers and four service chiefs; and a Development Control Committee (DCC), which is subordinate to the ECC and tasked to implement the nuclear development directive of ECC. The DCC was also chaired by the prime minister and comprised four service chiefs and four heads of scientific organizations.

The SPD was already functioning by this time in the JSHQ. The SPD constituted the second tier of the NCA. The third tier of the command system constitutes the three services' strategic forces commands, which exercised training and administrative control of nuclear forces. The operational control of nuclear forces remained with the NCA, where all members would make decisions by consensus.

Prime Minister Sharif approved the proposal in principle but asked his foreign minister to examine it. Sharif's skepticism resulted from long-time fears of the military obtaining an overarching role in national security affairs. The military has been a long-time proponent of establishing a national security council at the apex of power to ensure an institutional forum to discuss serious national issues.

As long as President Musharraf stayed in office, the president of Pakistan was the Chairman of the NCA, and the prime minister was the Vice Chairman. This structure was promulgated in the NCA Ordinance on December 13, 2007, and later approved by Parliament in 2010.[43] In February 2008, elections brought civilian government back to power. In August 2008, Musharraf resigned under pressure of impeachment from the elected parliament, and this formally ended a prolonged transition from a hybrid system into a fully democratic parliamentary system. As a result of the 18th Amendment to the Constitution, executive power returned to the prime minister, who is now the Chairman of the NCA.

Before the military takeover and formulation of the SPD, the nonaccountability of the A. Q. Khan network and weak oversight resulted in the loss of control of procurement activities and illicit trade in nuclear weapons.[44] The existence of diffused authority and ambiguity in responsibilities over the nuclear procurement activities in the 1990s led to A. Q. Khan's freelancing. The beneficiaries of the proliferation network business were spread worldwide; in Pakistan, however, several individuals—including politicians, scientists, and civil and military bureaucrats—who were responsible for protecting the nuclear program took advantage of this profit-making enterprise.

Several complex factors contributed to this lack of oversight and control. The national nuclear program was freed of all bureaucratic hurdles and provided with sufficient autonomy for the scientific community; finance incentives and innovative financial means were created to lure suppliers and to ensure the continuity of the program; unfettered access was allowed to conceal and transfer the procured technologies within the country to reach their destinations safely; and a peculiar diffusion at the apex of political power allowed space for A. Q. Khan to exploit and conduct a lucrative trade in nuclear technology.[45]

With the military in control and an altered regional and international environment after September 11, 2001 (9/11), President Musharraf instituted a tight control on the nuclear program, and his efforts contributed in unraveling the A. Q. Khan network. He also shaped the nuclear command and control system, and ensured it was robust enough to withstand political shocks and to deal with Pakistan's nuclear posture in peace, crises, and war. Since the 1998 nuclear tests, Pakistani deterrent forces and its command and control structure have been tested under both regional crises and domestic violence.

GROWING ARSENALS, INTERNAL STABILITY AND PAKISTANI NUCLEAR MANAGEMENT

After 9/11, Pakistan once again became a front-line state and a conduit to the war against al-Qaeda and the Taliban in neighboring Afghanistan. As several hundred terrorists were killed and captured, billions in aid and investments poured into the country. The investments propped up Pakistan's national economy, which began to show impressive growth by 2005-06, averaging a 6.5-percent annual gross domestic product (GDP). Pakistan was declared a non-NATO ally, which brought international support and recognition for its role in the war against terrorism. During this period, Pakistan went through several crises, including a 10-month military standoff with India in 2001-02 and the unraveling of the A. Q. Khan network in 2004. Pakistan was caught between international appreciation for its vital cooperation against the War on Terror and global condemnation for its role in the proliferation of nuclear technology, which overshadowed the establishment of the nuclear command and control system.

The handling of the 2001-02 military standoff with India and the shattering of the A. Q. Khan network were two main crises that tested the efficacy of Pakistan's nascent command and control structure. The Pakistani military countermobilized in response to India's military mobilization in December 2001-January 2002, at a time when U.S military forces were deeply engaged in military operations around the Pakistani western border at Tora Bora (Operations TORA BORA and ANACONDA). The NCA tightly controlled the situation and ensured that no nuclear deployments or threats occurred throughout the military standoff, which lasted until October 2002.[46] The SPD successfully dispersed nuclear assets into silos and made them impenetrable, ensuring secrecy and invulnerability.

In 2004, when the A. Q. Khan crisis erupted, the SPD handled the inquiry and took swift and effective measures to shut down the network in concert with international efforts. The SPD's task was tough: It had to balance international cooperative expectations against domestic public opinion (many Pakistanis viewed A. Q. Khan as a national hero), while simultaneously preserving operational secrecy associated with Pakistan's nuclear weapons program. Western critics saw this balancing act as an attempt to hide the network activities from scrutiny, whereas domestic critics of Musharraf viewed A. Q Khan's public confessions as the scapegoating of a national hero in order to protect the military's alleged complicity in the Khan network. The SPD's primary tasks were to preserve operational security, protect classified aspects of the nuclear program, and determine the extent of the network and international damage to national interest. General Musharraf instigated a full inquiry, which led to arrests that included several military officials, scientists, and others. The SPD subsequently shared the findings of its inquiry with all concerned allies, particularly the United States, and cooperated with the IAEA in its investigation on the matter.[47] These two crises resulted in the maturation of the Pakistani command and control and accountability systems. The 2001-02 standoff galvanized Pakistani force postures, and the A. Q. Khan crisis, as well as other instabilities, resulted in formation of a dedicated Security Division under the SPD, which now has over some 20,000 dedicated troops under a carefully constructed nuclear security architecture.[48]

Musharraf Downfall and Internal Crises.

Since the spring of 2007, after years of stability and growth under the military rule of Musharraf, Pakistan's internal situation has deteriorated. In March 2007, President Musharraf fired the Chief Justice of Pakistan, which resulted in a civil society movement against him. In July, after months of deliberations, he approved a military operation against *Lal Masjid* (Red Mosque), a radicalized mosque, that unleashed a

Taliban-style vigilante movement in Islamabad. These two events triggered movements from both the liberal left and the religious right that were directed against President Musharraf. At one level, the civil society and judiciary weakened the grip of Musharraf on the state, while simultaneously, suicide terrorists struck with impunity in cities, bazaars, and mosques—targeting civilians, military intelligence officers, and their families. Combined with the spillover of the Afghanistan conflict into tribal areas, and the general radicalization of society, Pakistan became a tinderbox and has been unable to fully recover from it.

In December 2007, a new organization, the Tehrik-e-Taliban Pakistan (TTP), was formed in tribal areas, and, in the Swat valley, another radical organization with links to terror organizations and the Taliban took over the valley. Meanwhile, in Baluchistan Province, a separatist insurgency commenced after a Baluch leader, Akbar Bugti, was killed in a military operation. The Pakistan Army was now at war with radical and separate forces within the country, on its western borders. It was simultaneously caught between balancing two-front contingencies on the borders with India and Afghanistan, and maintaining internal stability. The army's dilemma was compounded from both man-made crises (political, sectarian and extremist violence), as well as natural calamities (floods and earthquakes). At the same time, as custodian of nuclear weapons, the military had a responsibility to the NCA. These were monumental tasks for the military, which was under constant pressure from the United States to do more on the terror front.

The drivers of Pakistani strategic anxieties are not just the security situation described above. Other factors have immensely contributed to them. First is the progressive downslide in U.S.-Pakistan relations. The relationship between the two countries had spiked to new heights of cooperation and amity in the first half of the decade after 9/11. Then it gradually began to spiral down for multiple reasons, leading to rapid deterioration after the Barack Obama administration came to power, but especially related to Afghanistan policy and distrust of each other.

Second is the outright strategic tilt to India, which Pakistan views as detrimental to its security, and, specifically, the nuclear deal offered to India. The nuclear deal, in Pakistan's view, is inherently discriminatory, and tantamount to appeasing a non-NPT member. India is veritably accepted as a de facto nuclear-weapons state that has no legal obligation to a NPT regime. From the Pakistani standpoint the deal frees up nuclear trade with India, which allows India to use domestic uranium resources entirely for dedicated military purposes, and international suppliers to trade in nuclear energy. Pakistan thus has stopped cooperation in international multilaterals forums. It had blocked the Fissile Material Cut-off Treaty (FMCT) negotiations at the Conference of Disarmament and ramped up its fissile production.

Third is the Indian military's continued pressure on the Pakistan military when the latter is engaged on multiple fronts, as described above. The pressure on Pakistan is manifested in several ways: India military exercises each year; the announcement of new military doctrines, such as limited war under nuclear umbrella (Cold Start) and its force posture; and modernization and deployment patterns directed toward Pakistani borders. Though India's public position is that it is modernizing in response to its own rise and against the perceived China threat, its physical manifestation and orientation are against Pakistan. Since Pakistani conventional forces are spread thin so as to balance all contingencies, Pakistan has clearly signaled lowering the nuclear threshold to deter any military adventure.

Pakistan's growing nuclear arsenals and upgrades in nuclear security are a result of the above circumstances, perceptions, and anxieties. The international community's focus is on a nuclear-armed country under internal stress and the threat of violent extremism, where growing arsenals and terrorism are at a dangerous crossroads. The Pakistani response is that it is cognizant of the dangers and that its organizational response, best practices, and measure of performance in nuclear security need to be weighed against the fears of insecurities.[49]

CONCLUSION

Despite a tumultuous political history and challenging security circumstances in which the Pakistani nuclear program progressed, there has not been any terrifying moment when there existed a danger of the nation losing control of its arsenals. From the early-1970s, when the weapons program commenced, it was directed from the highest political office in the country, from Z. A. Bhutto (1971-77) to Zia-ul-Haq (1977-88) to President Ghulam Ishaq Khan (1988-93).

The role of the COAS historically has been pivotal in Pakistani nuclear history. When Zia was both president and COAS, he did not involve the military institution in the nuclear oversight program, but in a support role. After Zia's death, President Ghulam Ishaq Khan made the army his right hand; he asked the COAS to help coordinate and support the program on his behalf until he departed office in 1993. President Ishaq Khan never trusted the political leadership with the sensitivity of the nuclear program. Fearing political uncertainty and the diffusion of authority, he handed over the responsibility to the Army, which gradually formalized its role until it took over power.

In this history, there were two especially important political transitions during which there could have been a control problem, but on each occasion, the military had an organizational system in place to prevent any such danger. The first was immediately after the sudden plane crash of President General Zia-ul-Haq, when the entire military leadership vanished, but the nuclear program came under the control of President Ghulam Ishaq Khan, who was a veteran insider and consistent member of the coordination committee for the nuclear program.

The second occasion was in July 1993, when both the president and prime minister left office after political infighting. President Ghulam Ishaq Khan was a veteran bureaucrat, who had seen the bulk of the nation's political history. In his wisdom, his last step as a public servant was to shift the sensitive responsibility to Army Headquarters, which was the most viable and robust national institution in Pakistan. Though this move deprived the oversight of elected representatives, which is the norm of all democracies, in hindsight, President Ghulam Ishaq Khan was proven right.

From 1993 until the military took over in 1999, the tussle between the president, prime minister, judiciary, and Army continued to keep national governance in turmoil. It was during this period when the A. Q. Khan network, hitherto contributing inward into Pakistani procurement activities, turned its activities outward. It took several years of effort after the SPD was formed and after the Khan network was revealed for complete control of all organizations to be made fully effective. As command and control evolved, a more scientific methodology of material accountability and protection system was installed. The oversight mechanism that came into effect included strict access to control and personnel reliability programs. All these best practices were derived from cooperation with and training from the United States and other advanced nuclear countries. However, the nuclear security architecture in Pakistan and the oversight system established is indigenous, with an emphasis on cultural norms and national sensitivities.

The progress of the nuclear weapons program throughout this period remained firewalled from all political shocks. Though Pakistan's civil-military relations are still unsettled, the existing command and control structure is viewed as robust, institutional, and professional, and it has support across the entire political system.

During the 10-year period of democracy in the 1990s, the role of prime minister on nuclear control was a matter of controversy and power struggle. When the military coup occurred around the end of the decade, there was no ambiguity about where the apex of power rested. It took a decade to develop a robust command system, which transited to the civilian setup without any hiccups in 2008.

For over 4 years, since the return of representative government, Pakistan has undergone tremendous domestic tumult resulting from a series of regional crises and violent extremism—a democratic system facing multitudinous threats to its security. Meanwhile, Pakistan's nuclear capability and force goals have grown steadily, keeping pace with its rival,

India, where force modernization and strategic development in both the conventional and nuclear realms have significantly improved. Pakistan's nuclear force posture in part has been influenced by the lucrative nuclear deal granted to India by the United States. Above all, Pakistan went through a peaceful transition in 2008 for the first time in history, even though it had gone through violence and a domestic crisis that was unprecedented in its short history as a nation.

ENDNOTES - CHAPTER 5

1. Governor General Ghulam Mohammad removed Prime Minister Khwaja Nazimuddin in 1953. He removed Prime Minister Mohammad Ali Bogra in 1955. Next, Prime Minister Choudhury Muhammad Ali was removed in 1956. Prime Minister H. S. Suharwardy was the first prime minister after the 1956 constitution; he was removed in 1957. Prime Minister I.I Chundrigar replaced him for a short while in 1957. Finally, Prime Minister Feroz Khan Noon was removed by President Iskandar Mirza in 1958. President Mirza was removed by General Ayub, leading to the first military coup in 1958.

2. General Ayub Khan led the first military coup in October 1958 when he removed President Iskander Mirza; General Yahya Khan replaced Ayub Khan in March 1969; Zia-ul-haq deposed Prime Minister Zulfiqar Ali Bhutto in July 1977; and General Pervez Musharraf deposed Prime Minister Nawaz Sharif in October 1999.

3. In May 1988, President General Zia-ul-Haq removed Prime Minister Muhammad Khan Junejo; in July 1990, President Ghulam Ishaq Khan sacked Prime Minister Benazir Bhutto. President Ghulam Ishaq Khan sacked Prime Minister Nawaz Sharif in April 1993, and then President Farooq Leghari removed Prime Minister Benazir Bhutto from power.

4. Author's interviews with former politicians, bureaucrats, military officials, and scientists between 2005 and 2006 are unanimous on this question. Former PAEC Chairman Ishfaq Ahmad

(1991-2001) told the author that the classified nuclear program was never short of funds under all regimes, since Zulfiqar Ali Bhutto and every national institution in the country is the stakeholder in the nuclear program.

5. After the 1958 military coup, Ayub Khan dissolved the first constitution in 1956 and replaced it with the 1962 constitution, ushering in the presidential form of government. That included the introduction of a basic democratic system—the "Electoral College"—comprised of locally elected members who voted for the president. He nevertheless handed over power to General Yahya Khan, whose martial law lasted until the end of his presidency in 1971. Zulfiqar Ali Bhutto brought in the parliamentary form of government under the new 1973 constitution, which is still effective. General Zia-ul-Haq made the 8th amendment to the constitution, which retained the parliamentary system but made the president all powerful, with the authority to dissolve the assembly—essentially making the prime minister subordinate to the president. In 1997, Nawaz Sharif won a two-thirds majority in the parliament; he promptly clipped presidential powers with the passage of the 13th amendment to the constitution, once again returning all powers to the prime minister and reducing the authority of the president to merely a ceremonial one. General Musharraf then introduced 17th amendment, which returned powers to the president so he could dismiss the prime minister and dissolve parliament. Once Musharraf was ousted, President Asif Zardari reverted the powers back to the prime minister under the 18th amendment to the constitution.

6. Pakistan now has a functioning parliamentary form of government, strengthened with the 18th amendment to the constitution. However, the current president, Asif Ali Zardari, also retains the leadership of the ruling political party—the PPP. By doing so, he has the authority to fire any incumbent minister, including the all-powerful prime minister, who serves at the pleasure of the party leader. As president of the country and chairman of the political party in power, the president thus retains de facto power and influence, even though de jure parliamentary powers are with the prime minister. In practice, the troika of power is still in effect at the apex of country governance.

7. According to Pakistan's 1973 constitution, a parliamentary form of government has the prime minister as the chief executive with the power to run the country. In the 1970s, after seven amendments to the constitution under Bhutto, the prime minister became the most powerful office, with only nominal powers residing in the president. In 1985, General Zia-ul Haq initiated the 8th amendment to the constitution, as quid pro quo for restoration of the parliament, which gave him the powers to dissolve the parliament and the government. Successive presidents used this power four times in a row (1988, 1990, 1993, and 1997) to remove the civil government. Prime Minister Nawaz Sharif then introduced the 13th amendment to the constitution, which made the prime minister all-powerful again. Once again, a military coup removed him from power. In a repeat of history, Musharraf brought back presidential powers through the 17th amendment upon restoration of democracy in 2002. When he was ousted from power, the 18th amendment to the constitution brought back the powers to the prime minister.

8. Until November 2007, General Musharraf was both the president and army chief, so the unity of command rested in his office, and continued with him as civilian president until August 2008. After Musharraf resigned, President Asif Ali Zardari became the head of the National Command Authority (NCA), but he also voluntarily gave his powers as head of NCA to the prime minister in deference to the reform and reintroduction of the parliamentary form of government. This form was later promulgated after the 18th amendment to the constitution, which—for the fourth time—came back to the prime minister.

9. "NA passed National Command Authority Bill 2009," *Daily Times*, January 29, 2010, available from *www.dailytimes.com.pk/default.asp?page=2010%5C01%5C29%5Cstory_29-1-2010_pg7_5*.

10. Pervaiz Iqbal Cheema, *Pakistan's Defense Policy 1947- 58*, New York: St Martin, 1990, p. 85. The division of army units, ordnances, and infrastructure was always viewed as unfair in Pakistan. In general, the distribution of finance, defense, and administrative assets was among the bitter part of the tragedy that accompanied the bloody partition. Border disputes and the fate of the princely state of Jammu and Kashmir were two major blows that were, and remain, at the root of India- Pakistan rivalry.

11. Hasan-Askari Rizvi, *The Military, State and Society in Pakistan*, Lahore, Punjab, Pakistan: Sang-e-Meel Publications, 2003, pp. 3-24.

12. This term is a euphemism for the institutional role of the military and refers to the combination of armed forces, intelligence, and civil bureaucrats whose interests and line of thinking are supported by a strategic community composed of retired civil bureaucrats, military leaders, scientists, and academics backed by right-leaning conservatives.

13. Munir Ahmad Khan, "Nuclearisation of South Asia and its Regional and Global Implications," *Regional Studies,* Vol. XVI, No. 4, Autumn 1998, p. 11.

14. Zulfikar Ali Bhutto, *If I am Assassinated . . .*, New Delhi, India: Vikas Publishing House Pvt. Ltd., 1979, p. 137.

15. *Ibid.* Also see Feroz Hassan Khan, "Nuclear Proliferation Motivations: Lessons from Pakistan," in Peter Lavoy, ed. *Nuclear Weapons Proliferation in the Next Decade*, New York: Routledge, Taylor and Francis, 2007, p.71.

16. Author's interview with the late Agha Shahi, Islamabad, June 19, 2005. Also see Farhatullah Babar, "Bhutto's footprints on Nuclear Pakistan," *The News,* April 4, 2006.

17. Craig Baxter, ed. and annotated, *Dairies of Field Marshall Ayub Khan, 1966-1972*, New York: Oxford University Press, 2007, p. 55.

18. Southeast Asia Treaty Organization, Central Treaty Organization.

19. Khan, "Nuclear Proliferation Motivations," p. 505.

20. Author's interview with Dr. Ishfaq Ahmad, former Chairman PAEC (1991- 2001), Islamabad, December 20, 2005.

21. Article on Zulfiqar Ali Bhutto's Press Conference of May 19, 1974, *The Pakistan Times,* Lahore, Punjab Province, Pakistan, May 20, 1974.

22. Author's interview with PAEC scientists, civil and military officials from 2005 until 2011, during the author's research.

23. Lahore was brought under martial law in 1953, when sectarian riots to declare the Ahmadi community as non-Muslim went violent, forcing the army to step in. That event foreshadowed martial law in 1958.

24. Bhutto, *If I am assassinated*, pp. 135-137.

25. *Ibid.*

26. Major General Imtiaz Ali was posted back to the army to become Commandant of School of Infantry and Tactics, from where he eventually retired. Throughout the reign of General Zia-ul-Haq, the president's chief of staff coordinated the nuclear supervisory board.

27. Dr. Abdus Salam, a Nobel laureate, who helped lay the foundation of the nuclear program, had recruited several hundred scientists and technicians in the PAEC. Zia suspected all of them to be secretly Ahmedis, who were not considered loyal enough to be involved in the classified program. This bigoted approach affected the classified nuclear program, as many individuals were sidelined because of mere suspicion until they could be cleared after scrutiny. This was a sort of criterion of the personal reliability program prevalent at the time.

28. Ghulam Ishaq Khan was a long-time civil servant and Zia's finance minister and later Chairman of the Senate. After the accidental death of President Zia, he became acting president of Pakistan; after the general elections of 1988, he was elected the President of Pakistan.

29. Pervez Musharraf, *In the Line of Fire: A Memoir*, New York: Free Press, 2006, p. 285.

30. Author's interview with General Mirza Aslam Beg, Rawalpindi, Pakistan, September 1, 2005.

31. Also see Devin T. Hagerty, *The Consequences of Nuclear Proliferation: Lessons From South Asia*, London, UK: The MIT Press, 1998, pp. 135-136.

32. In an interview with the ABC television network, Benazir Bhutto stated that she was kept in the dark about the country's nuclear program. Cited in Zahid Hussain, "Deliberate Nuclear Ambiguity," in Samina Ahmad and David Cortright, eds., *Pakistan and the Bomb: Public Opinion and Nuclear Options*, Notre Dame, IN: University of Notre Dame, 1998, p. 39.

33. Author's interview with General Mirza Aslam Beg, Rawalpindi, September 1, 2005.

34. *Ibid*. Also see Douglas Frantz and Catherine Collins, *The Nuclear Jihadist*, New York: Hachette Book Group, 2007, p. 181; and Hussain, "Deliberate Nuclear Ambiguity," p. 30.

35. Author's interview with General Beg. Also see Hagerty, *The Consequences of Nuclear Proliferation*, pp. 128-129.

36. Zia-ul Haq's restraint agreement was explained to the author in an interview with Lieutenant General (Ret.) Syed Refaqat Ali, Chief of Staff to President Zia-ul-Haq (1985-88) in Islamabad, December 19, 2005. Also See Dennis Kux, *The United States and Pakistan, 1947-2000*, Washington DC: Woodrow Wilson Center Press, 2001, pp. 257- 258.

37. In her speech before a joint session of Congress in June 1989, Prime Minister Benazir Bhutto said: "Speaking for Pakistan, I can declare that we do not possess nor do we intend to make a nuclear device. That is our policy." Benazir Bhutto, "The Policies of Pakistani Nuclear Problems and Afghanistan," *Vital Speeches of the Day*, June 7, 1989, p. 553.

38. The crises between the president and the prime minister had been brewing over the course of several months, especially after the sudden death, in January 1993, of COAS General Asif Nawaz, who had succeeded General Aslam Beg in August 1991.

39. Author's interview with Dr. Ishfaq Ahmad, Islamabad, December 20, 2005.

40. The author was posted to this new covert nuclear setup in November 1993 and served in the Combat Development Directorate and then (after the nuclear tests) in the Strategic Plans Division, which was formed as the nuclear secretariat; his setup was merged with this new organization.

41. In 1997, after a bitter struggle between the president, prime minister, and chief justice of Pakistan, the latter two had to resign from office, making the prime minister all-powerful. The Army refused to be drawn into the institutional struggle and allowed the parliamentary process to continue. In October 1998, the prime minister sacked General Karamat, and thus became even more powerful with no accountability. When the prime minister tried this move a second time, the military retaliated and overthrew the prime minister on October 12, 1999.

42. Joseph Cirincione, *Bomb Scare: The History and Future of Nuclear Weapons,* New York: Columbia University Press, 2007, p. 64.

43. *Dawn*, Pakistan, December 14, 2007. On January 2010, the Pakistani parliament passed the bill that endorsed the NCA and brought it under direct control of the prime minister. See Tahir Niaz, "NA Passes National Command Authority Bill 2009," *Daily Times,* available from www.dailytimes.com.pk/default.asp?page=2010%5C01%5C29%5Cstory_29-1-2010_pg7_5.

44. In October 2006, during a visit to the Naval Postgraduate School in Monterey, California, Lieutenant General Khalid Kidwai, Director General, Strategic Plans Division, admitted the failure of the state on oversight but forcefully denied complicity in the network.

45. For details, see *Nuclear Black Markets: Pakistan, A. Q. Khan and the Rise of Proliferation Networks, a Net Assessment,* International Institute for Strategic Studies Strategic Dossier, London, UK: International Institute for Strategic Studies, 2007.

46. In October 2002, elections were held in Pakistan, which brought civilian parliamentarianism into participation under the continued military-dominated system of governance. General Musharraf continued to serve as the president, and Prime Min-

ister Zafrullah Jamali was chosen by the parliament. This hybrid system of governance continued until the 2008 elections brought back civilian government, and the military withdrew from political administration.

47. Despite stiff opposition from the hardliners, Pakistan agreed to send samples of centrifuges to the IAEA to help it complete its investigation on the A. Q. Khan network's sales to Iran.

48. Adil Sultan, "Nuclear Weapons and National Security," *The Tribune*, May 27, 2012, available from *tribune.com.pk/story/384907/nuclear-weapons-and-national-security/*.

49. For a detailed analysis, see Feroz Hassan Khan, "Pakistan Nuclear Security: Separating Myths from Reality," *Arms Control Today*, Vol. 39, No. 6, July/ August 2009, pp. 12-20.

PART II:
LESSONS LEARNED

CHAPTER 6

THE CONUNDRUM OF CLOSE CALLS: LESSONS LEARNED FOR SECURING NUCLEAR WEAPONS

Reid B. C. Pauly
Scott D. Sagan

The case studies presented in this volume are valuable contributions to the literature on nuclear security, as they bring to light new evidence of instances when nuclear test sites, weapons in transit, and deployed weapons were threatened during times of political instability. The authors did not, of course, discover instances in which nuclear weapons were actually stolen or used by rogue officers, revolutionary mobs, or terrorists. So there is a significant puzzle about how best to interpret the "close call" incidents highlighted in these cases.

Organizational scholars James March, Lee Sproull, and Michal Tamuz have argued:

> The most obvious learning problem with near-histories [is] the necessary ambiguity of interpretation.... Every time a pilot avoids a collision, the event provides evidence both for the threat and for its irrelevance. It is not clear whether the learning should emphasize how close the organization came to disaster, thus the reality of danger in the guise of safety, or the fact that disaster was avoided, the reality of safety in the guise of danger.[1]

A "systems safety" approach to this conundrum, however, focuses not on the inherent ambiguity of nuclear close calls, but rather on three related details about the incident in question and the organization's reaction to it afterward. First, how close was the "close call?" Can one provide an assessment of the probability that the incident under investigation would have led, under somewhat different but plausible conditions, to the theft or use of a nuclear weapon? For example, if a nuclear power plant has five redundant safety devices and four fail, that is a closer call to an accident than if only two fail. Second, what "saved the day" and prevented unauthorized individuals from getting control of a nuclear weapon? To the degree that the events were anticipated, and appropriate safety mechanisms were therefore built into the system, the incident should be placed on the safety, not the danger, side of the ledger. To the degree that the events were not anticipated, however, and good fortune, not good design, saved the day, a more pessimistic assessment is warranted. Third, what was learned from the incident? If the organization appropriately adjusted its policies and procedures after a close call, one should predict that the likelihood of a reoccurrence has decreased. If that is not the case, however, then one should predict that the likelihood of a second security incident, like the first one with similar risks, has not been reduced.[2]

This chapter will address each regional study through this lens of "normal accident theory" and organizational learning and will draw broader lessons for the security of nuclear weapons and material in each case. Unfortunately, the project authors do not always focus on these three dimensions of the problem in their case studies. Thus, we have provided our own assessment, when evidence exists or, alternatively, simply pointed out where more research is needed to provide an appropriate assessment.

RUSSIA

Nikolai Sokov provides accounts of procedural dilemmas and some cases of near-losses of control over nuclear weapons. The stories are chilling, but we lack crucial details. Did the tactical weapons on the aircraft in Baku in 1990 have Permissive Action Links (PALs) on them, and if so, how effective were the devices? (Even the best PALs are not a panacea, for they only delay the ability to use the weapon or the material inside it.) As far as we can tell from the Sokov chapter, the Soviet government had not pre-planned for the possibility of a large-scale insurrection on Azerbaijani territory, and the emergency withdrawal of the tactical weapons was an improvised security procedure. The Azerbaijan case also raises an important question about how to assess the probability of a system failure when there is deep uncertainty about what would have happened if the crowd had attacked the transport aircraft. A senior Department of Energy (DOE) official expressed his sense of the risks involved in such dangerous situations, and the need to avoid them, when he argued that, "Once the firefight starts, it is a crapshoot."[3] The 1990 incident also reveals the paradox of how efforts to protect weapons—transferring them to safer locations—can create vulnerabilities. Finally, Sokov could trace whether there was trial-and-error learning from the incident and whether subsequent operations to remove nuclear weapons from former Soviet republics were conducted under more effective operational security.

Sokov's research into the August 1991 coup attempt highlights the degree to which even sophisticated command and control systems are vulnerable to failure in times of political instability. His account implies that there was a combined technical and political checks and balances control arrangement under the Soviet Kazbek system: The General Secretary of the Communist Party held the authority and capability to launch nuclear weapons on his own, but only if the warning system had indicated that a U.S. attack was under way. If true, this description suggests that: a) the Soviet leader could not use nuclear weapons first; and b) the system was highly vulnerable to the risk of coup leaders' seizing and disabling Gorbachev's Cheget, as occurred in 1991.

The first point appears unlikely, however, since, according to David Hoffman, the General Secretary did have the authority to order a first strike.[4] The "check" in this case was that the General Secretary's permission order would have to be transformed into a direct command by the General Staff.[5] There is still ambiguity in the 1991 case about who had the authority versus the capability to launch nuclear weapons. But if Hoffman is right, it seems plausible that the coup leaders could have launched nuclear weapons on their own for the 3 days in August. Sokov's account demonstrates that the coup leaders were able to place elements of the Soviet nuclear arsenal in a heightened state of alert, but also suggests that personal intervention by some anti-coup officers (for example, Varennikov) could countermand their orders to specific units. The 1991 case is thus an illustration of the precarious "always/never" balance, whereby the loss of checks and balances in a command and control system increases the likelihood of unauthorized use.

PAKISTAN

Feroz Khan identifies Pakistan's Chief of the Army Staff (COAS) as a key stabilizing factor in the Pakistani nuclear weapons security system. Khan argues that the COAS played a key role in ensuring the undisrupted security of nuclear forces regardless of political posturing and the changes of leadership. We accept the notion that nuclear security procedures can be bolstered by decreasing their dependence on what could be rapidly shifting and unpredictable political conditions. However, many other questions about nuclear security in Pakistan were not sufficiently addressed. Pakistan has reportedly received nuclear security assistance from the United States but faces extreme challenges: the vulnerability/invulnerability paradox and insider threats.[6] The following issues merit further consideration.

First, is there an enduring risk of an Islamist coup? In 1995, the Pakistani Army arrested 40 officers who were implicated in a coup plot led by Major General Zahirul Islam Abbasi, who had alleged links to Islamic fundamentalist groups.[7] Another example came to light in June 2011, when Brigadier General Ali Khan was arrested in Pakistan on charges of suspected ties to Islamic fundamentalists.[8] If all authority and capability is in the COAS, and that officer is replaced by a military leadership with radical fundamentalist beliefs, would the lack of checks and balances actually make nuclear security more problematic in Pakistan?

Second, how effective is the Personnel Reliability Program (PRP) in Pakistan to address the insider threat? We lack evidence about the record inside the Pakistani Strategic Plans Division, but certainly the record inside the Pakistani personal security organizations does not engender confidence. In January 2011, Punjab Governor Salman Taseer was assassinated by one of his own bodyguards, who later told police that he had murdered the governor for his opposition to Pakistan's blasphemy law.[9] Two assassination attempts in 2003 against President Pervez Musharraf also involved insiders, though in these cases the security guards were not lone wolves but were tied to jihadist terror organizations.[10]

Third, how does Pakistan address the vulnerability/invulnerability paradox? When nuclear weapons are de-mated from delivery vehicles and locked inside a guarded facility, they are more secure from theft or seizure but more vulnerable to an enemy strike; when nuclear weapons are taken out of the base, mated with road mobile missiles, and dispersed into the country, they are less vulnerable to a first strike but more vulnerable to theft.[11] The insider threat problem and this vulnerability/invulnerability paradox could be mutually reinforcing in a dangerous way: As jihadist groups become more active in Pakistan, the likelihood of an Inter-Services Intelligence (ISI) supported group attacking India might increase. That event, however, would then increase the likelihood that Pakistani weapons would be taken out of more secure locations on military bases and deployed into the field.[12]

Finally, how will the likely deployment of tactical nuclear weapons and short-range missiles in Pakistan influence nuclear security? This trend puts pressures on commanders to delegate authority to launch down the chain of command, or worse, pre-delegate authority to launch. This is a situation that increases the risk of accidents and of unauthorized use.

CHINA[13]

Mark Stokes brings to light examples of the fracturing of Chinese command and control systems during the Cultural Revolution, most notably the conducting of a risky nuclear-tipped missile test in October 1966. Combined with the rise of internal and external security threats, this period of Chinese history proved to be a seriously unstable moment for nuclear security. Stokes asserts that China learned from its experiences during the Cultural Revolution, and has since prioritized security and safety over operational readiness, while maintaining a more centralized command and control system. Prioritizing safety and security over operational readiness is a choice that Stokes argues "could result in self-imposed constraints on the size of its arsenal." This is a key finding, but it is unclear whether Chinese nuclear doctrine or security concerns are the driving force behind the limited size of the arsenal. Above all, Stokes's case study is a prime example of his own conclusion that "No amount of physical security can shelter a nuclear arsenal from political chaos at the highest levels of government."[14]

FRANCE

Bruno Tertrais presents new evidence in his case study of Algeria in 1961 and is careful not to overstate the vulnerability of the French nuclear device. This is laudable, but was this a case of danger in the guise of safety? An assessment should address whether redundant safety mechanisms were in place and whether the key ones were designed into the system or were unanticipated or improvised. The French case demonstrates, like others in this volume, how the security of nuclear arsenals can depend on the personal loyalties of individuals in times of political instability. Thiry's decision not to side with the coup leaders was critical to the protection and eventual destruction of the nuclear device. The lesson from the Algerian case is not that there was no danger of a nuclear weapon falling into the wrong hands, but rather that the choice of whether or not the nuclear device would fall into the wrong hands came down to Thiry, who actively considered the request of the rebellious generals.

The Algerian case provides another important insight: The nuclear device to be tested was just that, a device, not a bomb. Tertrais makes clear that the device to be tested would not have been able to be detonated (at least not promptly) without the automatic arming mechanisms that were located at the testing tower. It is worth determining whether this setup was designed into the testing program to enhance nuclear security and safety, or whether it was done for reasons of technical convenience. It would also be helpful to know how often such redundancies were applied beyond the Algerian case.

JUST THE BEGINNING

These case studies focus on the record of close calls from the past. But this safety record may be less reliable as a guide for the future if new nuclear-weapons states have increased inherent risk characteristics. Unfortunately, two studies of such national risk indicators published by the World Bank and Polity IV database scores from 2009 and the 2012 Nuclear Threat Initiative (NTI) Nuclear Materials Security Index suggest that dangers are growing. Figure 6-1 visually compares current nuclear-weapons states and Iran on

World Bank indicators of control of corruption, political stability, and Polity IV scores. Taken as a whole, the nuclear powers and Iran fail to inspire confidence in every category. But the data clearly suggest that newer nuclear states pose higher challenges regarding such risk factors.

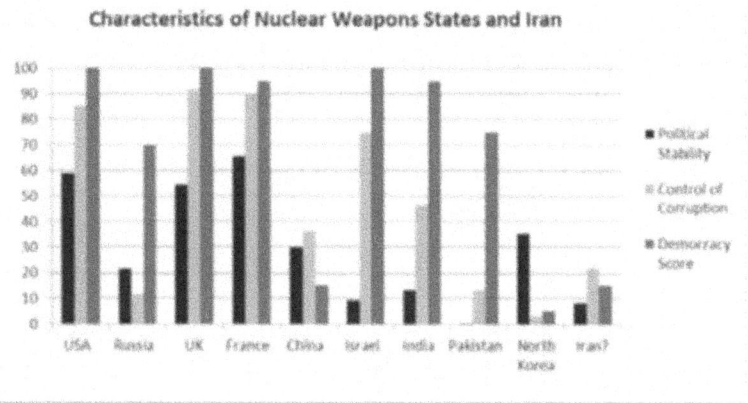

*Measurement for Democracy/Autocracy Score is Mean Polity IV 20-point score on a 100-point scale. Scores above 50 represent democracy; below 50 implies nondemocracy.

Source: World Bank, *World Governance Indicators, 1996-2007*, available from *info.worldbank.org/governance/wgi/index/asp*; Polity IV Project, *Political Regime Characteristics and Transitions, 1800-2007*, available from *www.systemicpeace.org/inscr.htm*.

Figure 6-1. Characteristics of Nuclear-Weapons States and Iran.

The Nuclear Threat Initiative published its Nuclear Materials Security Index in January 2012 (see Figure 6-2) and rightly emphasized problems of political stability and institutional corruption heavily in their "societal factors" category.[15] One glance at the Initiative's rankings reveals that there is nothing special about nations that actually possess nuclear weapons when it comes to nuclear materials security. Six out of the nine nuclear powers rank in the bottom third of states with weapons-usable nuclear materials, and none of them rank in the top 10. Of further note is that the overall score of every nuclear weapons state except North Korea is brought down by its scores in the societal factors category, which includes political stability and corruption indices. Potential future proliferants (e.g., Iran) exhibit similar patterns.

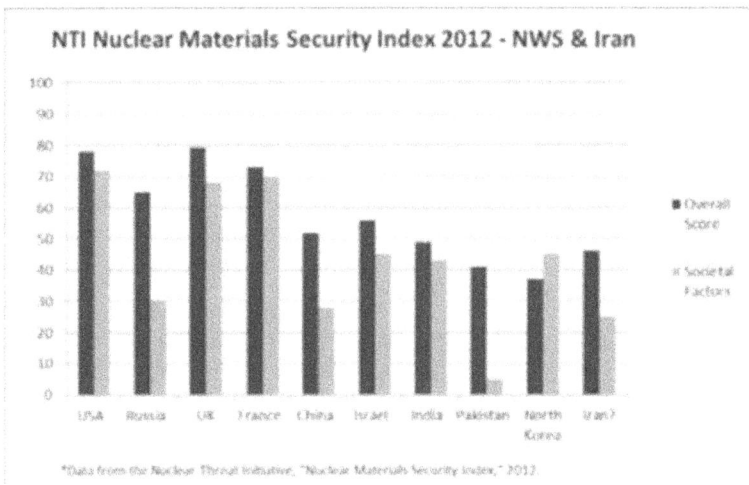

Figure 6-2. NTI Nuclear Materials Security Index 2012 - NWS and Iran.

OTHER CASES

This project has usefully encouraged research into events that have until now been shrouded in secrecy. There are, however, a number of other cases of nuclear close calls worth examining. First, an attack on the 42nd Field Artillery Brigade at the U.S. Army Base in Giessen, West Germany, on January 4, 1977, was reportedly carried out by The Revolutionary Cells (RZ), although the extent to which the stored nuclear weapons were targeted is unknown.[16] Second, the Japanese cult of Aum Shinrikyo is known to have sought nuclear weapons and biological weapons before settling for sarin gas. The extent of Aum's penetration of the Russian military, and its efforts to acquire nuclear materials through that pathway, remains understudied.[17] Finally, in 1981, four members of the Red Brigades kidnapped Brigadier General Dozier, North Atlantic Treaty Organization (NATO) Deputy Chief of Staff at Southern European land forces. They held him for 42 days, during which time they interrogated him about the location and security measures for nuclear weapons. The details of their plans remain largely unexamined.[18]

ENDNOTES - CHAPTER 6

1. James G. March, Lee S. Sproull, and Michal Tamuz, "Learning from Samples of One or Fewer," *Organization Science*, Vol. 2, No. 1, February 1991, p. 10.

2. Scott D. Sagan, *The Limits of Safety: Organizations, Accidents, and Nuclear Weapons*, Princeton, NJ: Princeton University Press, 1993, p. 47-52; and *Idem.*, "The Problem of Redundancy Problem: Why More Nuclear Security Forces May Produce Less Nuclear Security," *Risk Analysis*, Vol. 24, No. 4, 2004, pp. 935-946.

3. Sagan, "New Ideas for Strengthening the Design Basis Threat (DBT) Process," a report of the American Academy of Arts and Sciences' workshop on strengthening physical protection of nuclear weapons and materials, January 12, 2009.

4. David E. Hoffman, *The Dead Hand*, New York: Doubleday, 2009, p. 149.

5. *Ibid.*

6. Pakistan has received approximately $100 million's worth of technical assistance since 2001, according to David E. Sanger of *The New York Times*. See David E. Sanger and William J. Broad, "U.S. Secretly Aids Pakistan in Guarding Nuclear Arms," *The New York Times*, November 18, 2007.

7. John F. Burns, "Pakistan Arrests 40 Officers, Islamic Militant Tie Suspected," *The New York Times,* October 17, 1995.

8. Tim Lister and Aliza Kassim, "Arrest of Pakistani Officer Revives Fears of Extremism within Military," *CNN World*, June 22, 2011.

9. "Punjab Governor Salman Taseer Assassinated in Islamabad," *BBC News,* January 4, 2011.

10. Zahid Hussain, *Frontline Pakistan: The Struggle with Militant Islam*, New York: Columbia University Press, 2007, prologue.

11. Sagan, ed., *Inside Nuclear South Asia*, Stanford, CA: Stanford University Press, 2009, pp. 15-16.

12. There are two extremes in public discussions of Pakistani nuclear security. The extreme Western view claims that Pakistani forces are exceedingly vulnerable to seizure, exemplified by the *National Journal* article "Nuclear Negligence," by Jeffrey Goldberg and Marc Ambinder, who reported that nuclear materials in Pakistan were transported in unmarked civilian vans with negligible security in an attempt to hide their movements from the United States. See Goldberg and Ambinder, "Nuclear Negligence," *National Journal*, November 9, 2011, available from *www.nationaljournal.com/magazine/the-pentagon-s-secret-plans-to-secure-pakistan-s-nuclear-arsenal-20111104*. At the other extreme, some Pakistani officials make absurdly optimist claims about security. For example, the chairman of Pakistan's National Engineering and Scientific Commission (NESCOM), Samar Mubarakmand, claimed: "I will put a nuclear weapon on the road, you can keep it there for 10 months and I guarantee you that no one can use it or detonate it or cause any destruction from it." Samar Mubarakmand, "Capital Talk Special," *Geo TV*, March 5, 2012, available from *www.pakdef. info/forum/showthread.php?9214-Dr.-Samar-Mubarakmand-s-Inter-*

view-with-Geo-TV. Furthermore, in June 2011, Interior Minister Rehman Malik claimed that "[Pakistan's] nuclear weapons are 200 percent safe." See "Rehman Malik Assures Pakistan nukes are 200 Percent Safe," *Jagran Post,* June 5, 2011, available from *post. jagran.com/Rehman-Malik-assures-Pakistan-nukes-are-200-percent-safe-1307287729.*

13. The authors received this paper late, so could provide only a short assessment of its conclusions.

14. Mark Stokes, "Securing Nuclear Arsenals: A Chinese Case Study," Chap 3, this volume, p. 77.

15. The Nuclear Threat Initiative, *Nuclear Materials Security Index*, available from *www.ntiindex.org/*, 2012.

16. Wolfgang Kraushaar, "Im Schatten der RAF. Zur Entstehungsgeschichte der Revolutionären Zellen" ("In the Shadow of the RAF: The History of the Revolutionary Cells"), in Wolfgang Kraushaar, ed., *Die RAF und der linke Terrorismus* (*The RAF and the Left-terrorism*), Vol. I, pp. 583-601; and personal communications between Scott Sagan and Wolfgang Kraushaar, November 14, 2008.

17. For work on Aum's biological and chemical weapons programs, see Richard Danzig *et al.*, "Aum Shinrikyo: Insights into How Terrorists Develop Biological and Chemical Weapons," *Center for a New American Security Report*, July 20, 2011.

18. "Brig. Gen. James Dozier Rescued From Italian Terrorists," *Finding Dulcinea,* January 28, 2011, available from *www.findingdulcinea.com/news/on-this-day/On-this-Day--Gen--Dozier-Rescued-from-Italian-Terrorists-.html.*

CHAPTER 7

NUCLEAR COMMAND AND CONTROL IN CRISIS: OLD LESSONS FROM NEW HISTORY

Peter D. Feaver

The four case studies in this volume are usefully evaluated through two distinct lenses. First and foremost is the lens of theory: What do the case studies reveal about prevailing debates among theorists of nuclear proliferation, especially the optimist-pessimist debate? Second is the lens of policy: What do policymakers need to learn from the case studies?

WHAT DID WE KNOW AND WHY DID WE THINK WE KNEW IT?

For the theory lens, of course, what one sees depends on who is doing the looking. Some 2 decades ago, the field was locked in a dialectic over the consequences of proliferation. I identified at least four schools:[1] Paleo-pessimists, who thought that new nuclear states would be destabilizing because they would feature irrational leaders;[2] paleo-optimists, who thought new nuclear states would enhance stability because of the robustness of rational deterrence theory;[3] neo-pessimists, who thought that new nuclear states would be destabilizing because they would face daunting command and control problems;[4] and neo-optimists, who thought that new nuclear states would enhance stability because they would face easier command and control challenges and adopt safer measures to confront them.[5] There has been a vigorous theoretical debate in the intervening years, but most of it has focused on the determinants of proliferation—why and how a state develops nuclear weapons rather than to what effect.[6] Recently, however, the old optimist-pessimist debate has been revived by large-n studies of the effects of proliferation on the initiation and resolution of crises.[7]

A widely acknowledged limitation of the earlier literature was its near-total reliance on evidence from the two first nuclear powers—above all, the then-emerging and now-extensive record of U.S. nuclear history. The recent statistical studies, of course, address this problem to some degree, but in so doing, they introduce the inevitable limitations of large-n work—abstracting away granular detail about the way nuclear powers manage their nuclear arsenal and coding as similar cases that might have important, but fine-grained, distinctions. Significant empirical contributions have extended our understanding of relevant nuclear operations in other countries, approximating the granularity achieved decades ago in the U.S. and Soviet cases.[8] Yet, the four case studies commissioned for this project are an important step forward in this process of widening and deepening the public analysis of nuclear history and are especially valuable for zeroing in on a topic of special concern: nuclear security, specifically, the risks of accidental or unauthorized use of nuclear weapons arising out of a compromise in nuclear custody. Each of the case studies makes valuable contributions to that area by identifying lessons learned from the peculiar history of individual countries. The theoretical literature foreshadows what those lessons might be.

Optimists (whether paleo or neo) expect the cases to confirm several different expectations:

1. Regardless of what they say before they get nuclear weapons, states will recognize the distinctiveness of nuclear weapons.[9]
2. New nuclear powers will develop robust and careful procedures that minimize command and control problems.[10]
3. New nuclear states will adopt best practices, adapted to their specific needs.[11]
4. Apparent "near misses" will, upon closer inspection, turn out to be not such close calls after all.[12]
5. The nuclear command systems will bend and not break when stressed.[13]

Pessimists (paleo or neo), in contrast, expect the cases to confirm:
1. Wetware trumps software, which trumps hardware.[14] The effectiveness of technological devices will be determined by administrative procedures. The effectiveness of administrative procedures will be determined by the reliability of individuals tasked with implementing them.
2. Political and cultural factors will distort the normalizing and homogenizing logic of rational deterrence theory.[15]
3. Countries will undergo nuclear learning, involving trial and error.[16]
4. Material factors—such as the size of arsenal or financial constraints—will shape command and control choices, which may have downsides.[17]
5. The combination of complexity and unavoidable improvisation will result in "normal accidents."[18]

How do these expectations hold up in our cases?

RUSSIA

Nikolai Sokov analyzes a series of close calls during the breakup of the Soviet Union. None produced a catastrophic breakdown of the command and control system, and there were some aspects that reinforced the optimistic line. Yet, on balance, the post-Soviet experience seems to confirm the expectation of pessimists; Sokov echoes very closely the pessimist line: "... control of nuclear weapons in each case hung on a very thin thread, and next time we might not be as lucky."[19]

Optimists could read in Sokov's case one very important and reassuring fact: Political chaos can produce fissures in the military system without fracturing it. The nuclear custodians were touched by politics but also were inoculated with a professional sense that provided at least some immunity. But this immunity can be quite limited, for, as Sokov rightly emphasizes, this professionalism was forged in the context of loyalty to an existing state. If that state disappears, as happened to the Soviet Union, it is less clear what will be the object of professional loyalty.[20]

Optimists could also note how the prevailing international system, and not just the prevailing distribution of power, constrained the choices of emerging states in the post-Soviet region. The distribution of norms—by which I mean the relatively powerful nonproliferation regime—constrained the leaders' freedom to maneuver every bit as much as the distribution of power did, even in cases (like Ukraine) when the leaders clearly want to flout it. This normalizing influence is an important part of the optimists' model and operated to some degree in shaping the nuclear trajectories of the post-Soviet republics.

Finally, optimists would draw attention to the beneficial role played by the United States, especially in resolving tensions over Ukraine's erstwhile nuclear ambitions. This could cut both ways. On the one hand, this shows how influential third parties can play a beneficial role; on the other hand, it raises the question of how a less adept third party might have made things worse. But in most pessimistic accounts, third parties merely muck things up. It is the optimists who have high hopes for wise outsiders.

To my reckoning, however, the new dots Sokov uncovers fit much more neatly in a portrait of pessimism. I count at least eight that could have been torn from the pages of the older theoretical literature:

1. *Leaders worried and had reason to worry about the integrity of their command and control system.* Moreover, they did so despite having several key advantages that might not show up in other cases. First, except for the incidents with Ukraine, the leaders had clear conventional superiority and sufficient control of overwhelming conventional force so as to be able to assert dominance in a crisis. Second, they had fairly good trust in the actions of the United States, which played its role with particular deft and care. It is not too much of a stretch to imagine how both of those "silent variables" could be turned in a negative direction in a similar crisis with, say, Pakistan.

2. *Ad hoc fixes introduced other problems.* The rapid and improvised transfer of weapons outside of danger zones resulted in unplanned compromises in safety, such as poor inventory accounting and crowding that put environmental controls at risk.

3. *The problem of a transition in authority is a real one.* While acknowledged in the literature, the transition problem has been (comparatively) undertheorized.

Sokov suggests one interesting hypothesis based on his study: Transfers of authority arising out of even a peaceful dissolution of a state tend to be slow and uneven, resulting in fairly long periods during which there is a vacuum at the top of autonomous command elements. The longer this endures, the greater the chance that nuclear security and safety will be compromised.

4. *Some degree of loss actually happened.* The Soviet authorities believed they had lost at least some crucial aspects of nuclear command and control during the Ukrainian crisis: the capacity to implement the withdrawal of nuclear weapons. This did not mean they had lost all control over the weapons, but they lost the ability — or at least believed they had lost that ability — to take certain measures. More consequentially, there was genuine loss of legitimate political control over strategic nuclear forces during the 1991 coup; for a period of time, the coup leaders had what they needed to give what appeared to be authoritative orders to change alert levels and perhaps even to launch nuclear weapons.

5. *Control over the nuclear weapons became a totem of power that the new political authorities found irresistible.* How do you know you are in charge? Whether or not you have control over the most powerful weapons on your soil. Sokov makes the interesting observation that Ukrainian and Kazakh elites were "used to living in a nuclear state," and losing the prestige and influence that comes from holding that totem "is difficult to accept."[21] During the 1991 coup, control of the Cheget nuclear launch system was one of the most tangible, if short-lived, markers of the coup's early success.

6. *Outsized consequences flow from trivial mistakes.* An apparent error that resulted in Ukrainian officers' receiving an order intended for only Russian officers (to make a loyalty oath to Russia) resulted in the Ukrainian political leadership intervening to block the withdrawal of tactical nuclear weapons and taking steps to gain access to launch control systems of strategic weapons. This hard-to-predict chain of events is precisely the sort of normal accident in a complex system that Sagan highlighted in his study of the U.S. system.[22]

7. *Contradictions and conflicts between de jure vs. de facto arrangements are unavoidable and create secondary risks.* During the transition period following the collapse of the Soviet Union, the four nuclear weapons-holding states had a de jure arrangement that required the four leaders to confer by a secret communication channel before there was any use of a nuclear weapon. However, the de facto system allowed Russian President Boris Yeltsin to act without notifying the other three. This created pressure inside Ukraine to jury-rig a system that would restore Ukrainian de facto veto power. Out of this pressure came an effort by Ukraine to carve out zones of military autonomy within the chain of command where officers could and would resist higher Russian authorities.

8. *Military professionalism is partly a function of fiscal health.* The collapse of Soviet defense spending created perverse dynamics that undermined military professionalism, such as a burgeoning military trade union movement and the prospect of a disconnect between the nominal authorities (Russian) and the authorities actually able to provide pay and benefits (Ukrainian).

Of course, the case also re-inscribes the basic indeterminacy of the long-standing debate. Despite all of these problems, there was no breach of safety or security large enough to produce a catastrophe. Yet, Sokov is persuasive that there were close calls sufficient to motivate the pessimists.

FRANCE

The theme of an ambiguous close call is even more pronounced in the study of France's allegedly hastened nuclear test during the 1961 coup. Bruno Tertrais deals with the alleged problem head-on. Notwithstanding the strong claim by Brian Jenkins that the story is a myth,[23] Tertrais concludes that the conventional account is more true than not — that de Gaulle did order a hurried-up nuclear test in the midst of the coup, and the coup leaders did make at least some efforts to seize it for their own purposes. Tertrais amends the conventional account somewhat, claiming that the test was hastened primarily for the symbolic value of showing who was in charge rather than for preserving physical custody of the device and precluding the coup plotters from seizing it.[24] Moreover, weather proved a more significant factor in the timing of the test than did the machinations of the coup plotters or any alleged equivocation on the part of the local commanders.[25]

The French case provides some support for the optimist brief. According to Tertrais, senior French leaders responded to the crisis and quickly identified the need to deal with the nuclear issue. They were able to preserve command authority even in the face of a coup. De Gaulle was decisive, and the local authorities who had custody of the weapon ultimately followed his lead. Second, authorities exhibited a clear preference for fail-safe, and this pushed the system toward the "fail-impotent" side of the continuum. Probably because of the hastiness of the test, the detonation itself was a disappointing failure, with yields of only 5 percent of what had been planned.

At the same time, Tertrais finds greater support for pessimism:

1. *Hastily improvised measures resulted in serious safety and security compromises.* At a crucial point in the crisis, the nuclear device was transported to the test site not in the armed convoy—the convoy accompanied an empty truck—but rather in an engineer's 2CV compact car.

2. *Competing priorities for the weapon meant that security was not paramount.* The test was "hasty but not hurried," meaning that de Gaulle ordered that the test happen, not that the device be destroyed. If physical custody of the weapon was the preeminent concern, de Gaulle could have demanded an immediate test without regard to conditions that would allow for the test to be scientifically useful. Instead, he ordered an acceleration of the timetable, but one that would have allowed a successful test. Tertrais plausibly hypothesizes that this order demonstrates that de Gaulle's principal concern was the symbolic value of showing that he was still in control. However, the test ended up being a fizzle anyway, partly due to the decision to proceed even though the weather conditions were not ideal. Tertrais further (and just as plausibly) hypothesizes that this demonstrates that lower levels of command were concerned about physical custody. Moreover, the fact that local commanders ordered a fast test but not a test "as fast as possible" indicates that they themselves were conflicted.

3. *Uncertain communications contributed to uncertainty about nuclear security.* Tertrais says that satellite communications improvements make this less of a factor today, but I think it is just as possible for breakdowns to occur today.

4. *Complexity contributed to uncertainty.* Part of the crisis uncertainty arose out of the complex command arrangements established for managing nuclear weapons in peace time. There were regional commanders with responsibility for overall territorial security and for logistics support. There was a base commander responsible for base security and logistics. There was a test commander responsible for the test itself. Each had independent authority and channels of communication to higher authorities in Paris.

5. *Control of the nuclear devices was the key symbol of political power.* As with the Soviet case, the answer to the question "Who is in charge" was "He who has nuclear power." Intriguingly, unlike the Ukrainian leaders in the Soviet case, nuclear weapons were not seen as a preeminent concern for the coup plotters. The coup leaders did not time their coup nor organize their forces in a way that would maximize their opportunity to seize the nuclear device. Control over the nuclear device appeared to be an afterthought. Had it been a higher priority, the device might have been vulnerable. If the coup had succeeded, meaning that a controlling majority of French forces in Algeria sided with the coup leaders, it would have been quite possible to seize the device. However, they would have had only a device, not a usable weapon. It could only be detonated using the test equipment and would have required substantial re-engineering to be used in a different fashion. More probably, the device would have been a potent political symbol of power with potential blackmail uses.

CHINA

China has long been the optimists' favorite. If Mao managed the bomb safely, then why should we doubt that [fill in the blank] will do so? China's nuclear history does reinforce some optimistic conclusions, particularly the fact that until very recently, China opted for a comparatively small arsenal and avoided the escalatory arms race that captured the United States and the Soviet Union, along with the attendant crisis instability dynamics. With the caveat that we know far less detail about the China case than the U.S. or Soviet cases, Mark Stokes's case study reinforces another important optimistic insight: China has (apparently) consistently emphasized security over operational effectiveness—privileging the "never" rather than the "always" side of the command and control dilemma.[26]

On the other hand, at a crucial phase in its nuclear history, China underwent more internal turmoil than any other nuclear power (until the collapse of the Soviet Union). Stokes focuses on this period, the decade-long Cultural Revolution, and argues that it may have had a lingering, chastening influence on China's command and control choices.

Stokes's findings, indeed, seem squarely on the cutting edge of the half-full/half-empty balance that marks the theoretical debate:

1. *The cultural upheaval infected all phases of the nuclear system . . . but the patient survived.* The engineers and weapons designers split into the factions of the Cultural Revolution in 1966. Regional military commanders near key nuclear installations likewise factionalized, leading to a bloody crackdown and martial law.[27]

2. *Risky compromises were made in an ad hoc and possibly unauthorized manner . . . but no accident resulted.* In part due to a desire by the radicals to demonstrate revolutionary spirit in the nuclear realm, the Chinese conducted an especially dangerous test of a nuclear-tipped missile in 1966. While the test was successful, it involved flying the armed device over population centers and was seen by some as an unauthorized test.[28]

3. *Control of nuclear weapons featured centrally in the civil-military crisis of the quasi-coup of Lin Biao . . . but the authorized leaders prevailed.* While the struggle between Mao and his designated successor, Lin Biao, had multiple dimensions, what brought the matter to a crisis point was Lin Biao's unauthorized decision to move the People's Liberation Army to a higher state of readiness vis-à-vis Soviet forces. Stokes argues that Mao interpreted Lin Biao's actions as a "move to take control of nuclear weapons and leverage their political value as the basis for usurping Mao's power."[29]

4. *Traumatic formative experiences had a lingering effect on the command and control of the arsenal.* Because of the memory of this upheaval, Stokes argues, Chinese authorities centralized the nuclear storage and handling system and put it under very close party control and, moreover, instituted a relatively assertive (my word, not Stokes's) system that separated custodians from operators — and these choices remain operative to this day, as optimists would expect.[30]

PAKISTAN

Pakistan probably heads anyone's list of "states of concern" when considering the nuclear security issue. Feroz Khan's case study offers an optimistic take, even though he documents that Pakistan had the most convoluted political-military context regarding the pursuit of nuclear weapons of any of the cases under study. Despite that rocky history, so far as is known publicly, Pakistan has not had any close calls analogous to the ones covered in the other case studies.

Kahn bases his optimistic conclusion on the absence of evidence of accidents, as well as on Pakistani military professionalism, and claims "the existing command and control system [in Pakistan] is viewed as robust, institutional and professional."[31] Moreover, according to Kahn, the Pakistani case suggests the optimists' conclusion that birthmarks need not be birth defects. The Pakistani nuclear program was birthed in a system marked by political turmoil. Even so, the development of the Pakistani nuclear program continued on a fairly straight-line trajectory. Pro-nuclear leaders were able to make deals based on at least a modicum of nuclear restraint, and transitions in political authority—even very abrupt transitions—generated more or less orderly transitions in nuclear authority.

Yet, the case also provides some insights that meet pessimists' expectations:

1. *Control of nuclear weapons was control of government.* As with the other cases, one can trace who was the de facto power in Pakistan by tracing the line of power over the nuclear program. In a nuclear crisis, Pakistan is likely to face the same acute pressure to demonstrate that political leaders have control over nuclear weapons.

2. *A system that can produce the A. Q. Khan network was not a healthy system.* Despite high-level secret assurances to the contrary, Pakistan did produce the largest and most consequential illicit nuclear prolifer-

ation program: the A. Q. Khan network. It is not clear whether he relied on the permissive conditions of benign neglect, willful blindness, or some more proactive encouragement. Khan (the author) attributes the network more to perverse incentives to make the program financially sustainable and "a peculiar diffusion at the apex of political power" until the consolidation under Musharraf.[32] But what A. Q. Khan was able to do undercuts strong optimism.

3. *The absence of evidence is not necessarily evidence of absence.* The Iraq weapons of mass destruction (WMD) failure gave a bad odor to Donald Rumsfeld's insight about unknown knowns, but it does seem like Pakistan warrants a reapplication. Reports indicate that Pakistan's protocols involve transferring nuclear weapons in unmarked delivery vans without armed escorts in the convoy. This underscores that we are still learning new and unsettling details about Pakistan's nuclear custodial record.[33] In short, we may not know enough about the operational details in Pakistan to yet make a definitive judgment.

CONCLUSION: LOOKING THROUGH THE POLICY LENS

Early on in the academic debate, an important theory-praxis gap was identified. Even if the optimists were right in theory about how new nuclear states might behave, in practice U.S. policymakers might still oppose nuclear proliferation. To a policymaker, "system stability" meant "the United States cannot coerce that state because of mutual nuclear stalemate," and such a world would be undesirable for all sorts of other policy reasons apart from the likelihood of a nuclear war.[34] It behooves us, therefore, to explore whether there might be separate expectations of the cases from a policymaker's point of view. I suggest at least three:

1. The policymakers in the relevant historical episodes will not trust the functionalist logic of optimists—"It would be crazy if this were not so, so we can assume it is so." On the contrary, they will take pains to ensure that it is so rather than simply assume it.

2. The theorist's blithe "concentration of the mind" will be experienced as far more dire and alarming. As Sagan has observed, the airline passenger who survives a flight where the wing cracks, the engines fail, and the pressure system misfires, will be glad to be alive, but he will not celebrate the robustness of the airplane.[35]

3. In any crisis in which there is even a faint prospect of "loose nukes," that fact will be a central preoccupation for the players in the crisis, regardless of the other factors driving the conflict.

All of the cases seem to bear out these expectations, at least partly. The policymakers involved all considered nuclear security concerns to be high-priority problems, especially during a crisis. Without the benefit of hindsight and not knowing the benign outcome, the participants experienced the challenges as more dire than the clinical academic treatments might capture. Yet, the exposure to danger did not produce strong nuclear allergies. Pakistan's policymakers appear to embrace Khan's optimistic conclusions. France did not abandon its *force de frappe*. To be sure, all of the former Soviet Republics except Russia gave up nuclear weapons, but that seems largely due to international pressure, not to fears about managing nuclear security.

Moreover, the four cases highlight an aspect I had not noticed in the literature before: a convergence in expectations between pessimists, optimists, and policymakers that nuclear weapons will be sharp focal points during a crisis. It is not just that nuclear weapons concentrate the mind, as optimists expect. It is that in a crisis in which nuclear weapons are present, they concentrate the mind on the weapons: where they are, who has them, and what they can do with them.

The case studies also suggest that policymakers do not have enough information yet to handle their nuclear security responsibilities in an optimal fashion. In that spirit, I close with three specific recommendations for better securing nuclear assets now and in the future:

1. *Deepen the case studies of nuclear operations and, where appropriate, nuclear accidents.* Even a case as familiar and long-established as the French 1961 coup yielded new empirical insights and policy-relevant items of interest. I understand the politicians' concern about probing painful subjects, but the stakes warrant erring on the side of greater candor rather than ignoring problems that we hope we will not have to confront.

2. *Broaden the nuclear learning.* As I have argued elsewhere, the logic behind helping nuclear states improve their nuclear safety and security is pretty compelling and likely trumps other concerns once a state has crossed the weaponization threshold. States like Pakistan will be very suspicious of our help, understandably fearful that any such assistance is a Trojan horse for efforts to target and neutralize their arsenal. But an engaging exposure to the problems that other states have faced may be a compromise that even Pakistan authorities might consider.

3. *Make a virtue out of inevitability.* The case studies reached a consensus on at least one important point: The custody and control of nuclear weapons was, and thus likely will be, the symbol of governing authority. Acknowledging this has the perverse result of making the seizure of custody and control that much more valuable. But acting like it is not so is not a solution to the problem. Instead, perhaps, should we be more explicit, developing a policy that states that the safe and secure management of nuclear custody is the essential ingredient for any successful pretender to power? Such a policy might, on the margins, further incentivize states to take precautionary action to secure weapons, as France did, and to clarify more clearly the nuclear custodial line, as the former Soviet Union did not.[36]

ENDNOTES - CHAPTER 7

1. Peter Feaver, "Neooptimists and the Enduring Problem of Nuclear Proliferation," *Security Studies*, Vol. 6, No. 4, Summer 1997, pp. 93-125.

2. For a sample of paleo-pessimist thinking, see Lewis A. Dunn, *Controlling the Bomb: Nuclear Proliferation in the 1980s,* New Haven, CT: Yale University Press, 1982; Leonard Spector, *Nuclear Proliferation Today,* New York: Vintage, 1984; or Peter Lavoy, "The Strategic Consequences of Nuclear Proliferation: A Review Essay," *Security Studies*, Vol. 4, No. 4, Summer 1995, pp. 695-753.

3. For a sample of paleo-optimist thinking, see Kenneth Waltz, *The Spread of Nuclear Weapons: More May be Better,* Adelphi Paper Vol. 17, London, UK: International Institute for Strategic Studies (IISS), 1981; Idem., "Nuclear Myths and Political Realities," *American Political Science Review*, Vol. 84, No. 3, September 1990, pp. 731-745; Michael Intriligator and Dagobert Brito, "Nuclear Proliferation and the Probability of Nuclear War," *Public Choice*, Vol. 37, No. 2, 1981, pp. 247-259; and Bruce Bueno de Mesquita and

William Riker, "An Assessment of the Merits of Selective Nuclear Proliferation," *Journal of Conflict Resolution*, Vol. 26, No. 2, 1982, pp. 283-306.

4. For a sample of neo-pessimist thinking, see James Blight and David Welch, "The Cuban Missile Crisis and New Nuclear States," *Security Studies* Vol. 4, No. 4, Summer 1995, pp. 811-850; Peter Feaver, "Command and Control in Emerging Nuclear Nations," *International Security*, Vol. 17, No. 3, Winter 1992/93; *Idem.*, "Optimists, Pessimists, and Theories of Nuclear Proliferation Management," *Security Studies*, Vol. 4, No. 4, Summer 1995, pp. 754-772; *Idem.*, "Neooptimists and the Enduring Problem of Nuclear Proliferation"; Sagan, *The Limits of Safety: Organizations, Accidents, and Nuclear Weapons*, Princeton, NJ: Princeton University Press, 1993; *Idem.*, "The Perils of Proliferation: Organizational Theory, Deterrence Theory, and the Spread of Nuclear Weapons," *International Security*, Vol. 18, No. 4, Spring 1994, pp. 66-107; and Sagan and Kenneth Waltz, *The Spread of Nuclear Weapons: A Debate*, New York: Norton, 1995.

5. For a sample of neo-optimist thinking, see David Karl, "Proliferation Pessimism and Emerging Nuclear Powers," *International Security*, Vol. 21, No. 3, Winter 1996/97, pp. 87-119; Jordan Seng, "Command and Control Advantages of Minor Nuclear States," *Security Studies*, Vol. 6, No. 4, Summer 1997, pp. 50-92; and Bradley Thayer, "The Risk of Nuclear Inadvertence: A Review Essay," *Security Studies*, Vol. 3 No. 3, Spring 1994, pp. 428-493.

6. See, for example, Sagan, "The Causes of Nuclear Weapons Proliferation," *Annual Review of Political Science*, Vol. 14, June 2011, pp. 225-244; Jacques Hyman, "Theories of Nuclear Proliferation: The State of the Field," *Nonproliferation Review*, Vol. 13, No. 3, 2006, pp. 455-465; Hyman, *The Psychology of Nuclear Proliferation: Identity, Emotions and Foreign Policy*, Cambridge, MA: Cambridge University Press, 2006; Sagan and Alexander Montgomery, "The Perils of Predicting Proliferation," *Journal of Conflict Resolution*, Vol. 53, No. 2, April 2009, pp. 302-328; and Matthew Kroenig, *Exporting the Bomb: Technology Transfer and the Spread of Nuclear Weapons*, Ithaca, NY: Cornell University Press, 2010.

7. See Victor Asal and Kyle Beardsley, "Proliferation and International Crisis Behavior," *Journal of Peace Research*, Vol. 44, No. 2, 2007, pp. 139-155; Kyle Beardsley and Victor Asal, "Winning with the Bomb," *Journal of Conflict Resolution*, Vol. 53, No. 2, 2009, pp. 278-301; Matthew Fuhrmann and Sarah Kreps, "Targeting Nuclear Programs in War and Peace: A Quantitative Empirical Analysis, 1941-2000," *Journal of Conflict Resolution*, Vol. 54, No. 6, 2010, pp. 831-859; Robert Rauchhaus, Matthew Kroenig, and Erik Gartzke, eds., *Causes and Consequences of Nuclear Proliferation*, Routledge, 2011; and Kroenig, "Nuclear Superiority and the Balance of Resolve: Explaining Crisis Outcomes," *International Organization*, Vol. 67, Issue 1, January 2013, pp. 141-171.

8. The best of these are James Wirtz, Lavoy, and Sagan, *Planning the Unthinkable: How New Powers Will Use Nuclear, Biological, and Chemical Weapons*, Ithaca, NY: Cornell University Press, 2000; and Hans Born, Bates Gill, and Heiner Hänggi, *Governing the Bomb: Civilian Control and Democratic Accountability of Nuclear Weapons*, Oxford, UK: Oxford University Press, 2010.

9. Waltz, *The Spread of Nuclear Weapons*.

10. *Ibid.*; and Karl, "Proliferation Pessimism and Emerging Nuclear Powers," p. 94.

11. *Ibid.*

12. Thayer, "The Risk of Nuclear Inadvertence," pp. 428-449.

13. *Ibid.*, p. 440.

14. Feaver, "Social Sources of Inadvertent Nuclear Use in the Former Soviet Union: Civil-Military Relations and the Black Market," in Carin Atterling Wedar, Intriligator, and Peeter Vares, eds., *Implications of the Dissolution of the Soviet Union for Accidental/Inadvertent Use of Weapons of Mass Destruction*, Tallinn, Estonia: Estonian Academy of Sciences, 1992.

15. Feaver, "Proliferation Optimism and Theories of Nuclear Operations," *Security Studies*, Vol. 2, No. 3/4, Spring/Summer 1993, pp. 169-174.

16. Feaver, "Command and Control in Emerging Nuclear Nations," pp. 170-74; and Sagan, *The Limits of Safety*.

17. Feaver, "Proliferation Optimism and Theories of Nuclear Operations," pp. 165-167.

18. Sagan, *The Limits of Safety*.

19. See Sokov chapter in this volume, p. 91.

20. See Sokov chapter in this volume. Moreover, the immunity arising from professionalism can push in positive or negative directions. Curtis LeMay made it clear that his professionalism would have led him to perform in certain escalatory ways if he had experienced an extreme crisis. Feaver, *Armed Servants: Agency, Oversight, and Civil-Military Relations,* Cambridge, MA: Harvard University Press, 2003, pp. 129-130.

21. See Sokov chapter in this volume, p. 119.

22. Sagan, *The Limits of Safety*.

23. Tertrais cites Brian Jenkins, *Will Terrorists Go Nuclear?* Amherst, NY: Prometheus Books, 2008, p. 144.

24. See Tertrais's chapter in this volume, pp. 41-42, 48.

25. *Ibid*.

26. See Stokes's chapter in this volume.

27. *Ibid*.

28. *Ibid*., p. 69-70.

29. *Ibid*., p. 74.

30. *Ibid*., pp. 74-75.

31. See Khan's chapter in this volume, p. 179.

32. *Ibid*., p. 172.

33. Goldberg and Ambinder, "The Pentagon's Secret Plans to Secure Pakistan's Nuclear Arsenal," *National Journal*, November 5, 2011, p. 1.

34. Feaver, "Optimists, Pessimists, and Theories of Nuclear Proliferation Management," pp. 770-771.

35. Sagan, *The Limits of Safety*, pp. 204-205, 248-249.

36. The proposal deserves more careful scrutiny than I can give it here. One perverse aspect of this proposal is that, had it been in place, it would have dictated that the United States recognize the 1991 Soviet coup leaders as the de facto government, given their temporary control over the arsenal. That was clearly not in the broader interests of the United States, and so was a strong argument against the policy. On the other hand, had the policy been in place and well-understood, it might have helped Gorbachev anticipate and take precautionary action.

CHAPTER 8

SECURING NUCLEAR ARSENALS IN TIMES OF POLITICAL TURMOIL: "TOP 10" LESSONS LEARNED

Gregory F. Giles

The views expressed herein are those of the author, not necessarily those of Science Applications International Corporation (SAIC) or its sponsors.

Each of the four case studies examined in this project—the erstwhile "nuclear coup" in French Algeria in 1961, the Red Guards uprising in China in 1967, the turbulence in Pakistan since the 1977 military coup, and the slide to dissolution of the Soviet Union during 1990-91—provides a fascinating account of how centralized control over nuclear weapons was more or less imperiled by political upheaval and the lengths to which political and military institutions had to go to keep the weapons out of the wrong hands. The lengths to which they went include hasty detonation of a nuclear test device, the use of deadly force to quell a rebellion by nuclear engineers, urgent redeployment of nuclear weapon components to secret locations, or the improvised use of bombers and cannon fire to exfiltrate weapons to more secure regions. The authors are careful not to exaggerate the risk of nuclear weapon seizure in these incidents; there is no public evidence that nuclear devices fell into the wrong hands. Nonetheless, there is ample cause for concern that the margin of security was uncomfortably thin.

Each episode carried its own complexities. The A. Q. Khan proliferation network that operated from

Pakistan for decades underscores that the customary focus on the security of weapons and delivery systems can leave a gaping hole in terms of access to nuclear weapons-related design information and production components. This control failure has helped fuel proliferation in Iran and North Korea. The Soviet case highlights the fact that nuclear launch authority can be rapidly misappropriated in a coup and that disputes over nuclear weapons control can be a leading indicator of the imminent collapse of a nation-state. The Algerian episode points to the pivotal role individual military commanders can play in determining whether rebels succeed or fail in bolstering their cause with a nuclear capability. The China case demonstrates how domestic political turmoil can leave an indelible impression on a country's nuclear custodians, such that centralized warhead storage becomes the overriding design principle.

This chapter briefly surveys the four case studies, highlighting key facets, major cross-cutting themes, lingering uncertainties, and potential "What ifs." Building on the studious efforts of the case study authors, it offers a "Top 10" list of lessons to be learned, as the global community seeks to come to grips with how to insulate nuclear weapons from what is likely to be recurring political turmoil over the next half-century.

THE FRENCH NUCLEAR COUP IN ALGERIA, 1961

Bruno Tertrais's original research has expanded our understanding of the so-called nuclear coup in French Algeria in 1961. The episode may come into sharper focus still as further details are unearthed. In any event, it is clear that the status of the nuclear device at the Reggan test site was a top priority for President Charles de Gaulle as the Algerian coup came to light, discussing it with the prime minister on April 22. Yet, the apparent urgency to test the device on April 24 was not explicitly linked to the coup in Elysee's communiques to the Atomic Energy Commission (*Commissariat à l'énergie atomique* [CEA]) or Reggan. Nor do we have any mention by the central authorities in Paris of taking all the steps necessary to prevent the device from falling into the rebels' hands. The apparent absence of contingency planning in the event the nuclear device fell into rebel control is notable. Unexplored options in this regard include reinforcing Reggan with loyalists, e.g., paratroops (depending on the French order of battle [ORBAT] at the time), conducting an air strike against the test facilities, or issuing instructions to CEA staff to destroy key components—e.g. neutron initiator, explosive lenses, etc. Normal bureaucratic procedures were not superseded. The April 23 directive merely reverted to the original "On or about April 24" test date that had been set on March 30, before more time was requested for technical preparation of the device. The bland communique from Paris on April 25 announcing the test also was indicative of a desire to downplay the risk of device seizure. But practically speaking—and contrary to the characterization made by Tertrais—de Gaulle *did* order the test to take place as soon as possible. Again, further official disclosures may clarify how much the risk of device capture weighed in the decision to speed up the test. Until then, we can reasonably conclude that the test date was hastily advanced, though the situation was not desperate. Here it is interesting to speculate to what extent de Gaulle's behavior reflected a political imperative, as well as a cultural predilection, to convey self-confidence in a crisis.

By contrast, the nuclear device and impending test event was not a premeditated priority for the coup generals (e.g., Raoul Salan and Edmond Jouhand) who were anti-nuclear, but rather a target of opportunity. There was some, but generally poor, rebel awareness of the device (including the Radio-Algier account of whether the device components had already been sent to Reggan; Maurice Challe's seemingly accidental discovery of the test via the NOTAM [Notice to Airmen]; and Pierre Billaud's interrogation by rebel forces in Algiers and subsequent clearance to proceed to Reggan). Nonetheless, Challe sensed an opportunity for exploitation when he issued his April 23 directive to Jean Bastien Thiry not to explode his "little bomb," directing him to "Keep it for 'us,' it will always be useful." Challe's reference to "always" suggests intent to retain the device indefinitely. It is thus evident that the rebels were improvising and were ignorant of technicalities that could render the device inoperative after a certain "expiration date" (e.g., the reliability of the neutron initiator decreased over an extended period), particularly if they were cut off from CEA expertise.[1]

In hindsight, Challe was overconfident that he had Thiry's loyalty. There is no evidence that Challe had a contingency plan to prevent a test he had not authorized. He apparently made no effort to cut Reggan's communication links with Paris, nor to cast doubt on who was responsible for the test. Presumably, the coup was already unraveling at that point, but such a counterclaim might have provided a last-ditch effort to rally forces to the rebels' cause or at least cast doubt on de Gaulle's span of control.

The Algerian episode underscores that the leading rebel generals were not enamored with nuclear weapons, nor did they see any dignity to be had in nuclear blackmail. This nuclear disdain was likely a pivotal factor in preventing a compromise of nuclear control in 1961. Now that nuclear weapons have been more widely socialized in the intervening half-century, it remains an open question as to whether future rebels in a nuclear-armed state would be similarly disinclined to exploit any nuclear devices within their reach.

A key facet of the Algerian episode is the extent to which Thiry really delayed the test. Was it even 24 hours? After all, the order from Paris to test had been received on April 23, and accounts suggest that, probably on the morning of April 24, Thiry decided to test the following day; he ordered troops to the field the afternoon of the 24th. Since the neutron initiator had yet to be completed on the 23rd, was a test on the 24th even technically possible? If not, the case for Thiry's prevarication becomes slim.

Nor did Thiry seem to perceive an urgent need to scuttle the device. There was evidently no such indication in the Elysee directive on April 23, nor was there any indication from Challe the same day that he was sending forces to, or ordering the armored forces at, Reggan to ensure compliance with his test suspension order (assuming such links to the armored units existed at the time). This contrasts with Etienne Viard and other CEA staff at Reggan "urging" Thiry—as if he was procrastinating—to proceed with the test to prevent the rebels from acquiring a bargaining chip. It is not unreasonable to postulate that in times of political turmoil, bureaucratic figures and entities will "default" to standard operating procedures—in this case, proceeding with the usual test preparations, albeit on a compressed schedule.

But how are we to explain why the test was not postponed as weather conditions at Reggan deteriorated on April 25? Under such circumstances the test normally would have been delayed; Thiry had the authority to do so but opted not to exercise it. Thiry's decision to proceed perhaps reflects his recognition that the coup was destined to fail. After all, he had contradictory test orders from Paris and Algiers, yet appeared more concerned with the consequences of disappointing the former.

We are left to ponder how the outcome of the coup might have differed if Thiry had immediately (i.e., on April 21-22) and unequivocally sided with the rebels. Tertrais expresses his skepticism in this regard. But since France did not test its next nuclear device until November 1961, might there have been a window when the Algerian rebels had a nuclear advantage over the French mainland, which might have been exploited to rally more support to their cause?

What if Reggan's communications had been cut with Paris (i.e., Elysee, Ministry of Defense, and CEA)? How might that have changed crisis decisionmaking? Would de Gaulle's dramatic television speech on April 23 have been as effective if the rebels were believed to have control of the nuclear device? If the links had been cut, would de Gaulle have known of CEA loyalists (Viard *et al.*) at Reggan and been able to count on them to sabotage the device so that he could call a rebel nuclear bluff? Would the French president have continued to keep Washington in the dark,[2] or been forced to bring it into confidence and request assistance in recovering the device?

Here, we might assert that French nuclear command and control "failed safe" by good fortune, not design. Such a characterization is not unreasonable, given the relative immaturity of France's nuclear weapons program at the time. Still, while not necessarily feeding alarmist interpretations (which no doubt are further attenuated by the passage of time), the Algerian nuclear situation was perhaps more tenuous, more susceptible to transformation, than appreciated. Indeed, the chapter could support such an interpretation, since, as pointed out, in reforming French presidential authority the following year, de Gaulle perceived the need to ensure that he would have sole authority over the employment of French nuclear weapons.

THE LEGACY OF CHINA'S CULTURAL REVOLUTION ON NUCLEAR WARHEAD SECURITY

Mark Stokes calls attention to the upheaval in Chinese society caused by the Cultural Revolution of 1966-76 and the way it impacted China's approach to nuclear warhead security. As with France, China's crisis over nuclear weapons control came very soon after its entry into the nuclear weapons club. However, the Cultural Revolution provided a distinct challenge to nuclear weapons control in that revolutionary ardor and its disruptive effects were being actively promoted by the central political authority, Mao Zedong.

As Stokes recounts, this political disturbance quickly made its way into China's nuclear weapons complex. Scientific and technical cadres who designed and built the country's nuclear weapons were soon pitted against one another, not just ideologically, but physically. The country's youth, stirred up by Mao, organized into the Red Guards paramilitary units and sought to forcibly take control of nuclear weapons facilities in Harbin. One such radical group from a nuclear weapons plant, 221 Factory, occupied a provincial newspaper office in February 1967; its forcible eviction by the People's Liberation Army (PLA) resulted in the deaths of 169 people. Such was the uprising's threat to China's nuclear weapons production and testing facilities that senior PLA officers warned Mao they would forcibly take control of the sites if he did not rein in the Red Guards.

A particularly disconcerting aspect of the Cultural Revolution was the ideological pressure the Red Guards exerted over nuclear weapons policy under the premise that radicalism and atomic weapons were similarly explosive and both should be fully and expeditiously unleashed. This led to a risky operation wherein China's fledgling nuclear command flight-tested a nuclear-armed ballistic missile over populated portions of the country en route to its detonation in the western Xinjiang Province. We can only speculate to what extremes the Red Guards might have applied their nuclear ardor had they gained direct control over China's nuclear weapons complex. The episode may yet provide clues as to what we might expect in the event revolutionary Iran manages to acquire a nuclear arsenal of its own.

Stokes reconstructs how this period of domestic political instability helped shape China's approach to nuclear warhead security and the prominent role 22 Base has played in this regard. It is striking in that, for the first 35 years of China's nuclear force, control over warheads was maintained by 22 Base under the aegis of the PLA's National Defense Science and Technology Commission; that is, outside the delivery system chain of command. It was not until the Cultural Revolution fully receded in 1979 that 22 Base was subordinated to the Second Artillery Corps; even then the separation between warhead custody and delivery systems was maintained.

While Stokes is careful to note the influence of external factors—namely, deteriorating relations with Moscow in the 1960s—he observes that the chaos unleashed by the Cultural Revolution prompted China's nuclear custodians to centralize nuclear warhead storage at the 22 Base underground complex in Taibai. It is from here that nuclear warheads are "loaned" out in small numbers to Second Artillery missile regiment storage facilities, where they are kept physically separated from the missiles, the better to reduce vulnerabilities to political instability in a given region. Indeed, this emphasis on centralized control and both physical and organizational separation between warhead and launcher comes at the price of increasing China's vulnerability to a disarming first strike. To compensate, China relies on opacity to keep its adversaries guessing as to the precise details of warhead and launcher status and location. Indeed, the legacy of the struggle for control over China's nuclear complex during the 1960s is the enduring reluctance of the Chinese leadership to accept numerous offers from the United States to embrace greater transparency as a means of building nuclear stability.

POLITICAL TRANSITIONS AND NUCLEAR MANAGEMENT IN PAKISTAN

Feroz Khan's chapter traces the impact of national leadership turnover on Pakistan's nuclear weapons program. It observes that there were two "political transitions during which there could have been a control problem [President Zia's death in 1988 and the joint resignation of the prime minister and president in 1993], but on each occasion, the military had an organizational system in place to prevent any such danger."[3] Upon closer inspection, and not unlike in the Algerian case, this system seems to be a default mechanism rather than a plan. Moreover, this assertion seems to be contradicted by the observation that "It took a decade to develop a robust command system, which transited to the civilian [leadership] . . . in 2008."[4]

There are, unfortunately, critical gaps in the account to support the chapter's conclusion. Specifically, who were the key figures and what were the decisionmaking processes by which Pakistan violated its secret agreement with the United States not to produce highly enriched uranium (HEU), conduct the 1998 nuclear tests (also, technically a breach of the U.S. accord), and redeploy nuclear weapon components following the September 11, 2001, attacks by al-Qaeda against the United States?[5] Additionally, elaboration is needed on how Pakistan's nuclear "command and control [has been] tested under regional crises and domestic violence."[6] Were there incidents that challenged nuclear command and control (C2) in some fashion?

Notably, the chapter does not delve deeply into the A. Q. Khan debacle, asserting that the nuclear weapons program "remained firewalled" from political turmoil. The chapter contends that the Khan network operated "[b]efore the military take over and formulation of [the Strategic Planning Division] SPD." Yet, Iran has documented with the International Atomic Energy Agency (IAEA) that its first dealings with the network took place in 1987, a decade after General Zia's coup and while he was still in power, and continued through at least 1995, 2 years after then-President Ghulam Ishaq Khan transferred the nuclear dossier to Army General Headquarters (GHQ).

Also, the chapter makes no reference to Sultan Bashiruddin Mahmood, a former high-ranking Pakistan Atomic Energy Commission (PAEC) official who engaged in nuclear weapons consultations with Osama bin Laden.[7] In this regard, there is a tendency to understate the role of informal knowledge on the part of the Pakistan military, while claiming its ignorance of the Khan network. Historically, it is noted that the military was "well aware" of the nature of the nuclear program in the 1970s, even if it lacked details.[8] From 1988 on, the COAS started managing nuclear development on behalf of the president.[9] A. Q. Khan has asserted that the Pakistan Army leadership was well aware of the nuclear assistance his laboratory was providing to Iran and North Korea and provided material support.[10] Given the influence of the Pakistan Army and that the GHQ was the agreed locus and coordination of resources for the nuclear weapons program, how is it that the military did not have the legal authority to intervene in the autonomy of the scientists until after Musharraf's coup in 1998?

Further, Bashiruddin's Islamic "charity," Ummah Tameer-e-Nau, included retired Pakistani generals. If the Pakistan military was also unaware of Bashiruddin's nuclear freelancing, the claims that nuclear command and control was under firm control ring hollow. In spite of the Bashiruddin "surprise," there are hints that religious radicalization was considered a threat to Pakistan's nuclear C2 as early as 1977 and became a de facto selection criterion for personnel.[11] But the subject is not adequately addressed, and so we can form no opinion as to how robust the nuclear C2 system is against radicalized insiders.

The issue of Benazir Bhutto's access to the nuclear weapons program is contentious,[12] and the chapter could benefit from greater balance. Namely, the assertion that Bhutto was excluded from the program only after receiving the Central Intelligence Agency (CIA) briefing in June 1989 does not explain why she was not granted access to Kahuta, e.g., beforehand.[13] Since President Ghulam Ishaq Khan retained the secret nuclear files throughout Nawaz Sharif's first term as prime minister from 1990 to 1993 (turning them over to GHQ in 1993, only as a result of being forced to retire), a pattern of prime ministerial mistrust and, at best, selective access to the nuclear dossier is evident.

Notably, Pakistan's Western-trained civilian scientists became convinced that in an environment of competing demands on scarce resources, nuclear energy development would take place only if they could interest the national leadership in developing nuclear weapons. This was a sad and misguided rationale. As Khan's chapter notes, during the military rule of 1958-71, Pakistan's Army leaders expressed no such desire. Rather, the leading driver of nuclear weapons development was a civilian, Zulfiqar Ali Bhutto, who came to power in 1971. Bhutto enlisted the material support of the Army in the nuclear weapons program following the loss of East Pakistan, but kept decision-making in civilian hands until he was deposed in a military coup led by General Zia in 1977.

The chapter cites bureaucratic competition as a driver of Pakistan's nuclearization, but the theme warrants further consideration. For instance, how much did competition between Munir Khan and A. Q. Khan influence the pace and scope of fissile material production and delivery system development?

THE DISSOLUTION OF THE SOVIET UNION

Nikolai Sokov's chapter identifies at least three cases of potential loss of nuclear weapons control as the Soviet Union collapsed. It took nearly 5 years (1991-96) for control of all Soviet nuclear weapons to be fully restored by Moscow. Nearly a third of Soviet successor states had nuclear weapons on their territory when the Union of Soviet Socialist Republics (USSR) collapsed, posing complex challenges for centralized control. Sokov underscores the importance of nuclear custodians' loyalty to their mission, even if not to the political leadership, to weather this political storm.

Azerbaijan Seizure Attempt.

The hurried withdrawal in January 1990 of nuclear warheads for air defense missiles stationed in Azerbaijan (possibly in response to a firefight at a Baku nuclear weapons depot), seemingly required technical and procedural improvisation. Cannon fire was needed to ensure that the bombers carrying the warheads could escape intruders who had penetrated the airbase perimeter and blocked the runway. Given the hasty nature of this operation, it is not likely that any plans existed to exfiltrate stolen nuclear weapons.

Sokov notes that this episode triggered a massive withdrawal of tactical nuclear weapons to the territories of Russia, Belarus, Kazakhstan, and Ukraine by the spring of 1991—which occurred in almost complete secrecy. He further observes that the downside of this improvisation was inadequate record keeping; weapons were transferred to almost random facilities, resulting in safety problems as the maximum number of warheads per bunker was exceeded, and personnel had trouble maintaining controlled environments inside—a problem not resolved for another 15 years.[14] So how dedicated were the custodians and political authorities beyond physical consolidation of nuclear weapons? How high a priority was nuclear weapons safety?

1991 Coup.

Sokov's account of the 1991 coup against Soviet President Mikhail Gorbachev adds important detail that makes it clear that control of the entire Soviet nuclear arsenal was compromised. Strategic and tactical nuclear forces were put on high alert by the coup leaders in a dramatic fashion, with nuclear weapons being uploaded to theater-level strike aircraft and associated launch codes distributed for the first time in memory; Northern Fleet submarines were being readied to launch their nuclear missiles from pierside, if so ordered. This heightened nuclear alert was lowered before long, and the coup quickly unraveled, but the potential for an international nuclear crisis was undeniable.

In juxtaposing the 1991 Soviet coup with the French coup that preceded it by 3 decades, we see that whether a country is a nascent or mature nuclear weapons state, who has control over nuclear weapons inevitably colors the struggle for national political control. De Gaulle moved quickly to deny his rebellious generals in Algeria access to a nuclear test device by expending it. The Soviet coup plotters immediately seized Gorbachev's portable communication device, or "Cheget," to deepen his physical isolation and circumvent unsympathetic senior officers in the nuclear chain of command. They then activated the nuclear force to warn off any would-be interventionists and signal a return to Soviet assertiveness, but in so doing, they seriously increased the risk of inadvertent nuclear escalation.

As Sokov explains, the nature of the Soviet command and control system meant that simply by isolating the Soviet president from his Cheget, the coup leaders had achieved launch authority over the nuclear arsenal. The responsiveness of the nuclear forces to the high alert order indicates that nuclear units were accepting direction from the coup leaders. We can only speculate how the crisis may have spiraled if the United States had responded in kind to the Soviet nuclear alert and if the political crisis in Moscow had endured. Sokov further points out that while presidential security and communication systems were immediately revised after the coup failed, certain political vulnerabilities in the Cheget system remain, a symptom of the trade-offs between a system designed to ensure a nuclear response in the event of a nuclear attack and one optimized to ensure nuclear lockdown in the event of domestic political turmoil.

Collapse of the USSR.

The ensuing collapse of the Soviet Union by late-December 1991 underscores that nuclear weapons control is a function of time: The longer political uncertainty exists, the greater the chance political authorities will lose control over nuclear weapons. Moreover, Sokov keenly explains how loss of control over nuclear weapons can precede national dissolution. It was clear that Moscow perceived it had lost control of nuclear weapons — in terms of physical withdrawal to the territory of Russia — some months before the USSR was dissolved.

Notably, the risks of nuclear dissolution of the Russian Federation were anticipated by Russian academics in October 1991. It seems likely that given the prevailing political turbulence, academic thinking outpaced the Russian government in this regard. This, in turn, begs the question of whether it is possible for governments to plan for nuclear control arrangements in the event the state itself dissolves. To their further credit, Russian academics also foresaw the military-technical, intelligence, and economic risks of dependency in the event the Soviet nuclear enterprise was divided up among successor states.

Adding a more complex twist in October 1991 — that is, prior to the dissolution of the Soviet Union, Ukraine sought to ensure that nuclear weapons stationed on its territory could not be launched by Moscow. In November-December, Ukraine's leader requested a study of whether such weapons could be used for the purposes of *deterring* Russia. Divided loyalties among the technical experts conducting the assessment seem to have biased the results against the feasibility of such a move. Also prior to Soviet dissolution, Ukraine allegedly was able to obtain nuclear weapons maintenance and refurbishment manuals from a Russian nuclear weapons lab. This reflects the risks of political ambiguity and "bureaucratic autopilot."

Further compounding matters, in February 1992, Ukraine halted the withdrawal of tactical nuclear weapons from its territory. Sokov points out that technically Ukraine was believed to be capable of assuming operational control over nuclear weapons in just 9 months. Kiev then engaged in a concerted propaganda effort to persuade Soviet forces on Ukrainian soil to switch allegiances, luring all the strategic rocket and air force delivery units by April 1992. Two nuclear weapon custodial units at Ukrainian air bases followed suit in 1993. Sokov observes that, in effect, it was left to the discretion of individual military units and even individual officers to whom they would grant control over nuclear weapons. Ukraine lacked access to the weapons arming codes, however, and targeting information had been removed from air-launched cruise missiles (ALCMs) by the 12th Glavnoye Upravleniye Ministerstvo Oborony (GUMO)[15] prior to the shift in allegiance. Underscoring the risks of national dissolution, permissive action links were the only element of C2 not controlled at the unit level.

Political maneuvering was pervasive as Moscow struggled to retain full control over Soviet nuclear forces. In April 1992, Belarus demanded compensation and security guarantees from the West to relinquish nuclear weapons on its soil. Russia, for its part, overstated its degree of control over the former-Soviet nuclear stockpile to discourage U.S. interference in its discussions with former Soviet republics. The temptation for central authorities to exaggerate their control over nuclear events is not limited to the Russian leadership (witness the assurances by Tokyo, Japan, that the situation at Fukushima was under control). We can expect to see this kind of behavior in future nuclear control crises and should be prepared to challenge it head on, through private and official channels, backed by sustained media scrutiny.

Sokov observes that the disintegration of central authority creates a legal and psychological vacuum for the military. It also creates a political void that the military may seek to fill. For 2 to 3 months, two of the three suitcases containing nuclear launch codes, including one allocated to the civilian leadership — that is, the minister of defense—were controlled by General Boris Shaposhnikov, who then tried to assert himself as equal to a head of state and to dictate nuclear weapons policy to the political leadership. Retaining military unity was a core concern for Shaposhnikov and his military cohorts vis-à-vis the political leadership. Preserving military unity would likely be a top priority in future nuclear state dissolutions, and political authorities will need to address this concern quickly to dissipate any momentum toward military dictatorships. Keeping a close watch on potential Shaposhnikovs is a prudent task in this regard.

The Suitcase Nuke Saga.

Disturbingly, Sokov points outs that a thorough inventory of Soviet tactical nuclear weapons withdrawn to Russia in 1992 was not undertaken by Moscow until 1996, and even then, only in response to allegations that Chechnyan rebels had acquired portable, so-called suitcase, nuclear weapons. It took another 5 years for the 12th GUMO to reveal that all such portable nuclear devices had been eliminated, with confirmation by head of the State Security Council Denisov, not coming until 2004. This provides further evidence that the less "sexy" aspects of nuclear weapons control, storage and accountability are a weak link in Russian nuclear control, and likely elsewhere. Indeed, the United States is not immune in this regard, as evidence by the unauthorized and unwitting relocation of nuclear weapons aboard a B-52 bomber in 2007.

"TOP 10 LESSONS" FOR THE CONTROL OF NUCLEAR WEAPONS DURING POLITICAL TURMOIL

Insight: Political ambiguity and "bureaucratic autopilot" invite the loss of nuclear weapons control.
- Because no special concern was voiced or emergency measures directed by Paris, the Reggan test site followed standard (albeit accelerated) operating procedures in the midst of a coup, which posed a threat of nuclear seizure.
- Just prior to the dissolution of the USSR, Ukraine allegedly was able to obtain nuclear weapons maintenance and refurbishment manuals from a Russian nuclear weapons lab—the better to help it hold on to Soviet nuclear weapons and use them to deter Moscow.

Lesson #1: It is better for a National Command Authority to make the "Commander's Intent" known—that is, to err on the side of explicit and extraordinary instructions to nuclear entities—and to have in place authorities, regulations, and procedures to curtail nuclear flows in times of domestic political crisis.

Insight: Freelancing by scientists in the nuclear weapons complex is no less threatening than loss of command over a weapon by the military and may pose a greater control challenge to countries where the military is the dominant state institution.
- A. Q. Khan is a "poster child" in this regard.

Lesson #2: Controls over nuclear weapons-related technology, materials, and scientific and technical expertise need to be as stringent as the weapons and delivery systems themselves. This calls for an integrated, "whole of government" approach to security all along the nuclear weapon life cycle, and probably bears socialization amongst the nuclear-weapons states to hedge against cultural idiosyncrasies. The Pakistan case study indicates it was not until 1998 that the military believed it had the authority to challenge the autonomy of nuclear scientists—quite late in the Pakistani nuclear weapons program.

Insight: Because nuclear accounting lacks sex appeal, it tends to be neglected and erodes nuclear control.
- A thorough inventory of Soviet tactical nuclear weapons withdrawn to Russia in 1992 was not undertaken by Moscow until 1996, and even then, only in response to allegations that Chechnyan rebels had acquired portable, so-called suitcase, nuclear weapons.
- It took another 5 years for the 12th GUMO to reveal that all such portable nuclear devices had been eliminated, with confirmation by the head of the State Security Council Igor Denisov not coming until 2004.
- With regard to Pakistan, Feroz Khan noted the highly technical nature of the nuclear dossier, prompting the COAS to turn it over to the Army's Corps of Engineers.
- The United States has not been immune from inadequate nuclear accounting, as the Minot Air Base incident makes perfectly clear.

Lesson #3: Nuclear-weapons states must actively promote strict nuclear accountancy using a variety of tools (e.g., measure of performance standards, budgetary resourcing, career development, and organizational autonomy). This is a legitimate subject of military to military and laboratory to laboratory dialogues. A benchmark for success in this regard is when we see not only nuclear missiles in parade on national independence days, but also, right behind them, a parade float carrying the nuclear "bean counters." The banner on such a float might read, "Not only do we possess nuclear weapons, but we know where all of them are."

Insight: Central authorities will tend to overstate their degree of control over nuclear weapons during a political crisis.
- Political motivation: To discourage meddling by outsiders (e.g., Russia).
- Cultural motivation: To save face.
- Personal motivation: To convey self-confidence (e.g., de Gaulle).
- This is a phenomenon not limited to the case studies (i.e., Japan and Fukushima, the United States and the Minot incident).

Lesson #4: We can expect to see this kind of behavior in future nuclear control crises and should be prepared to challenge it head on, through private and official channels backed by sustained media scrutiny. This might have unintended consequences, but on balance, probably serves the cause of nuclear accountability and crisis stability.

Insight: It is unrealistic to expect central authorities to plan for the control of nuclear weapons after their own demise.
- Is it possible to design in advance a nuclear fail-safe model for political dissolution without being unduly fatalistic, unpatriotic, or treasonous? For example, where is the plan for controlling America's nuclear arsenal in the event the United States collapses?

- Even in a deep political crisis, state mechanisms are slow to react (e.g., Russia).
- It was Russian *academics* who, in October 1991, were identifying the nuclear implications of the collapse of the USSR and even the Russian Federation.

Lesson #5: It likely falls to quasi- or non-state entities to take up these tasks, using a variety of analytical techniques (including alternative futures and gaming), to be poised to assist governments in times of crisis.

Insight: In the event of the political dissolution of another nuclear-weapons state, rival political authorities will enter a competition to win the loyalty of personnel in direct control of nuclear weapons.

- Russia vs. Ukraine, 1992; to a lesser degree, Algeria, 1961.
- To what extent have there been negotiations among Pakistan's Corps Commanders and the Strategic Plans Division during times of political turmoil?
- As political authorities struggle to retain or achieve control, unbiased technical advice on nuclear matters (i.e., what is or is not feasible, desirable) will be in short supply (e.g., Ukraine).

Lesson #6: The international community should consider ways to influence this contest to ensure responsible and reliable nuclear weapons control in the event of future state collapse. Because the granting of control over nuclear weapons could be left to individual military units and even individual officers, our intelligence communities should be prepared to "reach out and touch" key people.

Insight: Military institutions abhor political vacuums and can leverage their control over nuclear weapons in an attempt to fill them.
- For Pakistan, this phenomenon is probably just reinforcement of Army preponderance, which is why the question of whether the generals can countenance real civilian control is an interesting one.
- For 2 to 3 months, two of the three "Chegets" containing nuclear launch codes, including one allocated to the civilian leadership—that is, the minister of defense—were controlled by Shaposhnikov, who then tried to assert himself as equal to a head of state and dictate nuclear weapons policy to the political leadership.

Lesson #7: Whether the military emerges from a nuclear control crisis as a dictatorship bears close watching. Preserving military unity will be a "hot button" issue for this group, suggesting that any armed forces restructuring should be done with great care and accompanied by mechanisms to establish or reinforce civilian control. Keeping a close watch on potential Shaposhnikovs is a prudent task in this regard.

Insight: Approaches to nuclear weapon design and maintenance will impact the feasibility of nuclear successor states preserving, in an operational sense, their nuclear inheritance.
- Limited value of the test device at Reggan.
- Russian and Chinese warhead shelf lives.
- Economic viability of successor states.

Lesson #8: We should anticipate how these technical, operational, and economic constraints might affect future nuclear inheritances in regions of concern, such as the Korean Peninsula.

Insight: In the event of nuclear dissolution, there will be no quick routes to final agreements regarding the disposition of inherited nuclear weapons.
- Rapid dissolution of the USSR led to hasty, generalized agreements.
- Ukraine shows that underlying rivalries and insecurities among successor states can turn nuclear rejection into nuclear retention.

Lesson #9: The cases of Ukraine, Belarus, and Kazakhstan should be further scrutinized to develop a playbook of specific obligations regarding the disposition of nuclear weapons to be sought in future contingencies.

Insight: The military tends to be seen as the safekeeper of nuclear weapons during political upheaval.
- The main theme of the Russia and Pakistan case studies.
- Algeria, 1961: Just how much did Thiry waver in conducting the test?

Lesson #10: The extent to which the military can be counted upon to preserve control of nuclear weapons during political crises is a function of many influences, including prevailing patterns of civil-military relations and the technical sophistication or maturity of the arsenal in question. It is not clear that the armed forces provide the only solution; other domestic custodians may be more appropriate (e.g., civilian-scientific control or a super-elite military unit effectively outside the military chain of command, such as China's 22 Base). More novel approaches may also merit consideration (e.g., international safekeeping).

ENDNOTES - CHAPTER 8

1. Polonium-210, used in nuclear weapons as a neutron initiator, has a half-life of 138 days, eventually decaying to lead-206. See "Factsheets and FAQs: Polonium-210," *International Atomic Energy Agency*, available from *www.iaea.org/Publications/Factsheets/English/polonium210.html*.

2. As Tertrais observed in his chapter:

The details of the Reggan events remained secret for several weeks, and there is no evidence that the United States, for instance, was aware in real time of what was going on at Reggan in April 1961. No mention of the episode is made in the studies of U.S. archives done by French experts. See Vincent Nouzille, *Des secrets si bien gardés: Les dossiers de la Maison-Blanche et de la CIA sur la France et ses présidents 1958-1981* (*The Secret So Well Kept: Records of the White House and CIA on France and Its Presidents 1958-1981*), Paris, France: Fayard, 2010; and Vaïsse, *Comment de Gaulle fit échouer le putsch d'Alger*. No U.S. official analysis of the events has been found by this author. A declassified 1964 CIA study entitled comments on each French test, but the description is excised in the declassified version. See Central Intelligence Agency, *The French Nuclear Weapon Program*, OSI-SR/64-10, March 27, 1964, available from *www.foia.cia.gov/docs/DOC_0001522915/DOC_0001522915.pdf*. Brian Jenkins had access to other previously classified documents and confirms that no mention of the test appears in any of them. Personal communication with the author, March 2012.

3. See Khan's chapter in this volume, p. 178.

4. *Ibid.*, p. 179.

5. "Pakistan Moves Nuclear Weapons," *The Washington Post*, November 11, 2011, available from *www.washingtonpost.com/ac2/wp-dyn/A9038-2001Nov10?language=printer*.

6. See Khan's chapter in this volume, p. 172.

7. See, for example, "Rogue Scientists Gave Bin Laden Nuclear Secrets," *The Telegraph*, December 1, 2001, available from *www.*

telegraph.co.uk/education/3291277/Rogue-scientists-gave-bin-Laden-nuclear-secrets.html.

8. See Khan's chapter in this volume, p. 156.

9. *Ibid.*, p. 162.

10. See A. Q. Khan's 13-page "confession," available from *www.foxnews.com/world/2011/09/15/aq-khans-thirteen-page-confession/.*

11. Ghulam Ishaq Khan was a long-time civil servant and Zia's finance minister and later Chairman of the Senate. After the accidental death of President Zia, he became acting president of Pakistan; after the general elections of 1988, he was elected the president of Pakistan.

12. The author interviewed General Beg in Rawalpindi in 1993.

13. See, for example, Pervez Hoodbhoy's account, available from *tribune.com.pk/story/325571/the-bomb-iran-saudi-arabia-and-pakistan/.*

14. See "Rossiya Perevypolnila Plany po Sokrashcheniyu Yadernogo Oruzhiya" ("Russia Has Exceeded the Plan for Reduction of Nuclear Weapons"), *RIA-Novosti*, June 22, 2005, available from *rian.ru/politics/20050622/40566772.html*; and Nikolai Poroskov, "Takticheskii Yadernyi Kozyr" ("A Tactical Nuclear Ace"), *Vremya Novostei* (*News Time*), September 7, 2007.

15. Glavnoye Upravleniye Ministerstvo Oborony, or Main Directorate of the Ministry of Defense.

CHAPTER 9

BEYOND CRISES: THE UNENDING CHALLENGE OF CONTROLLING NUCLEAR WEAPONS AND MATERIALS

Matthew Bunn

The case studies presented in this volume are invaluable contributions to thinking about an important aspect of the nuclear danger—the potential for loss of control as states with nuclear weapons go through periods of political turmoil and unrest.

From Sokov, we have the alarming spectacle of military forces digging a trench in the runway with cannon fire to scare off a crowd in order to fly nuclear weapons away before armed gangs arrive and seize them. From Tertrais, we have a situation full of uncertainty over which group of generals those with control of a nuclear weapon to be tested will be loyal to—and then the nuclear core being driven across the desert in a *deux chevaux*. From Stokes, we have the world's only case of an armed nuclear missile being fired over a long range and then detonated—and word of radical factions among nuclear custodians squabbling with other factors over control of key nuclear facilities. From Khan, we have a more reassuring argument that Pakistan's seemingly endless political turmoil has never seriously threatened its nuclear control, though well-organized attacks on heavily guarded strategic targets such as the Rawalpindi General Headquarters and the Mehran Naval Base—apparently with insider help—inevitably raise worries about the possibility of similar attacks on nuclear facilities.

But in a way, each of these case studies is the beginning, not the end, of a history. They open intriguing and important questions, but do not provide the answers we need to understand the full implications of these events. In most of these cases, we do not know in detail how close the nation came to losing control of nuclear weapons, what actors might have been attempting to get them, or what these actors' plans might have been.

One thing seems clear: Political chaos, turmoil, and insurgency in a state armed with nuclear weapons are extraordinarily dangerous things. Removing nuclear weapons from regions that may be vulnerable to such turmoil, providing multiple layers of security for nuclear weapons, and doing everything possible to strengthen governance and reduce the chances of turmoil in states with nuclear weapons all seem to be urgent tasks. Today, they may be most urgent in the very different cases of North Korea—whose dictatorial regime surely cannot last forever (though analysts have been saying that for 2 decades)—and Pakistan, where substantial security measures must protect against extraordinary threats from possible insiders, from outsiders, and from both working together. In both cases, how to accomplish the tasks of strengthening governance and reducing the chance of loss of control remain very much open questions.

But I would argue that the cases presented here tell only a small part of the history of nuclear security. They focus only on security for nuclear weapons, not nuclear material, and only on moments of turmoil and crisis, which are blessedly rare.

The broader story is that securing both nuclear weapons and weapons-usable nuclear material has been a difficult challenge throughout the nuclear age, in normal times and in crisis. Indeed, the nuclear thefts that have genuinely occurred have been of weapons-usable nuclear materials, not nuclear weapons (fortunately), and they have not occurred in the midst of political turmoil. If we want to understand the risks of nuclear theft—the central issue nuclear security measures are designed to address—we need to look beyond the windows we have peered through at this workshop.

REAL THEFTS, ATTACKS, AND INTRUSIONS: SOME CASES

Theft of highly enriched uranium and plutonium, the essential ingredients of nuclear weapons, is not a hypothetical worry—it is an ongoing reality. The International Atomic Energy Agency (IAEA) has documented some 18 cases of theft or loss of plutonium or highly enriched uranium (HEU) from 1993-2007 that were confirmed by the states concerned. See Table 1.[1] (These cases involving real weapons-usable nuclear material are only one small part of the broader phenomenon of illicit trafficking of nuclear and radioactive materials; the IAEA has reported hundreds of situations involving other materials.) Three of these cases (New Jersey, in 2005; Fukui, Japan, in 2005; and Hennigsdorf, Germany, in 2006) involve inadvertent loss, leaving 15 involving instances of intentional theft and smuggling. Of those, five involve less than a gram of material, and are included here only because of the possibility that these are samples of larger stocks available to the smugglers—as smugglers often claim is the case.

Date	Location	Material Involved	Incident Description
5/24/1993	Vilnius, Lithuania	HEU/ 150 g	4.4 t of beryllium including 140 kg contaminated with HEU were discovered in the storage area of a bank.
3/?/1994	St. Petersburg, Russian Federation	HEU/ 2.972 kg	An individual was arrested in possession of HEU, which he had previously stolen from a nuclear facility. The material was intended for illegal sale.
5/10/1994	Tengen-Wiechs, Germany	Pu/ 6.2 g	Plutonium was detected in a building during a police search.
6/13/1994	Landshut, Germany	HEU/ 0.795 g	A group of individuals was arrested in illegal possession of HEU.
7/25/1994	Munich, Germany	Pu/ 0.24 g	A small sample of PuO2-UO2 mixture was confiscated in an incident related to a larger seizure at Munich Airport on 1994-08-10.
8/10/1994	Munich Airport, Germany	Pu/ 363.4 g	PuO2-UO2 mixture was seized at Munich airport.
12/14/1994	Prague, Czech Republic	HEU/ 2.73 kg	HEU was seized by police in Prague. The material was intended for illegal sale.
6/?/1995	Moscow, Russian Federation	HEU/ 1.7 kg	An individual was arrested in possession of HEU, which he had previously stolen from a nuclear facility. The material was intended for illegal sale.
6/6/1995	Prague, Czech Republic	HEU/ 0.415 g	An HEU sample was seized by police in Prague.
6/8/1995	Ceske Budejovice, Czech Republic	HEU/ 16.9 g	An HEU sample was seized by police in Ceske Budejovice.
5/29/1999	Rousse, Bulgaria	HEU/ 10 g	Customs officials arrested a man trying to smuggle HEU at the Rousse customs border check point.
12/?/2000	Karlsruhe, Germany	Pu/ 0.001 g	Mixed radioactive materials including a minute quantity of plutonium were stolen from the former pilot reprocessing plant.
7/16/2001	Paris, France	HEU/ 0.5 g	Three individuals trafficking in HEU were arrested in Paris. The perpetrators were seeking buyers for the material.
6/26/2003	Sadahlo, Georgia	HEU/ ~170 g	An individual was arrested in possession of HEU upon attempting to illegally transport the material across the border.
3/?/2005 to 4/?/2005	New Jersey, USA	HEU/ 3.3 g	A package containing 3.3 g of HEU was inadvertently disposed of.
6/24/2005	Fukui, Japan	HEU/ 0.0017 g	A neutron flux detector was reported lost at an NPP.
2/1/2006	Tbilisi, Georgia	HEU/ 79.5 g	A group of individuals was arrested trying to illegally sell HEU.
3/30/2006	Hennigsdorf, Germany	HEU/ 47.5 g	Authorities discovered trace amounts of HEU on a piece of tube found amidst scrap metal entering a steel mill.

Table 1. HEU and Plutonium Incidents Confirmed to the ITDB, 1993-2007.

Unfortunately, after 2008, the IAEA stopped issuing public updates of this list of HEU and plutonium incidents. This does not mean, however, that incidents stopped occurring. The Georgian government has confirmed that in March 2010, Georgian agents seized approximately 18 grams of HEU just below 90-percent enrichment from smugglers who crossed into Georgia from Armenia. The smugglers reportedly claimed that more was available.[2] In June 2011, authorities in Moldova arrested six people who reportedly had 4.4 grams of weapons-grade HEU. The smugglers claimed to have access to nine kilograms of HEU, which they were willing to sell for $31 million. Moldovan officials report that "members of the ring, who have not yet been detained, have one kilogram of uranium." This case appears to involve a real buyer–still at large–and the possibility that there are kilograms of weapon-grade HEU in the smugglers' hands, making it potentially the most serious case in years.[3]

In addition to these cases confirmed to the IAEA, there is strong evidence that a number of additional thefts have occurred—including confessions and convictions for some of the perpetrators—which the states concerned have not confirmed to the IAEA. In particular, there was a well-documented theft of 1.5 kilograms of 90-percent-enriched HEU in 1992 (described in detail below), and two thefts from Russian naval facilities in 1993 that are not included in the IAEA database. Thus, there appear to be approximately 20 well-documented cases of actual theft and smuggling of plutonium or HEU in the public record.[4] At the classified level, the U.S. Government regards a significant number of additional cases as confirmed.

To these cases of actual theft and smuggling of plutonium and HEU must be added a substantial number of attempts, attacks, and intrusions that have taken place over the years. These include, among others: the still-unexplained apparent loss of hundreds of kilograms of HEU at the Nuclear Materials and Equipment Corporation (NUMEC) in the mid-1960s (which the balance of the evidence suggests was a theft by senior facility officials on behalf of Israel);[5] a 1982 incident in which an insider at the Koeberg nuclear power plant in South Africa planted and detonated explosives on the steel pressure vessel (before fuel had been loaded, intended only to raise alarm, not to spread radioactivity);[6] incidents in 2001 in which terrorist teams carried out reconnaissance at Russian nuclear weapons storage sites, and apparently also on nuclear weapon transport trains;[7] and a 2007 intrusion in South Africa in which two teams of armed men attacked the Pelindaba site, where hundreds of kilograms of HEU are stored (with one of the teams penetrating a 10,000 volt security fence, disabling intrusion detectors, going to the emergency control center and shooting a worker there after a struggle, and departing without ever being engaged by site security forces).[8]

In short, the threats are out there. In a world that includes terrorists with global reach, effective nuclear security and accounting measures are needed wherever nuclear weapons, plutonium, or HEU exist. All countries with such stockpiles on their soil should ensure that they are *at least* protected against a modest group of well-armed, well-trained outsiders; a well-placed insider; and both outsiders and an insider working together, using a broad range of tactics. Countries that face more substantial adversary threats—Pakistan being an obvious example—need to provide even higher levels of protection.[9]

Unfortunately, in many countries around the world, the security measures in place today are demonstrably not sufficient to protect against the kinds of threats terrorists and thieves have already shown they can pose. For example, a U.S. team visiting a foreign site with a Category I quantity of HEU from 2005 to 2010 found that there were no fences around the perimeter, no sensors to detect intrusions, no video surveillance systems to help guards assess the cause of alarms generated by sensors, and no vehicle barriers.[10] (It is a reasonable bet that this facility also did not have an on-site armed response team to protect it from armed attackers.) The U.S. team recommended that all of these basic security measures be put in place, which the country agreed to do. But when a team of congressional auditors visited in 2010-11, some of the improvements were still under way. The fact that such glaring weaknesses still existed at a site with Category I materials years after the September 11, 2001 (9/11), attacks speaks volumes about the urgent work still ahead to plug nuclear security weak points around the world. Indeed, I would argue that every country with nuclear weapons or weapons-usable nuclear materials—including the United States—has more to do to ensure that these items are effectively protected.

PUNCTUATING COMPLACENT EQUILIBRIUM: THE U.S. CASE

If political turmoil is not the most important driver of nuclear security problems, what is? In a word, complacency—the belief that nuclear terrorism is not a serious threat, and that whatever security measures are in place today are already sufficient. The history of nuclear security is a story of punctuated equilibrium, with long stretches of complacency and little change punctuated by moments when something—typically, a major incident of some kind—made it possible to move the system to a higher-security state, from which it would then begin to drift slowly into complacency again. The results of incidents and other events are mediated by the different political cultures and institutions in different countries, so that one country might react to an incident by establishing substantial new security rules, while another might react by having participants in the system offer explanations why it could never happen again.

For a brief picture of this kind of punctuated equilibrium, consider the history of nuclear security in the United States, which today probably has more stringent nuclear security rules and higher nuclear security expenditures than any other nation on earth. The Department of Energy (DOE) alone now spends some $1.8 billion a year on security, most of which goes to secure the nuclear weapons and weapons-usable materials it controls.[11]

From the beginning, the U.S. nuclear weapons program had substantial layers of security. But also from the beginning, there were serious weaknesses, highlighted by events such as the loss of nuclear weapon design information to the Soviet Union and driving the plutonium pit for the Trinity Test across the desert in an ordinary four-door Packard.

The first major puncture in the complacent equilibrium surrounding security for nuclear weapons was the 1960 visit by a team from the Joint Committee on Atomic Energy (JCAE) to bases in Europe where U.S. nuclear weapons were stored. They were appalled by the limited measures in place to prevent the seizure or unauthorized use of a U.S. nuclear weapon. At one base, for example, the team saw aircraft armed with fully operational U.S. nuclear weapons, ready to take off at a moment's notice, with foreign pilots. "The only evidence of U.S. control was a lonely 18-year-old sentry armed with a carbine and standing on the tarmac."[12] This led to the decision to develop and install the first primitive permissive action links (PALs) on U.S. nuclear weapons in Europe.

The situation with respect to weapons-usable nuclear materials was much worse. In the 1950s and 1960s, the Atomic Energy Commission (AEC) literally imposed *no rules at all* concerning how private companies with weapons-usable nuclear material had to secure such stocks, believing that because the material was valuable, companies would protect it adequately themselves.[13] Various authors pointed out that the consequences to society of the theft of enough nuclear material for a bomb were far greater than the financial value of the material, but logic was not sufficient to overcome complacency. Official government reports include photographs of items such as canisters containing 48 kilograms of HEU sitting on a dolly unguarded at an airport, waiting for a flight, or the exterior wall of a building that served as the principal barrier to accessing HEU that was so thin it could be cut open with tin snips.[14] The privately owned plutonium reprocessing plant at West Valley had many bombs' worth of separated plutonium on site, with only one guard during the day and none at night.[15] Nuclear material accounting was in its infancy and terribly inaccurate, and really tamper-resistant seals were not in use.

It was conditions such as these that existed at the Nuclear Materials and Equipment Corporation

(NUMEC) in Apollo, Pennsylvania, in the 1960s, when the poor accounting records that existed seemed to suggest that hundreds of kilograms of HEU were missing. I doubt we will ever know for sure, but the balance of evidence suggests that senior management of the facility stole a large amount of HEU and provided it to Israel.[16] (This reminds us that insider protection programs must include the senior leaders of a site among those they are designed to protect against.) Later in 1965, there was another large incident of HEU material unaccounted for (MUF) at the Nuclear Fuel Services (NFS) plant in Irwin, Tennessee [17]—a plant that continued to have problems for decades thereafter with MUFs larger than the statistical limits permitted.

The NUMEC and NFS episodes were another puncture for the complacent equilibrium. The AEC tightened material accounting rules, and designated Los Alamos as the lead laboratory to develop technology for nondestructive assay and other means of nuclear material accounting. Ironically, the development of many of the technologies used for international safeguards around the world today was initiated in response to concern about a possible theft in one unsafeguarded nuclear program on behalf of another unsafeguarded nuclear program. The AEC tasked an advisory group to review its safeguards program, and in 1967, the group recommended drastic improvements in security and accounting, warning—I believe, for the first time ever in a U.S. Government report—that terrorists might be able to get weapons-usable nuclear material and make a crude nuclear bomb.[18] Advocates within the AEC, notably Theodore B. Taylor, were pushing for action to improve nuclear security, and warning of a possible nuclear terrorist threat.[19] By 1970, the AEC finally issued requirements for private companies with weapons-usable nuclear material to provide some protection for it, though these initial regulations were quite weak.

The next puncture in the equilibrium came quickly: the Munich Olympics. Suddenly, the idea that a large, well-armed, and well-trained team could strike in the heart of a modern developed country was not a hypothetical worry but a stark reality. Congress held hearings that publicly chastised weak AEC security requirements, and the General Accounting Office (GAO) conducted a damning investigation. In 1973, the AEC imposed new nuclear security requirements and designated Sandia as the lead lab to develop and evaluate physical protection technologies. The Sandia experts began taking a systems engineering approach to security, carefully examining each pathway adversaries might use to get to a nuclear weapon and how it might be blocked, and found many gaping vulnerabilities in the security systems that existed at the time. As one of the grand old men of U.S. physical protection put it to me, "Before 1973, the only reason we never lost a nuclear weapon is that no one ever tried to take one."[20]

Throughout the 1970s, new challenges never let the system return to a complacent equilibrium. Growing public distrust of government and corporate assurances in general, and nuclear energy in particular; the debate over a plutonium economy, with the expectation that scores and eventually hundreds of plutonium-fueled reactors would soon be built and that tens of thousands of people would have direct access to separated plutonium; the Indian nuclear test in 1974; the continuation of international terrorist attacks (along with attacks and nuclear hoaxes within the United States); and a stream of investigations and analyses highlighting the dangers of plutonium and HEU and the possibility of nuclear terrorism combined to produce continuing public and government alarm. Indeed, provisions of the Energy Reorganization Act of 1974, which split the AEC, made it clear that Congress expected the new Nuclear Regulatory Commission (NRC) to take on the security issue immediately. By the end of the 1970s, the new DOE and the NRC had both, for the first time, established rules requiring that facilities have security measures in place able to provide protection against a specified "design basis threat" (DBT), and had begun performance tests including force-on-force exercises to test how well security systems worked in practice—ushering in the modern era of nuclear security.

With the Three Mile Island accident in 1979, followed by Chernobyl in 1986, and with the Cold War heating up, public attention turned to nuclear safety and nuclear war in the 1980s, and there was little public discussion of the danger of nuclear terrorism. Nevertheless, intensive congressional investigations of DOE security lapses (led by Rep. John Dingell); security tests in which security systems failed to protect against plausible adversary threats; and concern over truck bombs following the bombing of the Marine barracks in Lebanon in 1983 combined to drive further improvements in nuclear security. In 1985, then-Secretary of Energy John Herrington formed a "Special Project Team" to carry out a fast-paced review of security at all DOE facilities. The team found a wide range of vulnerabilities and made 94 recommendations for action. Over the next few years, DOE spent an estimated $1.5 billion upgrading physical security to implement these recommendations in an effort known as "Project Cerberus," named after the mythical guardian of the gates of hell.[21] Yet, within a few years complacency had crept back: Security budgets began to fall again, and DOE security managers warned that if immediate actions were not taken, nuclear weapons and materials could not be adequately secured.[22]

In 1996, DOE published *Plutonium: The First 50 Years*, an account of the U.S. plutonium inventory, which listed 2.8 tons of plutonium as officially unaccounted for. This was a remarkable confirmation of the results of decades-long complacency about material control and accounting in the U.S. nuclear complex.[23] Subsequently, a comparable report on the HEU stockpile reported 3.2 tons of HEU unaccounted for.[24] These amounts represent sufficient material for hundreds of nuclear bombs. It is very likely that some of it was lost to waste, some of it represented overestimates of how much material was produced in the first place, and none of it was actually stolen, but the accounting was so poor that we will never know for sure.

The next really dramatic puncture in the equilibrium was the 9/11 attacks. DOE and NRC ratcheted up their nuclear security requirements, new security performance testing programs were put in place, and more — which brings us more or less to where we are today. Events such as the inadvertent flight of the six warheads across the country suggest that in some areas, complacency is back.

It is important to understand that each of these improvements was resisted. Both industrial firms and operators of government facilities complained that the old approaches were enough, that the new requirements were needlessly expensive and burdensome, and that the threats were overstated. The firms and operators lobbied to weaken various proposed rules and procedures, and often succeeded. What is striking is that the degree of satisfaction with security measures already in place appears to be completely independent of what those security measures actually were; even when the AEC first required that transports of HEU and plutonium have at least a couple of armed guards, the industry complained that this was unnecessary and probably ineffective.[25] Nevertheless, over the years, the trend has been one of halting improvement in nuclear security over time, and industry has usually come eventually to accept and support the requirements.

The bad news in this story is that the richest and most powerful country on earth, with the most nuclear security experience, found achieving effective nuclear security to be an enormous challenge. Effective security took decades to accomplish—and remains in some respects unfinished—and it often took dramatic incidents such as major losses of nuclear material or terrorist attacks to lead to change.

The good news in this story is that on several occasions, "incidents" that could be generated by policy—congressional investigations, testing programs, analyses, and reviews—were sufficient to lead to important improvements in nuclear security. We are not doomed to wait until catastrophe strikes before nuclear security improvements are made. But how can policy drive such change more effectively in the future—in the United States and elsewhere?

OVERCOMING COMPLACENCY

For years, as this history was playing out within the United States, the U.S. Government has been seeking to convince countries around the world to improve nuclear security, with varying degrees of success. Policy tools have included attempting to negotiate treaties, such as the Convention on the Physical Protection of Nuclear Materials and its 2005 amendment; seeking ever-more-specific IAEA nuclear security recommendations, such as the recent revision of Information Circular 225 (INFCIRC/225, the IAEA physical protection recommendations referenced in many nuclear supply agreements); and pursuing technical cooperation to upgrade security—as in the Nunn-Lugar program and larger related efforts funded by the National Nuclear Security Administration. Other tools include helping to consolidate dangerous nuclear stocks to fewer locations, for example, by converting HEU-fueled research reactors and removing their HEU; passing United Nations Security Council Resolutions (UNSCR), such as UNSCR 1540, which legally obligates all countries to provide "appropriate effective" security and accounting for whatever stockpiles they may have; and, most recently, the nuclear security summit process, which brings dozens of heads of state together to commit to take action to improve nuclear security.[26]

What the United States has been seeking to do, in effect, is to accelerate this process of punctuated equilibrium, to convince countries to improve their nuclear security faster and more extensively than they otherwise would have. While each of these efforts has had its value, I believe the time has come for the United States and other countries to take on the driving cause of weak nuclear security—complacency—more directly.

The fundamental key to success in improving nuclear security and preventing nuclear terrorism is to convince political leaders and nuclear managers around the world that nuclear terrorism is a real and urgent threat to *their* countries' security, worthy of a substantial investment of their time and money. These countries must also be convinced that actions on their part are necessary to reduce the risk—something many of them do *not* believe today. If they come to feel that sense of urgency, they will be likely to take the needed actions to prevent nuclear terrorism; if they remain complacent, they will not. Some of the critical work of building this sense of urgency is already being done; the Nuclear Security Summit made some inroads in convincing some policymakers that the threat of nuclear terrorism was real, as has the Global Initiative to Combat Nuclear Terrorism. But much more needs to be done if President Barack Obama's objective of ensuring effective security for all vulnerable nuclear weapons and weapons-usable materials worldwide is to be achieved.

There are three layers of complacency that must be overcome: (1) the belief that terrorists could not plausibly make a bomb; (2) the belief that nuclear security measures are already adequate, so terrorists could not plausibly get the materials needed for a bomb; and, (3) the belief that even if terrorists could get nuclear material and could make a crude bomb, it is a U.S. problem, not one other countries need to worry about very much.

President Obama should work with other countries to take several steps to overcome this complacency and build the needed sense of urgency and commitment as described below.[27]

Joint Threat Briefings and Assessments.

Upcoming summits and other high-level meetings with key countries should include detailed briefings for both leaders on the nuclear terrorism threat, given jointly by U.S. experts and experts from the country concerned. These would outline the very real possibility that terrorists could get nuclear material and make a nuclear bomb, the global economic and political effects of a terrorist nuclear attack, and steps that could be taken to reduce the risk. U.S. briefings for U.S. and Russian officials highlighting intelligence on continuing nuclear security vulnerabilities were a critical part of putting together the Bush-Putin Bratislava Nuclear Security Initiative. With some key countries, the United States should seek agreement to draft joint assessments of the threat, following on the recent nongovernmental U.S.-Russian assessment.[28]

Intelligence Agency Discussions.

In many countries, the political leadership gets much of its information about national security threats from its intelligence agencies. It is therefore extremely important to convince the intelligence agencies in key countries that nuclear terrorism is a serious and urgent threat—and that plausible actions, taken now, could reduce the risk substantially. During the second George W. Bush term, DOE intelligence was actively working with foreign intelligence services to make this case and to build cooperation against the threat. This effort should be renewed and expanded to include focused efforts by the Director of National Intelligence, the Central Intelligence Agency, and other U.S. intelligence agencies as well.[29]

The "Armageddon Test."

President Obama should direct U.S. intelligence—possibly working in cooperation with agencies in other countries—to establish a small operational team that would seek to understand and penetrate the world of nuclear theft and smuggling. The team would be instructed to seek out sources willing to sell nuclear material for a bomb. If they succeeded, this would dramatically highlight the continuing threat, and potentially identify particular weak points and smuggling organizations requiring urgent action. If they failed, that would strongly suggest that terrorist operatives would likely fail as well, building confidence that measures to prevent nuclear terrorism were working.[30]

Nuclear Terrorism Exercises.

Building on the exercise program that has begun in the Global Initiative to Combat Nuclear Terrorism, the United States and other leading countries should organize a series of exercises with senior policymakers from key states. These exercises should have scenarios focused on: the theft of nuclear material; the realistic possibility that terrorists could construct a crude nuclear bomb if they got enough HEU or plutonium; the difficulty of stopping them once they had the material; and, the degree to which *all* countries would be affected if a terrorist nuclear bomb went off.[31] Participating in a realistic exercise can reach officials emotionally in a way that briefings and policy memos cannot. A program of such exercises should become a central element of the Global Initiative.

Fast-Paced Nuclear Security Reviews.

The United States and other leading countries should encourage leaders of key states to pick teams of security experts they trust to conduct fast-paced reviews of nuclear security in their countries, assessing whether facilities are adequately protected against a set of clearly defined threats—such as a well-placed insider, or two teams of well-armed, well-trained attackers. In the United States, such fast-paced reviews after major incidents such as 9/11 have often revealed a wide range of vulnerabilities that needed to be fixed.

Realistic Testing of Nuclear Security Performance.

The United States and other leading countries should work with key states around the world to implement programs to conduct realistic tests of the ability of nuclear security systems to defeat either insiders or outsiders. Failures in such tests can be powerful evidence to senior policymakers that nuclear security needs improvement.

Shared Databases of Threats and Incidents.

The United States and other key countries should collaborate to create shared databases of unclassified information on actual security incidents at both nuclear sites and at non-nuclear, guarded facilities, which offer lessons for policymakers and facility managers to consider in deciding on nuclear security levels and particular threats to defend against. The World Institute for Nuclear Security (WINS) could be a forum for creating one version of such a threat-incident database. In the case of safety, rather than security, reactor operators report each safety-related incident to groups such as the Institute of Nuclear Power Operations (the U.S. branch of the World Association of Nuclear Operators), and these groups analyze the incidents and distribute lessons learned about how to prevent similar incidents in the future to each member facility—and then carry out peer reviews to assess how well each facility has implemented the lessons learned.[32]

THE PATH FROM HERE

There is a great deal to be done to ensure that effective and lasting security and accounting are in place for all nuclear warheads and weapons-usable nuclear materials around the world. Nuclear security, like nuclear safety, will require constant vigilance and a focus on continual improvement—as long as nuclear weapons and weapons-usable materials continue to exist.

The case studies in this volume have made a valuable contribution to understanding how states have handled these matters in decades past. But there is much yet to be done to understand the history of nuclear security. To find the most effective policies to strengthen nuclear security worldwide, we need to know:

- Why have different countries made very different decisions about what nuclear security and accounting rules to put in place?
- What factors have led countries to change their nuclear security and accounting practices?
- What factors have been the most important obstacles to, and constraints on, such changes?
- What approaches can best strengthen secu-

rity culture, convincing all key staff of nuclear operations to take security seriously and constantly seek ways to improve it?
- What measures could best ensure that once effective nuclear security and accounting measures and strong security cultures have been put in place, they are sustained for the long haul?

Once we have learned some of the answers to these questions, we will be in a better position to judge how countries might best be convinced to make decisions that would drastically reduce the danger that nuclear weapons or the materials needed to make them could be stolen and fall into the hands of terrorists.

ENDNOTES - CHAPTER 9

1. International Atomic Energy Agency, "IAEA Illicit Trafficking Database Fact Sheet," Vienna, Austria: IAEA, 2008, available from *www.iaea.org/newscenter/features/radsources/pdf/fact_figures2007.pdf*. As of early-2012, this was the last of the annual editions of this fact sheet, which included a table detailing the HEU and plutonium incidents.

2. See, for example, Desmond Butler, "Georgia Details Nuclear Smuggling," *Associated Press*, November 7, 2010; and Julian Borger, "Nuclear Bomb Material Found for Sale on Georgia Black Market," *The Guardian*, November 7, 2010. Georgian President Mikhail Saakhashvili publicly confirmed the seizure had taken place on the margins of the nuclear security summit in April 2010. See Julian Borger, "Nuclear Summit Told How Georgia 'Foiled Plot to Sell Weapons-Grade Uranium'," *The Guardian*, April 13, 2010, available from *www.guardian.co.uk/world/2010/apr/13/nuclear-summit-georgia-uranium-plot*.

3. Committee on Foreign Relations U.S. Senate, *Enhancing Non-Proliferation Partnerships in the Black Sea Region: A Minority*

Staff Report, Washington, DC: Government Printing Office, 2011, available from *wid.ap.org/documents/np-minority-report.pdf.*

4. "Illicit Trafficking in Radioactive Materials," in *Nuclear Black Markets: Pakistan, A. Q. Khan and the Rise of Proliferation Networks: A Net Assessment,* London, UK: International Institute for Strategic Studies, 2007.

5. For a useful recent account, see Victor Gilinsky and Roger J. Mattson, "Revisiting the NUMEC Affair," *Bulletin of the Atomic Scientists,* Vol. 66, No. 2, March 2010, pp. 61-75.

6. For a detailed account, based on interviews with the perpetrator, see David Beresford, *Truth is a Strange Fruit: A Personal Journey Through the Apartheid War,* Auckland Park, South Africa: Jacana Media, 2010, pp. 102-107. I am grateful to Tom Bielefeld for providing this reference.

7. The incidents involving storage sites were confirmed by Colonel-General Igor Valynkin, then commander of the 12th Main Directorate of the Ministry of Defense (the 12th GUMO), which guards and manages Russia's nuclear weapons; the incidents involving the transport trains were reported by the Russian state newspaper. See Pavel Koryashkin, "Russian Nuclear Ammunition Depots Well Protected—Official," *ITAR-TASS,* October 25, 2001; "Russia: Terror Groups Scoped Nuke Site," *Associated Press,* October 25, 2001; Vladimir Bogdanov, "Propusk K Beogolovkam Nashli U Terrorista"(A Pass to Warheads Found on a Terrorist), *Rossiskaya Gazeta,* November 1, 2002.

8. For a summary and relevant sources, see Matthew Bunn, *Securing the Bomb 2008,* Cambridge, MA: Project on Managing the Atom, Harvard University; and Nuclear Threat Initiative 2008, available from *www.nti.org/securingthebomb.*

9. For a more extended argument for such a global baseline design basis threat, see Matthew Bunn and Evgeniy P Maslin, "All Stocks of Weapons-Usable Nuclear Materials Worldwide Must be Protected Against Global Terrorist Threats," *Journal of Nuclear Materials Management,* Vol. 39, No. 2, Winter 2011, pp. 21-27.

10. U.S. Congress, *Nuclear Nonproliferation: U.S. Agencies Have Limited Ability to Account for, Monitor, and Evaluate the Security of U.S. Nuclear Material Overseas*, GAO-11-920, Washington, DC: Government Accountability Office, September 2011, p. 23. When congressional investigators visited the site in 2010-11, they observed that the facility now had an armed guard; that a 12-foot perimeter fence was under construction; that a fence with motion detectors was being built around the entire facility; new access control measures had been put in place; and the central alarm station had been hardened. They were told that remote monitoring systems had been installed in key areas in response to the U.S. recommendation.

11. *FY 2013 Congressional Budget Request: Other Defense Activities, Departmental Administration, Inspector General, Working Capital Fund, Safeguards and Security Crosscut, Pensions*, Washington, DC: Department of Energy, February 2012, pp. 209-220.

12. Peter Stein and Peter Feaver, *Assuring Control Over Nuclear Weapons: The Evolution of Permissive Action Links*, CSIA Occasional Paper 2, Cambridge, MA: Center for Science and International Affairs, Harvard University, pp. 30-31. For a description of the JCAE's role in PALs in general, see Stephen I. Schwartz, "The JCAE and the Development of the Permissive Action Link," in Stephen I. Schwartz, ed., *Atomic Audit: The Costs and Consequences of U.S. Nuclear Weapons Since 1940*, Washington, DC: Brookings, 1998, pp. 514-515. See also Donald Cotter, "Peacetime Operations," in Ashton B. Carter, John D. Steinbruner, and Charles A. Zraket, eds., *Managing Nuclear Operations*, Washington, DC: Brookings, 1987.

13. William J. Desmond, Neil R. Zack, and James W. Tape, "The First 50 Years: A Review of the Department of Energy Domestic Safeguards and Security Program," *Journal of Nuclear Materials Management*, Vol. 26, No. 2, Spring 1998, pp. 17-22. The authors point out that the policy was that "SNM [special nuclear material] need be controlled only because of its intrinsic value . . . there were *no requirements* for nuclear material control or physical security for privately owned SNM" (emphasis added).

14. The first of these is in *Protecting Special Nuclear Material in Transit: Improvements Made and Existing Problems*, Washington,

DC: General Accounting Office, April 12, 1974, available as of October 26, 2004, from *archive.gao.gov/f0302/095909.pdf*, p. 19; the second is in *Improvements Needed in the Program for the Protection of Special Nuclear Material*, Washington, DC: General Accounting Office, November 7, 1973, p. 18.

15. See, for example, the discussion in John McPhee, *The Curve of Binding Energy: A Journey into the Awesome and Alarming World of Theodore B. Taylor*, New York: Farrar, Strauss, & Giroux, 1974.

16. Gilinsky and Mattson, "Revisiting the NUMEC Affair," pp. 61-75.

17. Desmond, Zack, and Tape, "The First 50 Years: A Review of the Department of Energy Domestic Safeguards and Security Program," presented at a workshop on *A Comparative Analysis of Approaches to the Protection of Fissile Materials*, Stanford University, July 28–30, 1997.

18. See Desmond, Zack, and Tape, "The First 50 Years." The result of the review was published in March 1967 as Ralph F. Lumb *et al.*, *Report of the Advisory Panel on Safeguarding Special Nuclear Materials*, Washington, DC: Atomic Energy Commission, 1967. One interesting aspect of this report was that it was written *before* the rise of the modern era of international terrorism, beginning after the 1967 Arab-Israeli war. The concern was probably provoked in part by the experience of the sophistication of Vietnamese guerillas in attacking U.S. bases and troops; it also came soon after NUMEC and just as the Nth-country experiment was showing that two or three people with no prior knowledge beyond physics could design a credible implosion-type bomb.

19. Taylor first raised his concerns in public, unclassified form in 1968, but the paper was little noticed. See Taylor, *Preliminary Survey of Non-National Nuclear Threats*, Stanford, CA: Stanford Research Institute, 1968. Later, Taylor publicized his concerns in interviews with a journalist; these first appeared as a series of articles in *The New Yorker*, and later in book form in McPhee, *The Curve of Binding Energy*.

20. Interview with J. D. Williams, September 2002.

21. See Committee on Energy and Commerce, *Nuclear Weapons Facilities: Adequacy of Safeguards and Security at Department of Energy Nuclear Weapons Production Facilities*, U.S. Congress, House of Representatives, 99th Congress, 2nd Sess., March 6, 1986; *Nuclear Weapons Facilities*, pp. 39-54; National Research Council, *Material Control and Accounting in the Department of Energy's Nuclear Fuel Complex*, Washington, DC: National Academy Press, 1989, pp. 30-31; John B. Roberts, II, "Nuclear Secrets and the Culture Wars," *American Spectator*, Vol. 32, No. 5, May 1999, pp. 34-39, 76.

22. By 1991, for example, DOE's annual report to the president on safeguards and security in the DOE complex was warning that "significant improvements must be made immediately"; by 1996, the annual report was warning of "severe budget reductions . . . which have undermined protection of special nuclear material." Both reports are quoted in the depressing appendix, listing reviews of DOE security in President's Foreign Intelligence Advisory Board (PFIAB), *Science at its Best, Security at its Worst: A Report on Security Problems at the U.S. Department of Energy*, Washington DC: PFIAB, June, 1999, available from *www.fas.org/sgp/library/pfiab/*.

23. See U.S. Department of Energy, *Plutonium: The First 50 Years: United States Plutonium Production, Acquisition, and Utilization from 1944 through 1994*, Washington, DC: DOE, 1996, available from *www.fas.org/sgp/othergov/doe/pu50y.html*. In 2012, an updated report reduced the amount of material unaccounted for – or "inventory differences," in the more neutral official term now used – to 2.4 tons, because some of the plutonium had been found in closing out Rocky Flats (0.3 tons) and some buildings at Hanford (0.1 tons). See U.S. Department of Energy, *The United States Plutonium Balance, 1944-2009*, Washington, DC: DOE, 2012, available from *fissilematerials.org/library/PU%20Report%20Revised%2006-26-2012%20%28UNC%29.pdf*.

24. U.S. Department of Energy, *Highly Enriched Uranium: Striking a Balance (Revision 1)*, Washington, DC: DOE, January, 2001, available from *www.fas.org/sgp/othergov/doe/heu/striking.pdf*. An update to this report is expected to be coming soon.

25. J. Samuel Walker, "Regulating Against Nuclear Terrorism: The Domestic Safeguards Issue, 1970-1979," *Technology and Culture*, Vol. 42, No. 1, January 2001, pp. 107-132.

26. For a summary of these various elements of the international regime and what has been accomplished in improving nuclear security, see Matthew Bunn, *Securing the Bomb 2010: Securing all Nuclear Materials in Four Years*, Cambridge, MA: Project on Managing the Atom, Harvard University, and Nuclear Threat Initiative 2010, available from *www.nti.org/securingthebomb*.

27. The following section is drawn from Bunn, *Securing the Bomb 2010*.

28. Matthew Bunn, Yuri Morozov, Rolf Mowatt-Larrsen, Simon Saradzhyan, William Tobey, Viktor I. Yesin, and Pavel S. Zolotarev, *The U.S.-Russia Joint Threat Assessment of Nuclear Terrorism*, Cambridge, MA: Belfer Center for Science and International Affairs, Harvard Kennedy School and Institute for U.S. and Canadian Studies, June 2011.

29. I am grateful to Rolf Mowatt-Larssen for discussions of this approach.

30. This concept was originally developed by Larssen. Care would have to be taken to structure the effort in a way that avoided creating perceptions of a market for nuclear material that might contribute to additional nuclear thefts.

31. The model would be the "Black Dawn" exercise organized by the CSIS (and sponsored by the Nuclear Threat Initiative) for key North Atlantic Treaty Organization (NATO) officials. For a description, see *Black Dawn: Scenario-Based Exercise*, Washington, DC: Center for Strategic and International Studies, 2004, available from *www.csis.org/media/csis/pubs/040503_blackdawn.pdf*.

32. See Joseph V. Rees, *Hostages of Each Other: The Transformation of Nuclear Safety since Three Mile Island*, Chicago, IL: University of Chicago Press, 1994.

ABOUT THE CONTRIBUTORS

MATTHEW BUNN is an Associate Professor at Harvard University's John F. Kennedy School of Government. His research interests include nuclear theft and terrorism; nuclear proliferation and measures to control it; the future of nuclear energy and its fuel cycle; and innovation in energy technologies. Before coming to Harvard, Dr. Bunn served as an adviser to the White House Office of Science and Technology Policy, as a study director at the National Academy of Sciences, and as editor of *Arms Control Today*. He is the author or co-author of 20 books and major technical reports (most recently, *Transforming U.S. Energy Innovation*), and over a hundred articles in publications ranging from *Science* to *The Washington Post*.

PETER D. FEAVER is a Professor of Political Science and Public Policy at Duke University. He is Director of both the Triangle Institute for Security Studies (TISS) and the Duke Program in American Grand Strategy (AGS). Dr. Feaver served on the National Security Council Staff as Special Advisor for Strategic Planning and Institutional Reform from June 2005 to July 2007, and as Director for Defense Policy and Arms Control from 1993 to 1994. He is the author of numerous works on American foreign policy, nuclear proliferation, information warfare, and U.S. national security. Among his recent publications is "American Grand Strategy at the Crossroads: Leading from the Front, Leading From Behind, or Not Leading at All," in *America's Path: Grand Strategy for the Next Administration* by the Center for a New American Security (May 2012).

GREGORY F. GILES is a Senior Director with Science Applications International Corporation (SAIC), where he advises U.S. Government decisionmakers on issues pertaining to Iran, nonproliferation, and deterrence. Mr. Giles has published widely and testified before Congress on these subjects. He has also lectured at the U.S. Air Force and Army War Colleges, the NATO Defense College in Rome, and at Saudi Arabia's Command and Staff College. Mr. Giles authored the path-breaking article, "Safeguarding the Undeclared Nuclear Arsenals," published by *The Washington Quarterly* in Spring 1993. He also wrote, "Command and Control Challenges of an Iranian Nuclear Force," in *Deterring the Ayatollahs*, The Washington Institute for Near East Policy, 2007 (available from *www.washingtoninstitute.org/uploads/Documents/pubs/PolicyFocus72FinalWeb.pdf*). Prior to joining SAIC, he worked as a staff assistant in the British House of Commons, the United Nations General Assembly, and the U.S. House and Senate.

FEROZ HASSAN KHAN is a former Brigadier General in the Pakistani Army and is currently a Lecturer in the Department of National Security Affairs and a researcher in the Center for Contemporary Conflict at the U.S. Naval Postgraduate School in Monterey, CA. Brigadier Khan is a former Director of Arms Control and Disarmament Affairs in the Strategic Plans Division, which is the secretariat of Pakistan's Nuclear Command Authority. He has held a series of visiting fellowships in several prestigious think tanks in the United States. Brigadier General Khan is the author of a variety of publications on nuclear arms control and nonproliferation issues in Pakistan, including the book *Eating Grass: The Making of the Pakistani*

Nuclear Bomb, Stanford, CA: Stanford Security Studies, November 2012.

REID B. C. PAULY is Scott Sagan's research assistant at the Center for International Security and Cooperation (CISAC) at Stanford University. Prior to joining CISAC, Mr. Pauly was a research assistant at the Ploughshares Fund in Washington, DC. Mr. Pauly graduated magna cum laude from Cornell University, where his honors thesis, "Containing the Atom: Paul Nitze and the Tradition of Non-Use of Nuclear Weapons," was awarded the Janice N. and Milton J. Esman Prize for Outstanding Undergraduate Scholarship. His thesis also won prizes from the Center for Strategic and International Studies and the Virginia Military Institute.

SCOTT D. SAGAN is the Caroline S. G. Munro Professor of Political Science at Stanford University, and a Senior Fellow at the Center for International Security and Cooperation at the Freeman Spogli Institute. Before joining the Stanford faculty, Dr. Sagan was a lecturer at Harvard University and served as a special assistant to the director of the Organization of the Joint Chiefs of Staff in the Pentagon. He has served as a consultant to the office of the Secretary of Defense and at the Sandia and Los Alamos National Laboratories. Dr. Sagan has authored and co-authored numerous works, including "A Call for Global Disarmament," in the July 5, 2012, issue of *Nature*; and "The Causes of Nuclear Weapons Proliferation," in the July 2011 issue of the *Annual Review of Political Science*.

HENRY D. SOKOLSKI is the Executive Director of the Nonproliferation Policy Education Center (NPEC) in Arlington, VA, and an Adjunct Professor at the Institute of World Politics in Washington, DC. He previously served as a military legislative aide and special assistant for nuclear energy affairs in the U.S. Senate, as Deputy for Nonproliferation Policy in the Cheney Pentagon, and as a member of the CIA's Senior Advisory Group. Mr. Sokolski also was appointed by Congress to serve on the Deutch WMD (weapons of mass destruction) Commission and the Commission on the Prevention of WMD Proliferation and Terrorism. He has authored and edited numerous books on proliferation, including *The Next Arms Race* (Strategic Studies Institute, 2012) and *Best of Intentions* (Praeger 2001).

NIKOLAI SOKOV is a Senior Fellow at the Vienna Center for Disarmament and Nonproliferation. He has worked at the James Martin Center for Nonproliferation Studies at the Monterey Institute of International Studies since 1996. Previously, Dr. Sokov worked at the Institute of U.S. and Canadian Studies, the Institute of World Economy and International Relations in Moscow, and the Ministry for Foreign Affairs of the Soviet Union and later Russia. He participated in START I and START II negotiations as well as in a number of summit and ministerial meetings. Dr. Sokov is the author of several books, over a dozen monographs, and more than 200 articles on arms control and international security issues.

MARK A. STOKES is the Executive Director of the Project 2049 Institute. A 20-year U.S. Air Force veteran, Mr. Stokes served as team chief and senior country director for the People's Republic of China, Taiwan, and Mongolia in the Office of the Assistant Secretary of Defense for International Security Affairs. He was also assistant air attaché at the U.S. Embassy, Beijing. Previously, he was vice president and Taiwan country manager for Raytheon International. He has served as executive vice president of Laifu Trading Company, a subsidiary of the Rehfeldt Group; senior associate at the Center for Strategic and International Studies; and member of the Board of Governors of the American Chamber of Commerce in Taiwan. He has published a variety of work on China and regional security issues, including *China's Nuclear Warhead Storage and Handling System* (The Project 2049 Institute, 2010).

BRUNO TERTRAIS has been a Senior Research Fellow at the *Fondation pour la Recherche Stratégique* (FRS), the leading French think tank on international security issues, since 2001. His past positions include Research Assistant, NATO Assembly; Director, Civilian Affairs Committee, NATO Assembly; Europe Desk Officer, Ministry of Defense; Visiting Fellow, the Rand Corporation; Head of Defense Policy Planning Unit, Ministry of Defense; and Special Assistant to the Director of Strategic Affairs, Ministry of Defense. Dr. Tertrais is a member of the International Institute for Strategic Studies (IISS) and the Global Agenda Councils of the World Economic Forum (WEF). He is also a member of the editorial boards of *The Washington Quarterly* and *Survival*. His recent publications include "The Demise of Ares: The End of War as We Know It?" in the Summer 2012 issue of *The Washington Quarterly* and *Pakistan's Nuclear Programme: A Net Assessment* (Fondation pour la Recherche Stratégique, 2012).

U.S. ARMY WAR COLLEGE

Major General Anthony A. Cucolo III
Commandant

*****

STRATEGIC STUDIES INSTITUTE
AND
U.S. ARMY WAR COLLEGE PRESS

Director
Professor Douglas C. Lovelace, Jr.

Director of Research
Dr. Steven K. Metz

Editors
Mr. Henry D. Sokolski
Mr. Bruno Tertrais

Editor for Production
Dr. James G. Pierce

Publications Assistant
Ms. Rita A. Rummel

*****

Composition
Mrs. Jennifer E. Nevil

www.ingramcontent.com/pod-product-compliance
Lightning Source LLC
Chambersburg PA
CBHW080533170426
43195CB00016B/2547